Transitive relation $\xrightarrow{BinRelation^{+}} \triangleq \xrightarrow{BinRelation} \cdots \xrightarrow{BinRelation}$

Total predicate

Isomorphic predicate

Codecharts

Codecharts

Roadmaps and Blueprints for Object-Oriented Programs

Amnon H. Eden

With contributions from Jonathan Nicholson

A John Wiley & Sons, Inc. Publication

Cover illustration:
Courtesy of Thal Kaminer

Library of Congress Cataloging-in-Publication Data:
Eden, A. H., 1967-
  Codecharts : roadmaps and blueprints for object-oriented programs / A.H. Eden ; with contributions from J. Nicholson.
    p. cm.
   ISBN 978-0-470-62694-8 (hardback)
 1. Computer software--Development. 2. Object-oriented programming (Computer science) I. Nicholson, J. (Jonathan), 1983- II. Title.
  QA76.76.D47E297 2010
  005.1'17--dc22
                           2010013941

Printed in Singapore

oBook ISBN: 978-0-470-89103-2
ePDF ISBN: 978-0-470-89102-5

10 9 8 7 6 5 4 3 2 1

Contents

Preface

In this book we set out to investigate some of the most difficult problems that software engineering faces. Although a young discipline, it nonetheless faces the most difficult challenges, as software is the most complex artefact ever crafted by humankind. As such, many of the problems can be traced to inadequate abstraction. Satisfying theoretical and practical demands in one visual, scalable, and decidable language has so far proven to be a genuine challenge. Any claim that one modelling language or one tool can be a "silver bullet" is patently false. Indeed, there are no silver bullets, and LePUS3, the language of Codecharts, is no exception.

As a first step in seeking a solution, we have set eight guiding principles of our design description language (Chapter 3). Jointly, these reduce the scope of our problem significantly. They leave much out. Nonetheless, we did discover that many of the problems in the theory and practice of software specification, verification, visualization, modelling, and design recovery have a common root. At their heart is the question of representation. Committing ourselves to these guiding principles has enabled us to tackle these difficult problems head on and reach a very useful result.

Is our task complete? Far from it. Additional cases need to be studied. And our attempt at formalizing our specification language is incomplete. In particular, our analysis of the mathematical properties of Codecharts is preliminary. To the eyes of the logician, the exhibition of this subject in this book is both inadequate and uninteresting, and the propositions and "proofs" we provide are sketchy and mathematically shallow. But this has been our conscious choice: The logician is not in our target audience; programmers and students of programming are.

At the time of writing this book, our research project is still in early stages. However, a controlled experiment conducted in our labs [Eden & Gasparis 2009] clearly indicates that a tool supporting automated design verification and software visualization with Codecharts, the Two-Tier Programming Toolkit, provides very significant productivity gains in key tasks in software development and maintenance. We therefore have every reason to believe that this book will help programmers overcome the difficult problems they encounter on a daily basis.

This work is intended to capture our research thus far, and as such we consider it far from final or static. We welcome all forms of feedback and comments, from typos to criticisms. Please contact us care of Wiley or via our website (www.lepus.org.uk) where we will publish book errata and other useful resources. Thank you.

AMNON EDEN and JONATHAN NICHOLSON

Colchester, Essex, England
October 2010

Acknowledgments

Many people deserve credit for making this book possible. First thanks go to Epameinondas Gasparis for all his diligent work and contributions over the years. Special thanks go to Yehuda Elkana who enlightened us; to Yoram Hirshfeld and Amiram Yehudai for their guidance in the initial stages of this project; and to Yossi Gil, in particular; for suggesting that LePUS can be used to model programs. Special thanks also go to Raymond Turner for helping us formulate the definitions and axioms. We also thank Rick Kazman, Peter Grogono, Kees Bleijenberg, and Ian Bayley for their feedback and David Lorenz for coming up with the idea of using triangles to model hierarchies.

We thank Christina Maniati for her permission to use her MSc dissertation as well as to our graduate students Olumide A. Iyaniwura, Gu Bo, Maple Tao Liang, Omololu Ayodeji, Dimitrios Fragkos, and Xu Yi, whose work contributed to the understanding and use of Codecharts. Thanks also go to all the graduate and undergraduate students who commented on early drafts of this manuscript.

This book is a product of research that was promoted in part by contributions received from a number of funding agencies: The Natural Sciences and Engineering Research Council of Canada (NSERC); The University of Essex, School of Computer Science and Electronic Engineering's Research Promotion Fund (RPF) and the Knowledge Transfer Innovation Fund (KTIF); Eshkol Fund, Israel Ministry of Science; and UK's Engineering and Physical Sciences Research Council (EPSRC).

We thank the staff of Wiley for their help and support, especially: George Telecki, Dean Gonzalez, and Lisa Van Horn. Finally, the authors wish to thank Naomi, Saul, Mary J. Anna, Becky, Marion, and Hugh for their support and inspiration.

Guide to the Reader

Let us clarify the charter and intended audience of this book.

Scope

This book shows using the language of Codecharts, called LePUS3, to capture and convey structural and organizational aspects of object-oriented programs at any level of abstraction. LePUS3 is a visual, formal design description language for representing (automatically verifiable) statements about programs encoded in languages such as Java, C++, C#, Smalltalk, Eiffel, Ada 95, CLOS, and Ruby. In particular, Codecharts are tailored to deliver roadmaps to large object-oriented programs, libraries, and frameworks as well as blueprints that articulate in precise terms nonfunctional specifications and design decisions such as design patterns. Codecharts are therefore committed to the building blocks of object-oriented design, which are, in essence, inheritance class hierarchies, sets of dynamically bound methods, and correlations amongst them. In addition, the language of Codecharts was tailored to meet a stringent set of guiding principles (described in Chapter 3), such as abstraction, scalability, rigor, and automated verifiability, while placing an emphasis on elegance and minimality.

The first part of this book demonstrates in detail how Codecharts can be used for documenting a program's structure and organization, for representing the properties of various components and how they relate to each other, and for representing design decisions of programs that are yet to be implemented, including design patterns and application frameworks. The second part of this book provides a mathematical foundation for Codecharts and discusses some rigorous means of reasoning about their relation to programs.

As a result of the language's guiding principles, LePUS3 can only be used to model *decidable* properties of object-oriented programs. Other kinds of specifications are therefore outside the scope of this book. These include specifications describing the design of programs that are not object oriented, architectural styles, and undecidable functional specifications such as temporal relations and certain behavioural specifications. Other languages and notations fit this purpose.[1]

Intended Audience of Part I

Part I of this book ("Practice") is primarily written for **computing professionals** who are dissatisfied with existing modelling and specification languages. Written to become readily useful to programmers and software designers who have no mathematical training, this part contains numerous examples drawn from Java's Software Development Kit (SDK), including the packages `java.awt`, `java.util`, `java.security`, `java.io`, `java.lang`, and `java.rmi`, as well as open-source and common programs, class libraries, and application frameworks in wide use, such as JUnit, JGraph, JDOM, Java 3D, and Enterprise JavaBeans. Special emphasis is placed in this book on precise modelling of common design patterns such as the Composite, Iterator, Factory Method, Abstract Factory, and Proxy patterns. No knowledge with these is expected, but experienced programmers stand to benefit most from this part of the book.

Programmers will find in this book a modelling language for effectively managing the complexity of programs written in Java, C++, C#, and similar object-oriented programming languages. You will also learn about a tool that can verify conformance of any Java program to Codecharts by a click of a button.

Software designers will find in this part powerful abstraction mechanisms that can express design decisions at any level of abstraction. The abstraction mechanisms described in the book are useful early and late in the software development life cycle: early, where premature commitment to implementation minutia is inappropriate, and in late stages of the development, where the size of the program requires the generation of program roadmaps at various scales. Software designers will also read about a tool that can generate Codecharts from plain Java source code (the Design Navigator).

Finally, **undergraduate students** of computer science taking courses in software engineering and programming can also learn from Part I of this book about a modelling and specification mechanisms that, within the language's scope, are more precise and more abstract than those taught in most universities.

This book does not teach programming or object-oriented design. A vast literature on these subjects is available, which is more suitable for students interested in learning these subjects.

Intended Audience of Part II

Part II "Theory" of this book is written for **graduate students** of computer science and **researchers** who study the subjects of software design,

---

[1]In particular, a more detailed comparison with the UML can be found in Chapter 4.

modelling, maintenance, evolution, specification, verification, and visualization. Written to provide sound means of reasoning about Codechart specifications, this part offers the mathematical foundation of Codecharts. It describes the precise meaning of Codecharts (a formal semantics) and defines formally the relation between specifications and programs. For individuals interested in the underlying mechanisms of reasoning about the design of object-oriented programs, this part demonstrates how intuitions about matters such as the relation between design patterns and Java programs can be formalized and propositions about them are proven. Knowledge of mathematical logic is not required for reading this part, but experience with it is likely to make this part easier to follow.

Codecharts

Propositions

Prologue

Chapter 1

Motivation

Existing means for representing design decisions are deeply flawed. These flaws are at the root of many of the common problems in software development and maintenance. Understanding these essential difficulties will motivate our presentation.

The history of software engineering is often told as the history of monumental failures. The very name of the discipline has been intimately tied with the "software crisis" [Naur & Randell 1969]: a syndrome associated with the abundance of ambitious software development projects which end up as "a monster of missed schedules, blown budgets, and flawed products" [Brooks 1987]. With time, pundits came to describe this on-going state of affairs as "software's chronic crisis" [Gibbs 1994] and even "software hell" [Carr 2004]. Indeed, even laymen have come to accept the fact that software used in daily life suffers from a higher rate of errors that any other commodity.[1] What explanations can be offered for this situation?

In "No Silver Bullet", Frederick Brooks [1987] attributes the difficulties that software development projects face to four inherent properties of their products: *complexity*, *conformity*, *invisibility*, and *changeability*:[2]

1. **Complexity.** By any measure, software systems are the most complex manufactured artefacts ever built by humankind—nuclear power stations, transatlantic jets and space stations notwithstanding. Many software systems are constituted of hundreds and thousands of components, each potentially manufactured by a different organization

---

[1]Indeed, end-user licence agreements for operating systems, word processors, databases, and other common applications commonly specify liability clauses that are more limited than any other form of technology.

[2] What follows is, although in the same spirit, on occasion somewhat of a liberal interpretation of Brooks.

---

or freethinking individual, consisting of computer instructions that measure in the millions of lines of code. The design and maintenance of such systems is therefore *inherently* difficult.

2. **Invisibility**. Software is invisible. What we think of as the programs is text, not matter embedded in space. Being invisible, program flaws are far from obvious and therefore particularly difficult to resolve.

3. **Conformance**. Designing and representing complex programs constitute one problem; enforcing conformance to design decisions is a different (but related) problem. It is of paramount concern because programs are "fragile": The smallest deviation can very often lead to catastrophic results.[3] Manual verification demands intensive manual effort and therefore is largely impractical. We conclude, therefore, that verification *must* be automated as much as possible. The problem of encoding design specifications in a form that can be verified fully automatically is therefore the central concern of this book.

4. **Changeability**. The pressure to change is greater for software than that applied to any other manufactured artefact. According to Lehman's [1996] first law of software evolution ("Continuing Change"), market forces dictate that a program must be continuously adapted or else it becomes progressively less satisfactory. And by the second law of software evolution ("Increasing Complexity"), as a program evolves, its complexity increases unless work is done to maintain it. Hence, maintaining conformance to design decisions throughout the life cycle of a program becomes even more pressing.

These properties of software are intimately interlinked. For example, *changeability* reinforces the need for *conformity*: Each time our program changes (a recurring event), we must ensure yet again that it conforms to its specifications.

Software's chronic crisis and the difficulties that these properties impose over contemporary software development technology have been the subject of intensive research in software engineering, modelling, evolution, visualization, reverse engineering, design recovery, formal methods, verification, and validation. Conferences, journals, books, and research budgets of unprecedented scope are concerned with various aspects of these problems. Evidently, the challenges they pose are far from trivial, and the demands they set are yet to be met. Indeed, the diversity and difficulty of the problems encountered led Brooks to entitle his article "No Silver Bullet": Easy solutions simply do not exist.

What, then, can be done to manage the complexity of software? How can programs be most effectively visualized? How can conformance to design decisions be enforced throughout the life cycle of programs and to the maximum possible extent? We believe that the answer to these questions lies in our choice of the language in which design decisions are encoded. In other words, the key problem is that of abstract representation of programs.

---

[3]To illustrate the chaotic nature of software, DeMillo et al. [1979] have even compared the complexity of software to that of the weather and suggested that butterflies' wings (single bits) can create storms (catastrophic failures).

    To be clear, the language we expect to encode design decisions is different from the language of implementing these decisions (the programming language). Indeed, programming languages deliver the most accurate and detailed specification of the *implementation*. Each programming language commits us to a specific set of abstraction mechanisms and affords us with a very specific range of possible insights to the design of software systems. But programming languages have already received much attention: Structural, object-oriented, functional, and logic languages are the subject of much theoretical analysis, and their use has benefited from years of rigorous analysis and protracted exposure to application. Instead, our interest lies with design description languages. By this term we refer to languages of representing, specifying, reasoning, and thinking *about* programs. There, we believe, lies the solution to many of the problems that plague software systems.

Chapter 2

Design Description Languages

Let us examine some of the vices and virtues of existing modelling and specification languages, thereby introducing some of the key terms in our discussion.

We take **software modelling** to be an activity concerned with representing descriptions of programs at some level (or levels) of abstraction. These descriptions are commonly called **specifications**. Specifications may represent programs, subprograms, libraries, application frameworks, design patterns, or categories of programs at many possible levels of abstraction. Class Diagrams, Interaction Diagrams, Data Flow Diagrams, and Statecharts are some of the most common forms of specification. The languages used for articulating them are commonly referred to as **modelling languages** but occasionally also as **specification languages**.

The division of labour between *modelling* and *specification* languages is not always clear, but specification languages (such as Z, B, CSP, and VDM) tend to be more rigorous and cater to a mathematical taste (in particular *formal specification languages*). Modelling languages such as the Unified Modelling Language (UML) and Data Flow Diagrams, on the other hand, emphasize practical benefits and intuitive appeal over mathematical rigour. Also, specification languages are more commonly used to express functional requirements, namely the behavioural demands set by its end user of the program under specification. We are concerned with nonfunctional specifications. Central to our interest are specification languages for software design, or *design description languages*.

We take a **design description language** to be any modelling or specification language that represents the nonfunctional specifications of software design. These statements may describe programs at any level of abstraction: strategic (or architectural) design, tactical design[1], and implementation minutia. For example, many *architectural description languages* (ADLs) can be used to articulate *architectural styles* [Perry & Wolf 1992; Garlan & Shaw 1993] such as Client-Server and Pipes and Filters. In contrast, *design pattern specification languages* [Taibi 2007] are formal design description languages tailored to represent design patterns.

The primary purpose of a design description language is to provide effective means of representing specifications for a range of purposes, which, broadly speaking, can be explained using either the *roadmaps* or the *blueprints* metaphors:

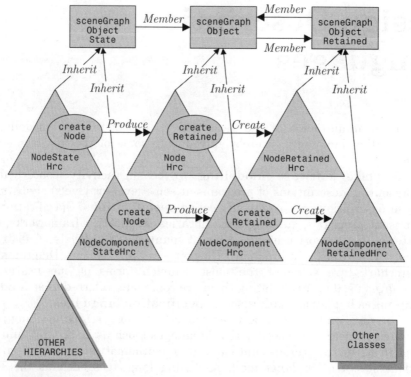

Codechart 1. A roadmap to the Java 3D API

- A **roadmap** to a program represents abstractions ("the design") of a completed implementation. Roadmap-like specifications document the program's structure and organization, representing the properties of various components and how they relate to each other. Roadmaps are useful late in the development process while maintaining, evolving, and attempting to reuse bits of the program. Roadmaps are useful in particular as a means of documenting class libraries offering reusable

[1]See Eden [2005] for a discussion in the distinction between strategic and tactical design.

services because they can help programmers find out how the library can be used and reused to develop new applications. Ideally, roadmaps are reverse engineered from the source code. For example, Codechart 1 demonstrates a roadmap to the Java 3D class library which was reverse engineered from the source code of the library.

- A **blueprint** of a program encodes the design decisions of a program that is yet to be implemented. Blueprint-like specifications may be used early in the development process as a means of recording and communicating design decisions. For example, software designers can use blueprints to convey their design decisions to the implementation team. Alternatively, blueprints can model design patterns or architectural styles, which are design motifs or *categories* of implementations which are characterised by a list of constraints. For example, in Chapter 11 we present Codecharts modelling the Composite and the Factory Method design patterns.

The blueprint and the roadmap are key metaphors in understanding what design description languages are for. A good design description language is one that lends itself to effective representation of software in the senses offered by both the roadmap and blueprint metaphors.

A *specification* in this context is therefore a roadmap or a blueprint articulated in a design description language. Whether they are represented verbally or visually, formally or informally, specifications communicate notions in the design of programs such as design patterns, architectural styles, application frameworks, and specific programs.

Having determined the terms to be used in our discussion, let us analyze some of the principal vices and virtues of existing design description languages.

2.1 THEORY VERSUS PRACTICE

We have only recently come to a realization of the mathematical and logical basis of computer programming: we can now begin to construct program specifications with the same accuracy as an engineer can survey a site for a bridge or road, and on this basis we can now construct programs proved to meet their specification with as much certainty as the engineer assures us his bridge will not fall down. Introduction of these techniques promises to transform the arcane and error-prone craft of computer programming to meet the highest standards of a modern engineering profession.

—C.A.R. Hoare [1983]

According to Robin Milner [1986], the problems related to the design of software systems can only be tackled successfully by combining theoretical investigation with practical experience:

The design of computing systems can only properly succeed if it is well-grounded in theory, and the important concepts in a theory can only emerge through protracted exposure to application.

Christopher Strachey [Malcolm & Goguen 1996] was even more explicit—the very reason why current approaches fail is because either they are impractical or they lack a sound theoretical underpinning:

> *It has long been my personal view that the separation of practical and theoretical work is artificial and injurious. Much of the practical work done in computing, both in software and in hardware design, is unsound and clumsy because the people who do it have not any clear understanding of the fundamental design principles of their work. Most of the abstract mathematical and theoretical work is sterile because it has no point of contact with real computing.*

The requirement that Strachey and Milner have expressed is not surprising. After all, the combination of theoretical insight with usability is the hallmark of every successful engineering discipline. Unfortunately, most existing design description languages are lacking at least one of these aspects.

Formal specification languages (e.g., [Hoare 1978; Milner 1982; Harel 1987; Murata 1989; Spivey 1992; Guttag & Horning 1993; Lamport 1994; Abrial 1996; Börger & Stärk 2003]) are normally based on a relatively well-understood mathematical theory. Specifications in such languages are therefore mathematical expressions. Unfortunately, formal specification languages have largely proven to be sterile. The reasons are, among others, because formal specification languages are largely found to be irrelevant to contemporary software design methodologies (e.g., object-oriented design), programming languages (e.g., Java, C++, C#, Smalltalk), and abstractions (e.g., design patterns). In addition, formal specifications normally consist of complex symbolic expressions, the articulation of which requires the kind of mathematical background which most programmers lack. For these reasons, formal methods are commonly dismissed as sterile and irrelevant.

A range of informal and semiformal modelling notations and languages are employed in industrial software development projects, including Type Diagrams, Data Flow Diagrams, and Flow Charts. Many of the most widely used notations are grouped under the UML [Object Management Group (OMG) 2005], including (what are sometimes colloquially known as) Class Diagrams, Package Diagrams, and Interaction Diagrams. Unfortunately, these notations are not based on a sound mathematical theory. While UML diagrams have intuitive appeal and a very rich vocabulary, they fail to provide an unambiguous account of what precisely is claimed by a diagram in one of these notations. Specifically, they generally lack rigorously defined criteria for satisfying these expressions by programs.[2] It is therefore largely impossible to determine whether a program meets its specification if it is encoded in a UML notation. For example, it is very difficult (or rather, impossible) to determine conclusively from a UML diagram whether the program being modelled satisfies the Factory Method design pattern (§15.2). Since practiced design description languages fail to marry theory and practice successfully, they also fail to determine the relation between specifications and programs unambiguously.

---

[2]This problem has not exactly been kept secret. For example, Martin Fowler [2004], a leading proponent of the UML, admitted that the absence of formal definitions "outside the UML rarefied world of the UML metamodel" is a serious shortcoming. Many others have listed the ambiguity of UML as a serious flaw.

We shall refer to the question concerning the precise relation between specifications and programs as the *verification question* [Wing 1990], summarized in Table 1. This book will provide clear criteria for answering it and sketch the operation of a tool which fully automates this process.

Table 1. The Verification Question

> Does program p *satisfy* specification Ψ ?

In addition, since the precise meaning of symbols is left undefined in most notations, reasoning over specifications is significantly hampered. For example, it is possible to determine whether every program which satisfies the Factory Method design pattern also satisfies the Abstract Factory (p. 208). As an outcome, not only do needless debates on these and similar matters consume much needed energy from practitioners who need them to communicate about software design, but also there is very limited use in principle for modelling tools. Indeed, what use is a specification if its meaning is the subject of so much speculation? In Chapter 18 we will demonstrate how questions about the relations between design patterns can be answered once they are modelled as Codecharts.

Since balancing theory and practice is our primary concern, the remainder of this book is divided into two parts: Part I focuses on the practical aspects of Codecharts whereas Part II focuses on the theory underlying this language.

2.2 DECIDABILITY

In computability theory, *full turing-decidability* (henceforth *decidability*) is an important property of languages.[3] Being concerned with specifications, we use this term in a rather specialized way. Loosely speaking, we say that a specification Ψ is **decidable** if the *verification question* (p. 11) for any program p can be answered by a computer program in a fixed (i.e., finite) number of computation steps (the precise number of which depends on the specification and the program). More precisely, a specification Ψ is *decidable* (also *fully decidable*) if and only if for each program p there is a natural number n such that the question whether p *satisfies* Ψ can be answered by a computer program in at most n steps. A specification language is decidable if all specifications that can be encoded in that language are decidable. The question of decidability is summarized in Table 2.

Table 2. The Decidability Question

> Can the verification question be answered by a program?

By definition, undecidable specifications cannot be verified automatically. Consequently, to ensure that a given implementation meets an undecidable

---

[3]See, for instance, Martin [1991] and Sipser [1997].

specification, in our organization we must hire specialists that attempt to prove their answer, commonly provided in what is referred to as *proofs of correctness*. For example, for some safety-critical applications such as those involved with the operation of space shuttles and medical equipment, a small army of mathematicians are hired to provide mathematical proofs that critical parts of the application satisfy their functional requirements. Such activities however are extremely expensive, time consuming, and fallible and can only apply under highly restrictive conditions. Correctness proofs can therefore only be afforded for minuscule segments of industrial software systems. Instead, most software manufacturers design extensive testing suits. Naturally, these do *not* guarantee a definite answer but at least provide a measurable amount of confidence in the "correctness" of a program. Others simply release unreliable, unstable, and largely unverified software.

Unfortunately, some of the most important functional requirements are undecidable. For example, specifications which require that a program does not "crash" or that it does not enter an infinite loop are, in the general case, undecidable. Consequently, most modelling and specification languages are undecidable. And if the relation between a specification and a program cannot be precisely established (which is not always the case for all design description languages), the *verification question* cannot be answered in principle, let alone established by a computer program. This is true for formal languages such as Z and VDM and for semiformal modelling languages such as Class Diagrams, Interaction Diagrams, and OCR.

Decidability is particularly important because of the problem of software *changeability*. During the evolution phases, as well as throughout their life cycle, programs mutate to some degree. Each change, no matter how slight, can potentially break the specifications carefully laid out by the designers. Consequently, verification needs to be conducted repeatedly throughout the life cycle of programs: for each release, each version, and each bug-fix and carried out as early during development as possible. Therefore, unless verification is automated, it is very difficult to enforce conformance to design specification. And, indeed, since most specifications are encoded in undecidable languages, in practice, design decisions are not adhered to. Consequently, the problems of insensitivity to the architectural specifications (*architectural drift*) and the problem of increasing departure from the intended design (*architectural erosion*) [Perry & Wolf 1992] have been observed to be most common.

We believe that many of the problems of software development technology can be attributed to the undecidability of their specifications, if any are at all encoded. Indeed, in the absence of automated verification, enforcing conformance is too expensive. In effect, specifications rarely serve as reliable *roadmaps* of the program. This also explains why reusing, evolving, and maintaining large programs have become extremely difficult.

2.3 ABSTRACTION

Without abstraction and idealization there is no systematization.

— John Searle

Today's software systems are the largest, most complex artefacts ever built by humankind, often compared to bridges and buildings. Kazman and Chen [2009] observe that many software systems are even more complex than ordinary cities, thereby comparing them to metropolises. The construction process of a metropolis is almost always undertaken while the remainder of the metropolis must continue to function as normal. It is therefore a prolonged, on-going, ad hoc, collaborative process that is rarely entirely planned and managed centrally, aims to reconcile conflicting and unfixed requirements, and leads to a constantly evolving product, many of whose dynamics emerge rather than being designed. In the construction of a metropolis, roadmaps serve as abstractions that reflect the general organization of the "implemented" parts of the metropolis, whereas blueprints lay out the plans for the parts that are under construction. Can a metropolis be built without blueprints? Can it evolve without current and correct roadmaps? Of course not, yet these are the conditions in which most programmers work. It is no wonder that the software systems we build are more dysfunctional and unreliable than any other engineered artefact. We programmers create our programs like an artist drawing one pixel at a time, and our programs are fragile as a consequence [Yudkowsky 2002]. Clearly, our tools and methodologies are inadequate to the task. We lack appropriate mechanisms of abstractions: a design description language that allows us to see what is essential to the representation without being distracted by everything else.

Abstraction is the cornerstone of computer science. It underlies the investigation in automata, programming languages, compilers, and software design. But abstraction does not underlie only the mathematical theories of computation. In practice, developing a functioning program is most often a matter of representing and applying abstractions of various levels. For example, operating systems abstract and hide much of the complexity of the set of physical resources available for common applications. In another example, high-level (compiled) programming languages provide a layer of abstraction over the complex sets of memory and computation resources that computing machines provide. Finally, the success of object-oriented programming can largely be attributed to the abstraction mechanisms they provide. Indeed, *encapsulation*, *inheritance*, and *dynamic binding* are the abstraction mechanisms that so far have provided the most effective means of representing and implementing software systems.

Table 3.   The Scaling Question

> How many levels of abstraction do specifications allow? May we use arbitrarily few symbols to model a program?

Scalability is the requirement from a language for representations modelling not only small but increasingly larger objects. Table 3 asks the basic scaling questions. A *scalable* design description language can represent not only toy programs but industry-scale software systems consisting of millions of lines of code. *Scalability* permits the language to model increasingly larger programs without modelling each and every element of the program. More precisely, a language *scales* to the extent that it can specify arbitrarily large programs using as few symbols as we wish. When modelling programs of such a large scale, the number of individual classes and methods can reach thousands. Diagrams using this many symbols have very little value. Consider, for example, the attempts to model large collections of classes depicted in Figures 2-1 through 2-3.

These examples illustrate the scaling problem arising from modelling large domains in terms of individual classes. Clearly, any attempt to model industry-scale applications and class libraries without using adequate abstraction mechanisms violates the Feynman–Tufte Principle (Table 7, p. 30). This, of course, applies not only to class diagrams but to *any* design description language, including LePUS3[4]. Scalability is therefore a paramount concern.

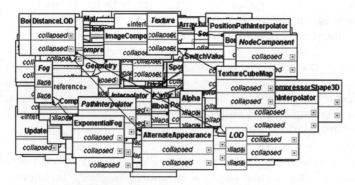

Figure 2-1. UML class diagram of Java3D 1.5 API generated using Fujaba Tool Suite 5 by reverse engineering the source code. Only very few of the classes in the library (the number of which exceeds a thousand) are discernible [Maniati 2008]

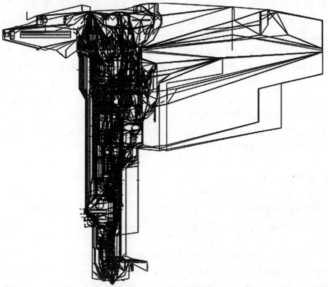

Figure 2-2. UML class diagram of Java3D 1.5 API generated using NetBeans 6.1 by reverse engineering the source code. The size of the diagram requires pixel scaling to an extent which renders the diagram unusable [Maniati 2008]

[4]As demonstrated by Codechart 67 (p. 108), which depicts the outcome of an attempt to model Java 3D in terms of the library's individual elements.

Figure 2-3. Class diagram of package `java.util` generated using Borland JBuilder 2005 Enterprise Edition by reverse engineering the source code. Even a class diagram modelling merely a few dozens of classes is too large to be practical [Gasparis 2009]

A possible technique for achieving scalability is to add to our language a symbol for each of your favourite modular units: packages, libraries, namespaces, subsystems, subprograms, processes, components, connectors, ports, and so forth. Each one of these is indeed an abstraction mechanism, but a very specific one. For example, visual tokens dedicated to modelling each one of these modular units exist in the UML, where any additional symbols can be incorporated using the "stereotype" mechanism. But bloated glossaries and lack of a formal semantics are not the worst consequences of such an approach. The examples depicted in Figures 2-1 through 2-3 demonstrate why specific abstraction mechanisms restricted to physical modular units such as packages and libraries are inadequate. The reason is because committing a notation to a set of symbols of any specific implementation artefact limits it to the level of abstraction of those artefacts. Is it sufficient to represent software systems at the highest level of abstraction (in terms of packages, subsystems, subprograms, etc.), and at the lowest level of abstraction (i.e., using the finest-grained symbols) in terms of millions of classes? The equivalent in cartography is to commit ourselves to the glossaries of maps at the 1:5000 scale alone. Such a commitment prevents the notation from being effective in modelling at other levels of abstraction.

In contrast to such notations, Codecharts offer the abstraction mechanisms that are required for modelling significant proportions of large programs. These abstraction mechanisms are demonstrated in Codechart 1 (p. 8), which models the same class library as attempted by Figures 2-1 and 2-2.

These advantages translate into more effective tool support for program visualization, amongst others. Consider, for example, Figure 2-4, which depicts a Codechart reverse engineered from the JGraph class library. Here, the visualization tool has been far more successful in reverse engineering an intelligible roadmap than the figures presented previously in this chapter. That success can first and foremost be attributed to the abstraction mechanisms that Codecharts provide.

In contrast with other notations, Codecharts take a more flexible approach which employs the notion of finite sets without being restricted to *any* particular number of entities therein and correlations between such sets. These sets include inheritance hierarchies consisting of any finite number of classes, finite sets of dynamically bound methods.

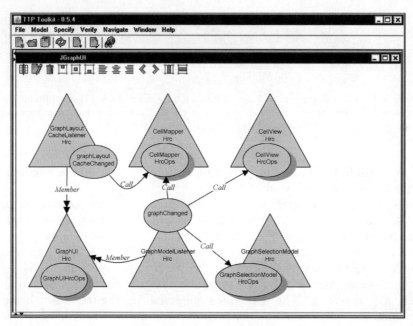

Figure 2-4. A Codechart offering a roadmap to the user interface classes in the JGraph class library, generated using the Design Navigator tool in the Two-Tier Programming Toolkit (§3.2) by reverse engineering in the source code

The next question is therefore: Which elements of object-oriented programs should be taken to be the minimal set of building blocks that provides us with adequate abstract mechanisms for our purposes? Since the set of elementary building blocks constitute the conceptual building blocks in the representation of the programs we shall refer to it as the ontological question, summarized in Table 4.

Table 4. The Ontological Question

> Which set of primitive building blocks of software design—and which combinations thereof—may be articulated in the design description language?

In Chapter 3 we describe exactly how the ontological question (p. 15) and the scalability question (p. 13) are answered by LePUS3, the language of Codecharts.

2.4 ELEGANCE

Beauty is in the eye of the beholder and what is pleasing is subjective. But elegance is not purely a matter of taste. Spelling out some the maladies that afflict software design, Tony Hoare [1975] has introduced the subject of *elegance* as follows:

We need a puritanical rejection of the temptations of features and facilities, and a passionate devotion to the principles of purity, simplicity and elegance.

Bertrand Meyer [1997] has famously mocked the inelegance of the Unified Modeling Language:

> *UML is in fact as complex as a big and cryptic programming language, with generous use of "$" and "#" and "·" and "*" and "solid triangles with no tail" and rectangles and diamonds and solid lines and dotted lines and solid ellipses and dotted ellipses and arrows of all kinds and keywords such as "const" and "sorted" (not to be confused with "ordered") and different semantics for a class depending on whether its name appears in roman or italics.*

However program specifications are represented, elegance depends on whether the appearance of the specification offers the (visual) cues that roadmaps and blueprints for programs are supposed to provide. Programmers often refer to the lack of such an intuitive link and to the problems of bloated glossaries as the Keyboard Safari Syndrome.

Let us illustrate this criticism using the roadmap metaphor: Roadmaps are useful because the set of symbols they use lends itself naturally to the kind of reasoning that drivers perform. When planning the trip from London to Liverpool, a driver rarely needs to consult with the roadmap's glossary because its visual appearance is intuitive: Thin lines stand for narrow roads, thick lines stand for motorways, petrol pumps stand for petrol stations, and so on. Can the same be said about specifications in common notations? Meyer begs to differ.

Specifications in design description languages are also subject to the demand for elegance: Ideally, program "roadmaps" should lend themselves naturally to the kind of reasoning that serves the majority of programmers and software designers.

A broad range of software modelling dialects and notations were aggregated under the umbrella of the Unified Modeling Language. Unfortunately, many of those who attempted to use, formalize, and provide tool support for any combination of these notations concluded that the diversity of its symbols is to its detriment. Not only that, but one needs to become an expert in the notation's Byzantine glossary, as Bertrand Meyer suggests. But there is hardly any sense in which diagrams offer at a glance a faithful picture that adequately visualizes the overall composition of the program. As a result, UML is rarely used as a language for program visualization. Table 5 summarises the core questions of elegance.

Table 5.   The Elegance Question

How many symbols are employed by the language? To what extent do these symbols reflect the nature of that which they represent?

Chapter 3

An Overview of Codecharts

The vices and virtues of existing modelling and specification languages examined in Chapter 1 motivate our choice of the underlying principles of LePUS3, the language of Codecharts, as follows:

1. Object-orientation
2. Visualization
3. Rigour
4. Automated verifiability
5. Scalability
6. Genericity
7. Minimality
8. Information neglect

Let us examine each one of these principles and illustrate how each manifests itself in Codecharts.

3.1 OBJECT-ORIENTATION

LePUS3 is an object-oriented design description language: It is a language of statements about the design of programs encoded in object-oriented programming languages called Codecharts. More specifically, we may divide the subjects of LePUS3 specifications into three broad categories:

1. **Programs and Class Libraries**. Codecharts can serve as roadmaps for existing implementations and blueprints for hypothetical ones encoded in various class-based programming languages. Verification proceeds by indicating the meaning of the terms in the symbols (e.g., what CollectionsHrc stands for).

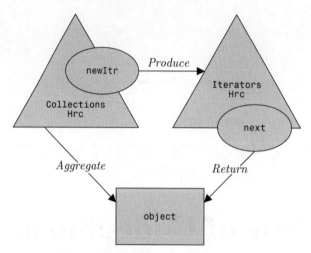

Codechart 2.   Collections and their iterators in `java.util` (Chapter 7)

2. **Design Motifs**. Codecharts were tailored to articulate object-oriented design patterns, in particular the Gang of Four design patterns (Chapter 11). Verification normally proceeds by indicating which parts of the program are intended to serve as the implementation of the pattern (e.g., which classes implement the *Iterators*).

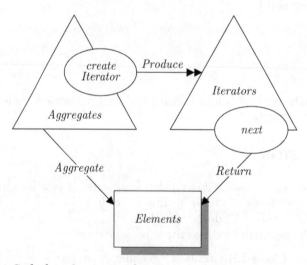

Codechart 3.   Iterator design pattern (§ 11.2)

3. **Application Frameworks**. The combination of constants (`testCase`, `setUp`) and variables (*userTest*, *FixtureClasses*) captures the interactions between the prefabricated (existing) and the user-defined (yet-to-be-implemented) elements in specifications of application frameworks. Verification normally proceeds by indicating how each variable is assigned its intended implementation.

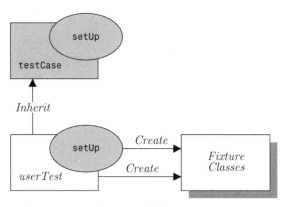

Codechart 4. Elements of JUnit

Presently, object-oriented languages are the most popular programming languages in academia and industry. But this is not the only reason for focusing on the object-oriented programming paradigm in this book. More importantly, the abstraction mechanisms underlying this programming paradigm offer the most effective means for constructing large, complex, and versatile software systems.[1] In other words, the tools that such languages provide offer the most promising instruments for addressing the problem of software complexity.

Let us consider abstraction mechanisms underlying the object-oriented paradigm and see how exactly they relate to LePUS3:[2]

(i) *Encapsulation* (also *modularity*) allows data and related operations to be divided into *classes*. Each class is a unit associated with a set of operations, referred to as *methods*. Classes and methods are therefore our primitive (or atomic) entities. In other words, Codecharts abstract programs in terms of classes, methods, and their properties as the elementary units in the representation.

(ii) *Inheritance* is a powerful abstraction mechanism which allows a class (the *subclass*) to be defined incrementally by importing data and operations from another (the *superclass*). Inheritance is also a mechanism of subtyping: Operations defined for a class are also defined for classes that inherit therefrom. Inheritance in LePUS3 has a special status, as a special symbol is reserved for sets of classes that constitute *inheritance class hierarchies* (§7.6).

(iii) *Dynamic binding* is a mechanism which allows the selection of the appropriate method to be called at runtime. In Codecharts, a special status is reserved to sets of methods that share the same *signature* (name and argument types) throughout an inheritance hierarchy, to which we refer as *clans* (§7.3).

---

[1]The numerous merits of object-oriented programming have been discussed extensively in the literature; see, for example, Wirfs-Brock et al. [1990].

[2] What follows are not definitions. We recommend Wirfs-Brock et al. [1990] and Craig [2000] as sources of detailed information about these terms.

These abstraction mechanisms motivate our answer to the *ontological question* (p. 15). In Table 6 we list the *building blocks of object-oriented design*, that is the rudimentary elements with which our descriptions are concerned and the means by which they are represented. Restricting ourselves to the list in Table 6 means that the only statements that can be represented using Codecharts are those that describe "things" made of one of the four categories of these specific building blocks. The advantages of restricting ourselves this way is the prospect of an *elegant* design description language (p. 17) that is committed to a *minimal ontology* (p. 15). The disadvantage is that Codecharts are not as expressive. In particular, our language cannot effectively model architectural styles or the design of programs encoded in other programming paradigms, such as functional, logic, and procedural programs.[3]

Table 6. Building-Blocks of Object-Oriented Design

- **Classes and methods** are the primitive, atomic entities of our representation. For example, the constant `testCase` in Codechart 4 (p. 21) stands for a class, whereas the superimposition of `setUp` over `testCase` stands for a method.

- **Relations** between entities are also represented. For example, the edge marked *Inherit* in Codechart 4 represents the inheritance (in Java: `extends`) relation between *userTest* and `testCase`.

- **Sets of classes/methods** are called higher dimensional classes/methods. For example, the variable *Elements* in Codechart 3 (p. 20) stands for a class of dimension *1* (a set of classes). Particular attention is given to sets of classes that constitute inheritance hierarchies. For example, the constant `CollectionsHrc` in Codechart 2 stands for the set of Java's collection classes. Also, sets of dynamically bound methods (*clans*) are also represented. For example, the set of methods with the signature `next()` that are defined in classes of the `IteratorsHrc` is represented in Codechart 2 by superimposing the signature constant (`next`) over the hierarchy constant (`IteratorsHrc`).

- **Correlations between sets** of classes/methods associate entities between the two sets. For example, the edge marked *Aggregate* in Codechart 2 specifies that every concrete class in the Collections hierarchy has an aggregate of type `Object`.

Finally, let us note that the term "object-oriented" has many different interpretations in the literature. These vary largely by the interpretation given in each programming language. Craig [2000] divides object-oriented programming languages into prototype-based and class-based languages. We

---

[3]Note that the programming language is not the only factor: One may write procedural programs in an object-oriented programming language such as Java. The design of such a program will not be amenable to representation in LePUS3.

shall focus our attention on the class-based languages: the bigger and more popular category of programming languages that includes Simula 67, Smalltalk (in its various versions), C++, Object Pascal, Beta, Java, Ada 95, CLOS, and C#. Nonetheless, since the term "object-oriented" is more widely recognized than the term "class-based", we shall employ the former even in contexts when the latter is more precise.

3.2 VISUALIZATION

The language of Codecharts, LePUS3, is a visual language for the same reasons that roadmaps and blueprints are visual: because visual cues offer effective representations of very complex objects and their relations. Like the languages of roadmaps and blueprints, the principle of visualization dictates that visual tokens (such as shapes and edges) and their visual properties (such as fill and shade) effectively capture and convey the subject of representation—in our case, modular units and their correlations. When used correctly, Codecharts are effective visualizations that allow us to "see" programs in any appropriate level of abstraction.

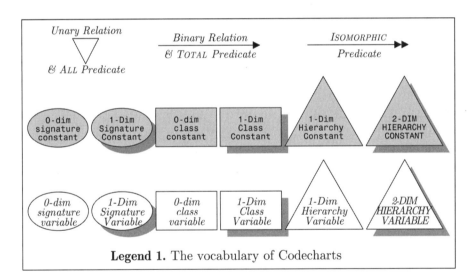

Legend 1. The vocabulary of Codecharts

There are many advantages to visual languages: First, diagrams are more intuitive than most formulas. Therefore, using it does not require special mathematical training. Furthermore, since specifications are Codecharts, they can also be used for the purpose of *program visualization*. That is, diagrams generated by reverse engineering the source code depict the program in various levels of abstraction.

For example, the Design Navigator [Gasparis 2009], which is part of the Two-Tier Programming Toolkit [ttp.essex.ac.uk], can generate visualizations of Java programs by analyzing their source code. Program visualization reverse engineering source code can significantly promote the understanding of the structure and organization of arbitrarily large programs. The tool can be used to unfold the organization of large collections of classes and methods in a gradual process of *concretization* [Gasparis et al. 2008], a step wise, user-guided process of refining each visualization—or any part thereof—using an effective tool such as the Design Navigator. Let us demonstrate the effectiveness of such a process with a specific example.[4]

The Closeable hierarchy in package `java.io` consists of all the classes and interfaces that inherit (possibly indirectly) from the interface `Closeable`. The Design Navigator can visualize the entire hierarchy using one symbol, a *hierarchy constant*, as demonstrated in Figure 3-1. The Codechart in this screenshot demonstrates the power of effective abstraction, hiding the richness of an entire hierarchy, and the notion of *scalability* that our design description language supports.

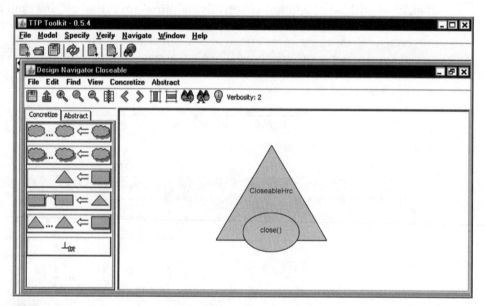

Figure 3-1.   Screenshot of the TTP Toolkit visualizing an abstraction of the Closeable hierarchy in package `java.io`

The Codechart in Figure 3-1 is only useful as a first abstraction. The Design Navigator may be used to *concretize* the `CloseableHrc`, a process which replaces any abstraction—essentially, any visual depiction of a set—with a finer grained and more detailed representation. For example, to reveal the organization of the classes that comprise this class hierarchy, the user clicks on the `CloseableHrc` symbol and then clicks on a *concretization operator*, the list of which appears on the left panel in Figure 3-1. The outcome of this process is demonstrated in Figure 3-2.

---

[4]Steps in this sequence were omitted from this description and the layout of the symbols in the figures have been adapted to this demonstration.

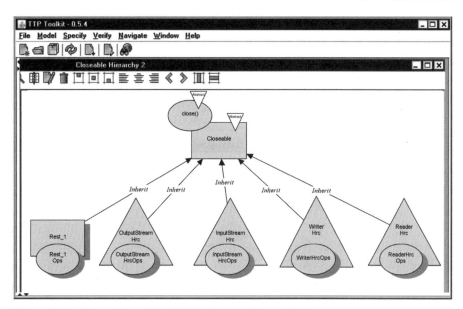

Figure 3-2. Screenshot of the TTP Toolkit visualizing a slightly more concrete representation of the Closeable hierarchy

The complexity of the Closeable class hierarchy further unfolds as we concretize the Codechart, demonstrating that the Design Navigator is indispensible in creating such representations. For example, after a number of "concretization" steps, the Design Navigator will break down each one of the hierarchies depicted in Figure 3-2 to several sets of classes and sub hierarchies, as illustrated in Figure 3-3.

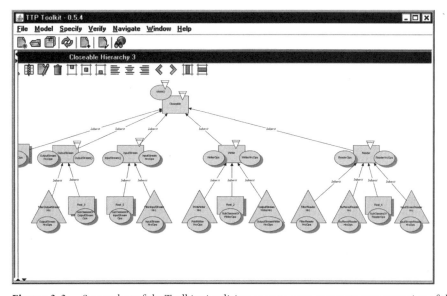

Figure 3-3. Screenshot of the Toolkit visualizing an even more concrete representation of the Closeable hierarchy

Rather than concretizing entire Codecharts, concretization can visualize the details of any part thereof. For example, Figure 3-4 depicts a Codechart produced by concretizing only the `OutputStreamHrc` hierarchy in Figure 3-3. The resulting Codechart details some of the subclasses of `OutputStream` and their methods. At this level, individual methods, classes, and relations become clearly visible.

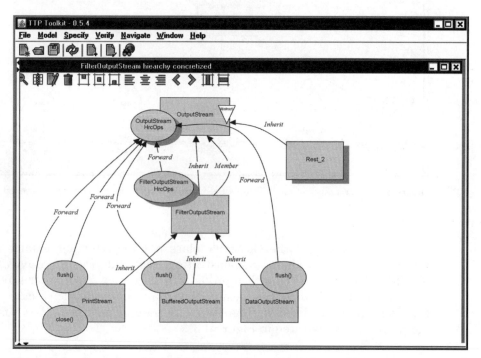

Figure 3-4.   Screenshot of the TTP Toolkit visualizing the subclasses of `OutputStream` in the Closeable hierarchy

3.3   RIGOUR

In §2.1 we emphasized the need to reconcile practical with theoretical demands. The first requirement from a sound scientific theory is mathematical rigour. But our theoretical demands are dictated by pragmatic concerns: Rigour prevents us from "unsound and clumsy" practical work done in computing (p. 9). Formalizing Codecharts equipped us with many insights into the properties of such formal languages, in particular, *decidability* (§2.2). Rigour affords clarity and confidence in reasoning at levels that otherwise cannot be achieved. Only precise definitions can ensure that designers and programmers indeed share the same understanding of specifications. Such confidence is essential for effective tool support in specification and verification. Indeed, the *verification question* (p. 11) demands that we define precisely the relation between specifications and programs.

Which mathematical framework offers us the most appropriate tools for unpacking our language? Robin Milner [1986] motivates mathematical logic as follows:

Almost everyone who builds computing systems is convinced that all systems design—software or hardware—needs to be done within a rich conceptual frame, which is articulated by rigorous methodologies. ... The conceptual frame provided just by programming languages is too narrow; a wider frame is needed in which to understand the specifications of systems and the methodology which articulates this understanding must be based on some form of logic.

For these reasons we choose to employ mathematical logic in defining LePUS3 as a formal specification language. Below we briefly recap elements in the formalization of LePUS3. A detailed and systematic presentation of LePUS3 as a formal language is given in Part II of this book.

A Codechart is a specification in LePUS3, which consists of a set of *formulas* that can be unpacked as *well-formed formulas* in the first-order predicate logic (FOPL). As a first-order language, symbols in the vocabulary of LePUS3 (Legend 1, p. 23) can be categorized by the conventional elements of formal grammars as follows:

- A *formula* (such as *Inherit*(*userTest*, testCase) in Codechart 4) is a combination of a *relation symbol* (such as *Inherit*) with one or more *terms* and occasionally also with a *predicate symbol*.
- *Terms* (constants and variables) stand for entities, such that:
  - (a) *0-dimensional terms* (such as *userTest* and testCase in Codechart 4) stand for individual entities, whereas
  - (b) *1-dimensional terms* (such as *Elements* and *Iterators* in Codechart 3) stand for sets of entities
- *Variables* (*userTest* and *Elements*) range over classes and methods whereas *constants* (testCase, setUp) stand for specific program entities.

An intuitive introduction to these symbols is given throughout Part I of this book. Although precise definitions are offered in the opening of each section, an informal tone is kept throughout this part. Part II offers a more rigorous approach to specifications, whereas formal definitions are summarized in Appendix II. More specifically, Part II offers a formal semantics for Codecharts, defined as finite structures in model theory. A decidable *abstract semantics function* maps every "program" (which is taken to be defined as an expression in the programming language) into a *finite structure* (Chapter 14). These can be enriched with higher order (namely sets of) classes and methods to become *design models*, which are axiomatized in the first-order logic.

In Part II of this book we also define precisely the relation between (the decidable, non-functional, LePUS3) specifications and programs. In particular, we can resolve conclusively the question of whether a particular program indeed constitutes an implementation of a specific design pattern as formalized in our design description language. We also show that automated verifiability affords us to delegate the responsibility for resolving such questions to a fully automated process. For example, in Proposition 3 (p. 186) we prove that package java.util *implements* the Iterator pattern, and in Proposition 4 (p. 186) we prove that package java.awt *implements* the Composite pattern; both of which can be automated using the Two-Tier Programming Toolkit (see next section).

Rigour also allows us to carry out some reasoning on Codecharts at a level of confidence that otherwise cannot be achieved. For example, in Part II we prove that any visual token can be safely removed from a chart without invalidating it (the principle of *information neglect*). We also prove a number of propositions concerning the relationships between design patterns. For example, in Proposition 5 (p. 203) we prove that the Iterator pattern is a "special case" of the Factory Method pattern (Iterator ⊨ FactoryMethod).

3.4 AUTOMATED VERIFIABILITY

Rigour enables us to use a mathematical theory to understand the properties of LePUS3, including the property of *decidability* (p. 11). Unlike most design description languages, LePUS3 is fully *turing decidable*. By this we mean that, at least in principle, the *verification question* (p. 11) can be resolved fully automatically. Loosely speaking, this notion implies that given a LePUS3 specification (a Codechart) S and a program p we can determine the maximal (computation) time and space resources which require a computer program to compute the answer to the question whether p *satisfies* S. In fact, not only can this be done in principle, but also it is easy to show that it can be done in a relatively short time.[5]

To answer the *verification question* (p. 11), we must establish formally the relation between specifications and programs. The relation between Codecharts and Java programs is formally established in Part II of this book. Specifically, in Chapter 9 we define a set of *truth conditions* under which a specification is *satisfied*: Each formula imposes a set of Tarski-like truth conditions on design models. A specification S is *satisfied* by program p if and only if a *design model* 𝔐 can be constructed such that 𝔐 is an appropriate representation of p and 𝔐 *satisfies* (the truth conditions in) S.

Having established these conditions, we can turn to the question of whether automated design verification is possible *in practice*. The Two-Tier Programming Project at the University of Essex has been concerned with investigating the feasibility of a tool implementing the verification algorithm. Our research has shown that, with a design model, the complexity of the verification algorithm is at most squared in the number of entities in the interpretation of the constants in a closed specification. In an open specification, the complexity is at most squared in the number of entities in the range of the assignment provided. Furthermore, we have implemented the verification algorithm in version 0.5.1 of the Two-Tier Programming Toolkit [http://ttp.essex.ac.uk/], which we shall simply refer to as the Toolkit (see §15.4). For example, at a click of a button, the Toolkit can establish whether a given Java 1.4 program *implements* the Composite design pattern. Verification of design pattern implementations typically requires less than a second to produce a definitive answer, as demonstrated in Figure 3-5.

---

[5]That is, in computational complexity that is squared in the size of the relations in the design model.

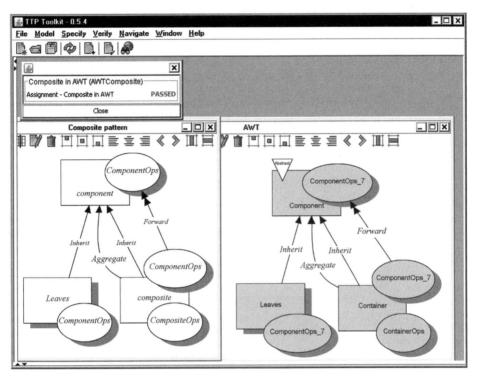

Figure 3-5.   Screenshot of the TTP Toolkit showing the results of verifying that package `java.awt` *implements* the Composite pattern (§15.3)

If violated, the Toolkit indicates which parts of the specification have been violated, thereby enabling the programmer to restore the consistency between design and implementation. In §15.4 we expand on this facility.

As a consequence of our commitment to automated verifiability (more precisely, to *decidability*), Codecharts cannot always be used in the same way as other design description languages. For example, the statement which requires that a certain event (creating an instance of class *a*) shall precede another (creating an instance of class *b*) under all possible executions, which can be articulated in modelling languages such as UML and formal specification languages such as Z, is undecidable and cannot be represented using a Codechart. Indeed, as a consequence of the decidability requirement, LePUS3 is unsuitable for representing a range of specifications concerning the behaviour of programs. In exchange for giving up such statements, Codecharts can be verified automatically. Have we made a wise choice?

To answer this question, let us return to our analysis of the inherent properties of contemporary software technology (Chapter 1). *Conformity* relates to the difficulty that arises from our inability to enforce specifications. Programs do not conform to our expectations at the most basic level because there are no effective tools that can help us enforce them. Undecidable modelling languages have so far crippled development and CASE tool manufacturers because, even if the meaning of specifications is well established, there can be no effective means for enforcing them.

And even when conformance is established for yesterday's software by whatever means (e.g., using testing and program inspection), *changeability* dictates that today's software may not conform to our specifications. Software is in a continuous state of flux. Inconsistencies between design and implementation must be detected early in the development process and repeatedly sought for throughout each and every stage of evolution. Such inconsistencies must be resolved by either fixing the implementation or changing the specifications. Unless the process is fully automated, problems such as *architectural erosion* and *architectural drift* are bound to arise.

Finally, automated verification is the ultimate tool for managing complexity. Only a continuous, repeated process of detecting and resolving inconsistencies between design and implementation can ensure that specifications are current and correct, thereby providing the kind of roadmaps for programs which are absolutely essential for managing the complexity of software systems of industrial scale.

3.5   SCALABILITY

A crucial trait of design description languages is their capacity for *abstraction* (p. 12), in particular their *scalability*, which we discussed extensively in Chapter 2 (see in particular p. 13). To ensure scalability we subscribe to the Feynman–Tufte Principle given in Table 7. Economy of expression is therefore a leading concern. By this criterion, a design description language is measured by its ability to represent "a lot of information" about a program compactly using as few symbols as possible.

Table 7.   Feynman–Tufte Principle

A visual display of data should be simple enough to fit on the side of a van.

Source: Shermer [2005].

In Codecharts we take scalability to require our design description language to allow effective representation of arbitrarily large systems with as few symbols as we choose. As we show in detail in §3.2, scalability is particularly useful in software visualization: Not unlike roadmaps, visual specifications generated by program visualization tools must be of any *scale*.

Scalability of a design description language is achieved, amongst others, by using abstractions that capture commonly recurring regularities in software design. For example, in Codecharts, the *ISOMORPHIC* predicate is particularly useful for conveying an abstract visualization of the one-to-one correlations between sets of methods. Consider, for instance, the use of this abstraction in modelling 23 of the methods[6] in class `java.awt.Container`, each of which forwards the method's arguments to a method with the same

---

[6]There are many more methods in classes `Container` and `Component` which match this description but only 23 of them fit here.

signature in class `java.awt.Component`. The *ISOMORPHIC* predicate symbol in Codechart 5a (a double-headed arrow) captures the regularity between each pair of methods with matching signatures concisely and precisely.

Scale in Codechart 5b is achieved using abstractions such as sets (shaded shapes) and the *ISOMORPHIC* predicate symbol (double-headed arrow). Specifically, the two sets of methods are represented by superimposing a representation of the set of their common signatures (`ContainerOps`) over a representation of the two classes (`java.awt.container` and `java.awt.component`). The 1 : 1 correlation between methods in both sets is specified by the *ISOMORPHIC* predicate symbol.

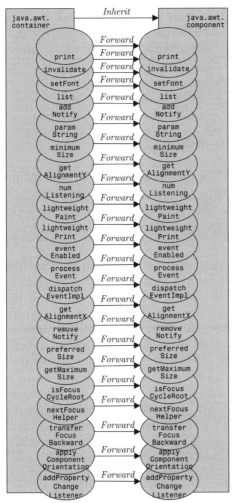

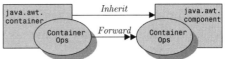

Codechart 5a. Each of the 23 individual methods in `Container` forwards the call to the method it overrides in `Component`

Codechart 5b. Each method in a set of methods in class `Container` forwards the call to the method it overrides in `Component`

3.6 GENERICITY

Genericity is a principle most commonly associated with the abstraction of type information in programming languages like Java and C++. But genericity also plays a very important role at the specification level. We consider the principle of genericity to be that principle which dictates the distinction between the representation of concrete programs and abstract ideas. It dictates an explicit distinction between constants and variables. This distinction has two uses: abstraction for early design and the distinction between specific programs and design motifs. Below we demonstrate these uses, whereas Chapter 9 is dedicated to explaining the genericity mechanisms in the language of Codecharts.

Premature commitment to implementation minutia is one of the costliest mistakes of inexperienced software designers. As a language for representing blueprints of programs, a design description language must therefore allow us to represent only the constraints we wish to impose on the intended implementation without committing us any more detail than absolutely necessary. This requirement is referred to as the principle of abstraction in early design (Table 8).

Table 8.   Principle of Abstraction in Early Design

A design description language should focus on specifying constraints, not implementation detail. It must offer the software designer the means to refrain from making premature commitments to implementations during the early design stages (the blueprint metaphor).

Some of the instruments required for representing the abstractions needed during early design, such as *higher-order terms* and *predicates*, have already been presented under the principle of *scalability* (§3.5). In addition, Codecharts may employ *variables* for describing nonspecific entities in the implementation. For example, in combination with the signature constant push, the variable *some* in Codechart 6 specifies that a class inheriting from Stack will eventually be implemented such that (a) it will contain a method that overrides Stack.push(), and (b) this method will contain a return statement with an expression of type Stack (or subtypes thereof). Note, however, that Codechart 6 does *not* commit us to any additional implementation detail: We are free to choose the name of that class, the number of levels of inheritance that separate it from class Stack, the number of fields and methods it implements in any way we see fit, and even the precise type of the return expression it contains (as long as it is a subtype of Stack).

Another shortcoming of informal modelling notations is their lack of clear distinction between specific implementations and abstractions, such as design motifs.[7] In the absence of *variables*, modellers resort to specific examples. Why exactly are such specifications inadequate?

---

[7]Which is not surprising given that most notations were tailored for the purpose of modelling specific programs.

In a nutshell, the level of abstraction that variables afford is indispensible if a line is to be drawn between a category of implementations—a design motif (such as a design pattern)—and programs. Consider, for example, the difference between the constant **testCase** in Codechart 4, which stands for a specific Java class called `TestCase`, and the variable *userTest*, which stands for some implementation chosen by the programmer that uses the JUnit application framework. *userTest* has no specific interpretation: Mapping it to class `MyUserTest` therefore constitutes the claim that class `MyUserTest` indeed satisfies the requirements that JUnit imposes on its clients. The introduction of variables therefore allows us to articulate specifications that are not tied in to a particular implementation.

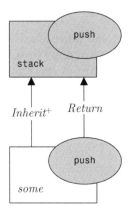

Codechart 6. Method Stack.push will be overridden by a method that returns an instance of Stack

The failure to distinguish abstractions from implementations is also a hindrance during early design stages, because it forces software developers to make premature commitments to implementation detail. Consider, for example, how to capture the design decision that "method `Stack.push()` will be overridden by a method that returns an instance of `Stack`" without prematurely committing to details such as which class defines the overriding method, how many levels of inheritance separate it from `Stack`, and what is the actual return type of the method `push`. Codechart 6 demonstrates how variables in our language provide the abstraction mechanism by which this statement is precisely captured without making neither one of these unnecessary commitments (see Chapter 12: Modelling early design revisited).

3.7 MINIMALITY

We seek to accommodate Tony Hoare's [1975] notion of *elegance* (p. 17) and thus have made every effort to reject of "the temptations of features and facilities", and adopt "a passionate devotion to the principles of purity, simplicity and elegance". In this spirit, the number of symbols in our design description language must be kept to a minimum, so long as it can be used to capture and convey the *building blocks of object-oriented design* (described on p. 22):

- *Individual classes* and methods are represented using *0*-dimensional terms.
- *Sets of entities* are represented using *1*-dimensional (shaded) terms.
- *Relations between entities* are represented using arrow-headed edges.
- *Correlations between sets* of entities are also represented using edges.

Consequently, the vocabulary of Codecharts consists of only 15 visual tokens, depicted in Legend 1 (p. 23).

3.8   INFORMATION NEGLECT

To be rigorously defined, a design description language must specify not only what each symbol represents but also what exactly the *absence* of information means. But while this issue may first appear insignificant, it can be the source of considerable ambiguity. Let us demonstrate this point with an example.

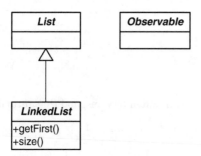

Figure 3-6.   A UML class diagram (Glossary: see p. 233)

Consider, for example, the class diagram in Figure 3-6: Does class Linked List inherit from Observable? Does LinkedList define more than two methods? Does a program which contains more than the three classes modelled in Figure 3-6 *satisfy* it? In which one of these cases does the absence of a representation stand for negative information, and in which does it not?

Since the language of class diagrams is not well defined, none of these questions have definite answers. Clearly, in some cases the absence of a symbol implies negative information (e.g., LinkedList does *not* inherit from Observable). In other cases it implies nothing (e.g., there may be other classes in the program). Finally, in some cases it is not at all clear whether the specification is complete or partial. For example, is the list of methods in LinkedList exhaustive?

The principle of *information neglect* dictates that the absence of information from a Codechart implies nothing (Table 9). In other words, each specification in our design description language merely imposes a set of constraints on conforming implementations, and if an element of the program is not represented, this should be taken to require its absence.

Table 9.   Principle of Information Neglect

> Absence of information in a specification does not imply negative information.

There is one interesting consequence for the principle of information neglect: Every Codechart can be simplified by removing symbols from it. Any program that satisfies the first Codechart will also satisfy the simplified Codechart. In other words, if the simplified Codechart is valid,[8] then it models a superset of the set of programs that the original Codechart described.

The principle of information neglect follows naturally from the principles of scalability and abstraction in early design. It greatly simplifies the semantics of the language. For example, it implies that the semantics are preserved by removing parts of the Codechart, namely by applying the operator of *abstraction viz. information neglect* (p. 202).

---

[8] For example, if a term is removed, then all formulas containing it must also be removed.

Chapter **4**

UML Versus Codecharts

Since the UML is the de facto industry standard modelling language, questions naturally arise about its relation to Codecharts. This subject has been treated in detail throughout our discussion in the properties of design description languages in Chapter 2 and in the guiding principles of Codecharts presented in Chapter 3. This chapter summarizes the similarities and differences between Codecharts and UML diagrams.

The UML is a rich and expressive set of notations designed to articulate a very wide range of functional and nonfunctional specifications of software as well as activities related to software development. Unlike Codecharts, the UML is not merely a *design description language* (Chapter 2), and it is not constrained to design decisions about object-oriented programs. Its charter is therefore significantly broader than that of Codecharts.

More to the point, the UML is not a formal language: It is not bound by the need for precision, nor is it restricted by the requirement for verifiability—and by implication, *automated verifiability* (§3.4). This freedom from rigour allows using the UML to articulate specifications for which any notion of design verification (let alone automated verification) is hard to conceive. For example, Use-Case Diagrams and Activity Diagrams are particularly effective in visualizing informal notions such as user requirements, whose representation often requires concepts that fall well outside the charter of any formal language. Furthermore, the UML's stereotype mechanism allows users to extend it in any way desired, offering the software engineer the flexibility required for capturing and conveying novel kinds of specifications without requiring attention to the precise meaning of any particular symbol. On the flip side, the same freedom entails the ambiguity from which UML suffers. Consider, for example, the ambiguity of whether symbols missing from the diagram imply negative information, discussed in detail §3.8. This ambiguity entails that tools that use UML for design verification and program visualization are inherently problematic.

Codecharts: Roadmaps and Blueprints for Object-Oriented Programs, by Amnon H. Eden
Copyright © 2011 John Wiley & Sons, Inc.

Even if the meaning of some UML diagrams can be determined in a fairly precise manner, UML diagrams are, by and large, *undecidable* (§2.2). In effect, this means that it is virtually impossible in principle to verify conformance to UML diagrams and it is impossible in principle to build a tool that can answer the *verification question* for such diagrams. Undecidability implies that UML diagrams can be very expressive in modelling scenarios and patterns of behaviour in programs. But it rules out automated verification, which means that conformance to specifications need be checked manually, an error-prone and expensive process that rarely takes place in reality.

Finally, the UML emphasizes expressiveness, offering versatile means for modelling specifications, whereas Codecharts are guided by the principles of *elegance* (§2.4) and *minimality* (§3.7). That is, where the UML is tailored to articulate an abudance of specific types of services and modules, such as packages (namespaces), libraries, subsystems, subprograms, processes, components, connectors, ports, and so on, the vocabulary of Codecharts (p. 23) is restricted to 15 visual tokens.

Given the differences in scope and formality, the UML and Codecharts seem far apart. A detailed comparison between the languages is therefore only appropriate when the languages are narrowed down to *design description languages* (Chapter 2) for object-oriented programs. That is, only a comparison between UML Class and Package Diagrams vs. Codecharts is meaningful. Below we sketch some of the obvious differences in modelling programs, design patterns, and application frameworks.

To compare the notations' capabilities in modelling programs, contrast Codechart 1 with the Class Diagrams in Figures 2-1 and 2-2 (p. 14), all of which were reverse engineered from the same source code [the application programming interface (API) of the Java 3D class library]. Clearly, the class diagrams are not usable because they attempt to visualize a large program in terms of individual classes. The only relevant means of abstraction that UML provides are packages. But Package Diagrams do not improve the situation because they are restricted to modelling relations between the physical units that Java packages and C++ namespaces offer.

This comparison demonstrates that Class Diagrams can effectively model the implementation minutia of small programs but also that the notation does not *scale* (§2.3). It illustrates a fundamental difference between Codecharts and Class Diagrams: In Codecharts, where the emphasis is on visualizing programs at *any* level of abstraction, sets of classes, methods, and class hierarchies can be depicted regardless of their size. Consequently, Codecharts are more scalable, and visualization tools supporting Codecharts can be more effective in reverse engineering roadmaps to large programs. Furthermore, Codechart abstraction mechanisms allow software designers to use it to articulate early design decisions without premature commitment to implementation minutia, a feat that is much less achievable in the absence of generic notions such as that of a set of classes and isomorphic relations. This explains why program visualization tools are not common in the industry and why the visualization tools rarely employ UML.

Finally, let us consider the matter of tool support. The conformance of a program to a Codechart can be verified fully automatically (§3.4). This, for example, can be done with the Toolkit for Java 1.4 programs. Conversely,

Class Diagrams are not formally defined, let alone automatically verifiable. For this reason, tools that claim to verify class diagrams largely end up verifying only a trivial subset of the notation.

To compare the notations' capabilities in representing design patterns, contrast the class diagram in Figure 4-1 with Codechart 7. Both describe the Composite design pattern (to which §11.1 is dedicated).

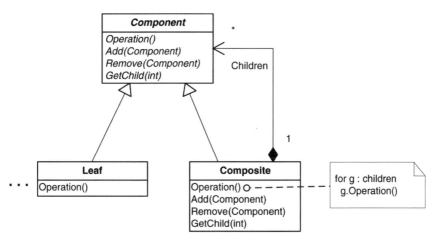

Figure 4-1.   The Composite pattern modelled in the UML's Class Diagram notation (Glossary: p. 233; adapted from [Gamma et al. 1995])

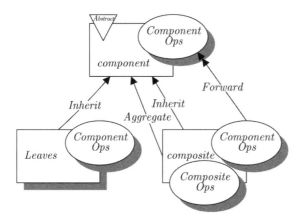

Codechart 7.   The Composite pattern in LePUS3

A number of obvious differences come to light from this comparison: Both diagrams attempt to depict the main *participants* in the pattern, which are classes and methods that play specific roles in the design motif that the pattern captures. But the UML depicts the Component participant as a class called Component, whereas the Codechart employs a variable for the purpose called *Component*. The difference is that a variable specifies unambiguously that any class may (in principle) play this role as long as it satisfies the formulas depicted in the Codechart. Next, observe that both diagrams seek to indicate that the Component class defines operations over the set of children (add, remove, getChild) and that these operations are overridden in the Composite class. The Class Diagram enumerates these operations, whereas the Codechart models them as a tribe (as a set of methods) of any size. The same applies to the number of Leaf classes (which can be one or more) as modelled in the UML using the informal ellipsis (...) notation, whereas in the Codechart it is modelled as a set of classes (*Leaves*).

Are these differences significant? The problem with the informal notation is that it leaves many questions unanswered: *Must all "leaf" classes inherit from Component?* (Yes). *Must all "leaf" classes override the methods in Component?* (No, they can inherit them). *Must all the Component operations that are overridden by the Composite class forward the call to the respective method in the children?* (Yes). *Are there only three operations over children?* (No). Answers to these questions are rigorously specified only when appropriate abstraction mechanisms are employed, such as sets of classes, sets of methods, and *isomorphic* predicate formulas.

Beyond these observations, the comparison brings to light a more fundamental difference between the notations. Symbols in Class Diagrams stand for elements of specific programs, whereas Codecharts subscribe to the principle of *genericity* (§3.6), setting apart symbols that model programs (*constants*) from symbols that model generic abstractions such as participants in design patterns (*variables*). Finally, our commitment to the principle of *automated verifiability* also dictates that the conformance of a program to Codechart 7 can be verified fully automatically.

Finally, let us compare the two notations' capabilities in documenting the use of application frameworks (see Chapter 10). Compare the Class Diagram in Figure 4-2 with Codechart 8. Both model some elements of Enterprise JavaBeans (to which §10.1 is dedicated). If a Class Diagram is used to demonstrate how programmers should write their code and how it should relate to the framework's classes, then only specific examples will do—classes Customer and CustomerHome in Figure 4-2. Such practice is likely to lead to confusion between the parts in the examples that programmers must replicate (in this case, a home interface must inherit from class javax.ejb.EJBObject) vs. the parts in the example that are merely demonstrative (everything else about class Customer). Codechart 8, on the other hand, uses variables to describe only the constraints over the user-defined classes without implying any irrelevant constraints. In large and complex application frameworks, where interactions between user-defined and prefabricated parts of the program can take a very complex form, the use of variables is indispensible (see, e.g., Codechart 85, p. 136).

Home Interface   **Remote Interface**

«interface»
javax.ejb.EJBHome

«interface»
javax.ejb.EJBObject

«interface»
CustomerHome

«interface»
Customer

Figure 4-2.   Enterprise JavaBeans™ (Table 11) elements in the UML (Glossary: p. 233, adapted from [Monson-Haefel 2001]). Classes CustomerHome and Customer are sample implementations of "home interface" and "remote interface"

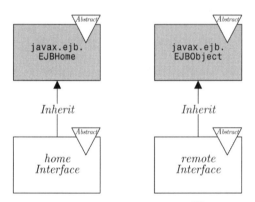

Codechart 8.   Enterprise JavaBeans™ (Table 11) elements in LePUS3. Variables (empty shapes) represent user-defined (yet to be implemented) entities whereas constants (filled shapes) represent prefabricated (fully implemented) entities

In conclusion, **UML Class Diagrams** and **Codecharts** are suitable for very different purposes. The appropriateness of each notation therefore depends on the circumstances in which they are used.

Chapter 5

Historical Notes

The subject of this book has occupied me from my first encounter with design patterns in the summer of 1994.[1] My experience as a professional software designer led me to recognize almost immediately that design patterns stand to become an important step in the advancement of software design.[2] Given their prominence in the literature on software design, I've chosen the problems of modelling design patterns and of providing tools supporting their implementation as the subject of my Ph.D. research.

At the time I knew of some formal languages, of logic languages, and of commercial object notations. So I expected to find that at least *one* of these languages offers mechanisms for representing patterns by means that are at once as well-defined as logic sentences and intuitive—preferably visual—not unlike the Object Modelling Technique [Rumbaugh et al. 1990] and the other modelling languages that were popular at the time. I was wrong. So I started with doodling little pictures with triangles for class hierarchies and ellipses for methods. That turned into the first version of LePUS, which became the subject of the second part of my Ph.D. dissertation [Eden 2000].

Through the years that followed I've learned of the many shortcomings of LePUS. It is unsuitable for modelling programs, only design patterns, which led to the distinction between *constants* and *variables*. The definitions of the language's constructs in higher order logic (HOL) were at once too much and too little: HOL was too powerful and the language's semantics were lacking. Yoram Hirshfeld, who at the time was my Ph.D. co-supervisor and logic teacher, suggested that LePUS could be redefined as a proper subset of the first-order predicate calculus. Assigning "precise" meaning to my doodles posed a new problem with every class-based programming language.

---

[1]This chapter was written by Amnon Eden in the first person.

[2]Indeed, the Gang of Four design patterns are the *raison d'être* for the first version of LePUS.

Codecharts: Roadmaps and Blueprints for Object-Oriented Programs, by Amnon H. Eden
Copyright © 2011 John Wiley & Sons, Inc.

Therefore, a definition of the language in the first-order logic was devised, finite structures were borrowed from model theory, and the relation between specifications and programs was defined using the abstract semantics function.

In 2003, after joining the University of Essex, I started the Two-Tier Programming Project aimed at further developing and providing tool support for LePUS. During his MSc research, my graduate student Notis [Gasparis 2004] investigated the visual properties of LePUS and suggested that the many different kinds of arrowheads employed at the time were confusing to the reader—a description which smacked of inelegance (see §2.4). All edge styles were therefore replaced with two, which stood for the two predicate symbols in the current version (*TOTAL* and *ISOMORPHIC*). The accumulation of these necessary changes warranted a change of name, so we chose to refer to it as LePUS2 [Gasparis 2006].

In 2006 we were joined by Jonathan "Mac" Nicholson, and together we set out to investigate a wider range of case studies and to provide a complete account for LePUS2 as a logic language. After arbitrating the balancing act between the objective of minimality and the complexity of the problem of modelling object-oriented design, we were left with a language that is at once well-defined and intuitive. Together we have written a detailed technical definition of our specification language [Eden et al. 2007] and called the revised modelling language LePUS3, the language of Codecharts.

Most importantly, the Two-Tier Programming Project has been concerned with proving that automated design verification is not only possible in principle but also feasible and useful in practical domains. Several MSc dissertations were dedicated to developing prototype tools and examining case studies corroborating this hypothesis. In 2006, Notis and Mac set out to integrate the prototype hitherto developed into a software specification, design verification, and visualization toolkit. At the end of 2007, version 0.5.1 of the Two-Tier Programming Toolkit was completed, and although the task undertaken has proven to be difficult, a few months afterwards it was made available for free download (http://ttp.essex.ac.uk/main/download).

Version 0.5.1 of the Toolkit has demonstrated that Codecharts of many class libraries and design patterns, which started their way as doodles, can be verified against Java programs by a click of a button, and this process can be optimised to last less than a second using only the average software and hardware available today.

This success made it apparent that Codecharts stood to offer, at least in part, a solution to some of the thorniest problems in software engineering. At last, programs can be visualized in a top-down, stepwise process of refinement of Codecharts that not only "fit on a side of a van" but also contain arbitrarily few symbols. The marriage between logic and as visual modelling does not seem quite as far-fetched as it did 11 years ago.

It is my hope that this book, together with the Toolkit, will make software modelling an easier and more manageable task.

Part I

Practice

The average mathematician should not forget that intuition is the final authority.

—J. Barkley Rosser

This part constitutes a gentle and largely informal introduction to our design description language. Its purpose is to introduce programmers and software designers to effective means of modelling programs and design patterns without requiring any mathematical training.

Throughout this part we will adhere to the following writing conventions:

- Starred sections (e.g., 6.4: * Modelling Implementation Minutia) include advanced reading which can be skipped without affecting the readability of most of the remainder of the book.

- Much of what will be presented is set outside the main text and captioned as follows: Legends introduce symbols, Codecharts are specifications in LePUS3, programs are valid expressions in a programming language, tables depict tabular information, and figures include anything else that need be set apart from the main text.

- Source code follows Knuth's conventions with keywords in **bold typewriter**.

- Codechart symbols (Iterator, JavaRMIImp) appear in Euclid typeface.

- When a new term is introduced or defined it appears in **bold typeface**

Chapter 6

Modelling Small Programs

The simplest Codecharts represent individual classes and methods, their properties, and the relations between them. This chapter introduces the reader to these symbols, depicted in Legend 2 (page 48), and demonstrates how they are used.

We begin with the example of the classes LinkedList and LinkedListItr and some of their interfaces in package java.util,[1] extracts from which are depicted in Program 1.

Program 1. Extracts from java.util

```
public interface Collection { …          public interface Iterator { …
    public Iterator newItr();   …            public Object next(); …


public interface List                    public interface ListIterator
    extends Collection { …                   extends Iterator { …


public class LinkedList                  class LinkedListItr
    implements List … {                      implements ListIterator { …
    public Iterator newItr() { …             public Object next() { …
    // produce a (new) instance              // iterate over a LinkedList
    // of LinkedListItr                       // return Object
```

Note: Identifiers were slightly altered for pedagogical purposes. For example, to prevent confusion with class Iterator, the signature of the various iterator() methods was changed (consistently) to newItr().

---

[1]Version 1.4.2 of the Java™ Software Development Kit [Sun 2003].

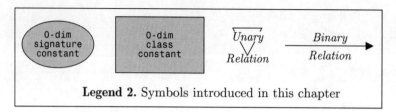

Legend 2. Symbols introduced in this chapter

Codecharts were tailored to overcome many of the limitations of existing modelling notations. By the principle of abstraction, Codecharts do not distinguish between classes and interfaces or between member and inherited methods. The notation *Inherit⁺* specifies that `LinkedList` inherits possibly indirectly from `Collection`. In addition, the principle of *information neglect* dictates that the absence of information about methods in class `List` does *not* imply that there aren't any. Finally, properties and relations specified using Codecharts have well-defined semantics.[2]

Consider, for example, Codechart 9, which models Program 1.

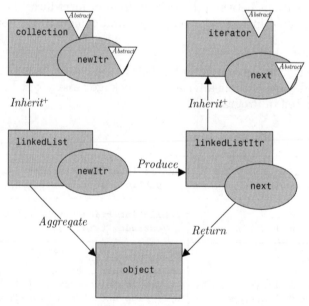

Codechart 9. Abstract and concrete collection and iterator in `java.util` (Program 1)

Note that methods are not represented as elements of a class or using a dedicated symbol. Instead, the method `LinkedList.newItr()` is modelled by superimposing the *signature constant* `newItr` over the *class constant* `linkedList`. The advantage here is that the symbol `newItr` is reused in representing methods `Collection.newItr()` and `LinkedList.newItr()`.

---

[2]These are discussed later in this chapter and determined formally by the *abstract semantics* function is discussed in the second part of this book.

Simple relations between classes and/or methods are modelled using arrow-headed arcs labelled with the appropriate relation name. For example, the arc marked *Return* connecting the (superimposition) term which stands for the method `LinkedListItr.next()` with the term which stands for class `Object` (Codechart 9) specifies that `LinkedListItr.next()` may return instances of class `Object` (or subclasses thereof). In the remainder of this chapter we define and introduce each one of these symbols.

6.1 MODELLING INDIVIDUAL CLASSES

We begin with class constants, the visual tokens used for modelling individual static types. In Java, types include classes, interfaces, primitive types, and array types. Other class-based programming languages offer different constructs which also serve as static types, all of which can also be modelled using class constants.

Formally, a *0*-**dimensional class constant** (Legend 3) is a term that represents a specific static type. As a convention, names of *0*-dimensional constants are written in lowercase fixed-size typeface (e.g., `collection`, `object`).

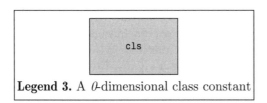

Legend 3. A *0*-dimensional class constant

In Java, *0*-dimensional class constants represent classes, such as `Vector` and `Object`; interfaces, such as `Collection` and `Comparable`; primitive types, such as `int` and `char`; and array types, such as `char[]`, as demonstrated in Codechart 10.

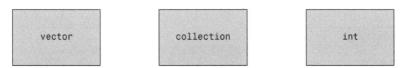

Codechart 10. A Java class (`Vector`), a Java interface (`Collection`), and a Java primitive type (`int`)

The reason for abstracting the distinction between classes, interfaces, and primitive types is because such a distinction is largely an implementation detail which rarely serves the software designer. Such abstractions help minimize the set of building blocks of object-oriented design (p. 22). If, however, such subtleties must be represented and enforced, then a dedicated *unary relation symbol* (see §6.3) such as *Interface* or *PrimitiveType* can be used.

Should we wish it to be spelled out, the precise meaning of `vector`, namely the mapping of the symbol `vector` to the class `java.util.Vector`, can be formally established using the *interpretation function* notation as demonstrated in Equation (1):

$$\mathcal{I}(\text{vector}) = \underline{\texttt{java.util.Vector}} \tag{1}$$

In accurate terms, interpretation functions map constants not to identifiers (e.g., `java.util.Vector`) or to other syntactic elements of the program but to *entities*, which are abstractions in its semantic representation. The precise nature of entities and their distinction from the source code are the subject of Chapter 14 in the second part of this book. During this part of the book we will treat **`java.util.Vector`** and `java.util.Vector` as virtually one and the same.

Note also that the interpretation function notation need only be used when the meaning of a constant is not self-evident. Wherever possible, we will stick to obvious constants and refrain from detailing the interpretation function except where it cannot be avoided (e.g., Chapter 7).

6.2 MODELLING INDIVIDUAL METHODS

To model methods we introduce *0*-**dimensional signature constants** (Legend 4a), a term which represents a specific method signature, namely method name and argument(s) type(s). A method in class-based languages such as Java is modelled by superimposing a signature constant over a class constant, representing that method with the specified signature defined in the specified class.

More precisely, the superimposition of a *0*-dimensional signature constant **sig** on a *0*-dimensional class constant **cls** is called a *0*-**dimensional superimposition term** (Legend 4b), symbolically transcribed as

$$\text{sig} \otimes \text{cls}$$

The term represents that method with signature **sig** which is also a member of (or inherited by) class **cls** (Definition V).

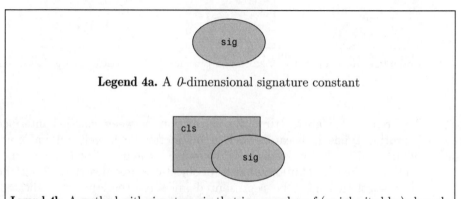

Legend 4a. A *0*-dimensional signature constant

Legend 4b. A method with signature sig that is a member of (or inherited by) class cls

For example, the method `Vector.size()` has the signature `size()`:

```
class Vector ... {
  public int size() {
    ...
  }
```

Method `Vector.size()` can therefore be modelled by superimposing `size` on `vector` as demonstrated in Codechart 11.

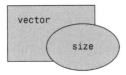

Codechart 11. Method `Vector.size`

Should we wish to do so, we may use the interpretation function notation to spell out what the θ-signature constant `size` stands for:

$$\mathcal{I}(\text{size}) = \underline{\text{size()}} \tag{2}$$

Equations (1) and (2) allow us to unpack the meaning ("interpretation") of the superimposition term $\text{size} \otimes \text{vector}$:

$$\mathcal{I}(\text{size} \otimes \text{vector}) = \underline{\text{java.util.Vector.size()}}$$

For example, since the three methods `Vector.size()`, `ArrayList.size()`, and `LinkedList.size()` share the same signature, the constant `size` can be reused in modelling each one of the methods, as demonstrated in Codechart 12. As no two methods can be defined in the same class with the same signature,[3] superimposing the same signature `sig` twice over the same class is a redundancy.[4]

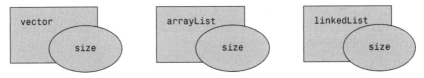

Codechart 12. One signature constant can be used to model many methods with same signature

Codecharts abstract away the distinction between modelling member and inherited methods. For example, although there is no `clone()` method defined in class `Vector`, a method with such signature is inherited from class

---

[3]This is not allowed by any class-based programming language and therefore is encoded as the *first axiom of object-oriented programming* (§17.3).

[4]In other words, that would constitute not an error but merely a duplicated representation of the same method.

Object. The (inherited) method can therefore be modelled using the term clone⊗vector, depicted in Codechart 13.

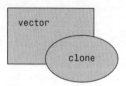

Codechart 13. A method with signature clone() is inherited by class Vector

Abstraction is the guiding principle in choosing not to distinguish between modelling member versus inherited methods. This information is abstracted because it is considered to be an implementation detail that is irrelevant to most design stages. For example, Codechart 13 merely specifies that objects of type Vector can be "cloned". Whether this method is implemented in class Vector or in one of its superclasses is abstracted away. Indeed, the precise location of the implementation does not affect the result of calling this method.

The *principle of information neglect* (p. 34) dictates that neglecting to specify in Codechart 13 other methods in class Vector does not imply that no such methods exist. Indeed, class java.util.Vector *implements* (or *satisfies*) both Codechart 11 and Codechart 13. More formally, the semantics of Codecharts demands that any program which implements Codechart 12 and Codechart 13 also implements Codechart 14, and vice versa.

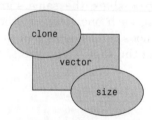

Codechart 14. Some methods in class Vector. Any program that satisfies Codechart 11 and Codechart 13 also satisfies Codechart 14 and vice versa

Finally, let us consider how methods in various class-based programming languages are modelled using Codecharts. In Java and Smalltalk, each method is associated with exactly one class. But this limitation is not imposed by other programming languages. For example, in C++ "global functions" are not associated with any class. Such methods can be modelled using a stand-alone signature, such as the global function sort in Codechart 15. In multiple-dispatch programming languages such as CLOS [Craig 2000], a method can be a "member" of one, two, or more classes, in which case it is modelled as method multiply in Codechart 15. In conclusion, methods are not thought of as elements of a class nor are they modelled that way. Instead, methods are thought of as independent entities. They can be associated with any number of classes, or possibly none—depending on the programming language.

Codechart 15. `sort` is a global function and `multiply` is a double-dispatch method

To summarize, in this chapter we have encountered three kinds of *0*-dimensional terms:

- Class constants (`cls`)
- Signature constants (`sig`)
- Superimposition terms of signature constants over class constants ($\text{sig} \otimes \text{cls}$)

Zero-dimensional terms represent individual entities in the programs. Terms that stand for sets of entities (called *higher dimensional terms*) are introduced in the next chapter. In the remainder of this chapter we consider how the *0*-dimensional terms introduced so far can be used in simple expressions called *ground formulas* to specify the properties of program entities and the relations between them.

6.3   MODELLING PROPERTIES

Ground formulas specify properties of classes and methods as well as the relations between them. We begin with the simplest formulas, called *unary ground formulas*, which are so named because they include only one argument.

More precisely, a **unary ground formula** (Legend 5b) is symbolically transcribed as

$$UnaryRelation(\,t\,)$$

where *UnaryRelation* is a **unary relation symbol** (Legend 5a) and t is a *0-dimensional term* (Legends 3 and 4). It specifies that the entity represented by t is in the unary relation *UnaryRelation* (Definition X). Unary relation symbols specify properties of an individual class or method. For example, the unary relation symbol *Abstract* is used in two formulas in Codechart 16: one to model the abstract class `AbstractList` and the other the interface `Collection`.

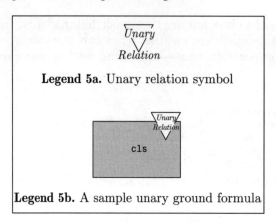

Legend 5a. Unary relation symbol

Legend 5b. A sample unary ground formula

The two formulas in Codechart 16 are symbolically transcribed as follows:

$$Abstract(\texttt{abstractList})$$

$$Abstract(\texttt{collection})$$

(3)

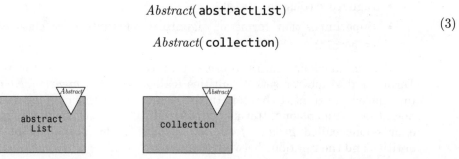

Codechart 16. AbstractList is an abstract class and Collection is a Java interface

The formulas in Codechart 16 consist of the combination of a relation symbol (such as *Abstract*) and a term (such as `collection`). The formula *Abstract*(`collection`) is called a *ground formula* because `collection` stands for an individual class (as opposed to a set of classes). It is called a *unary ground formula* because *Abstract* is a unary (one-place) relation symbol. We will continue to refine the notion of *formula* throughout this chapter, during which the notions of a formula and (unary and other) relation symbols will become clearer.

Note that, although the Java programming language distinguishes between abstract classes and interfaces, the choice between them is largely an implementation detail. Therefore, by the principle of abstraction in early design (p. 32), both are represented using the relation symbol *Abstract*. Note also that, by the *principle of information neglect* (p. 34), failing to include the *Abstract* symbol from Codechart 10 does not imply that Collection is *not* abstract.

The unary relation symbol *Abstract* can also be used to specify that a method is abstract (in C++ it is called a pure virtual function). For example, consider the problem of modelling the methods depicted in Program 2. To specify that `AbstractList.get(int)` and `Collection.size()` are abstract we use the formulas *Abstract*(`get`⊗`abstractList`) and *Abstract*(`size`⊗ `collection`) modelled in Codechart 17.

Program 2. Two Abstract Methods

```
public abstract class AbstractList … { …
   abstract public Object get(int); …

interface Collection {
   int size(); …
```

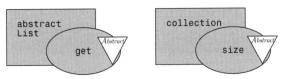

Codechart 17. The method with signature `get()` in `AbstractList` is abstract and the method with signature `size()` in `collection` is abstract

6.4 * MODELLING IMPLEMENTATION MINUTIA

The requirement for *abstraction* (p. 12) demands that design description languages allow software designers to focus on the essential elements in the program and avoid forcing them to commit themselves to the plethora of implementation minutia that programming requires. In particular, the principle of *abstraction in early design* (p. 32) dictates that a design description language should not force the software designer to make premature commitments to implementation detail. For this reason Codecharts abstract away many of the distinctions that are made by programming languages, such as the distinction made in Java between classes and interfaces and the distinction between member and inherited methods. Nonetheless, a case can be made for making subtle distinctions later in the development process. Indeed, there are circumstances in which seemingly subtle distinctions are in fact crucial. For example, it can be argued that the distinction between class methods (in Java: *static methods*; in C++: *static function members*) and the distinction between *classes* and *interfaces* are indispensable and must be clearly specified. Since Codecharts are not restricted to using any specific set of relation symbols, such distinctions are accommodated easily. Indeed, any relation is allowed *provided that it is decidable* (§2.2). For example, we may admit the unary relation symbols *Static* and *Interface*, as demonstrated for example in Codechart 18, to specify these distinctions explicitly.

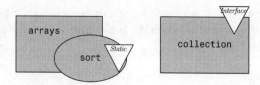

Codechart 18. The method with signature `sort()` in class `Arrays` is a Java "static" method and `Collection` is a Java "interface"

6.5 MODELLING SIMPLE RELATIONS

Directed edges represent relations between any pair of classes and methods and are appropriately called *binary* relation symbols.

More precisely, a **binary ground formula** (Legend 6b) is symbolically transcribed as

$$BinaryRelation(\,domain, range)$$

where *BinaryRelation* is a **binary relation symbol** (Legend 6a) and *domain* and *range* are *0*-dimensional terms. It specifies that the pair of entities represented by *domain* and *range* is in the binary relation (Definition II) *BinaryRelation*.[5]

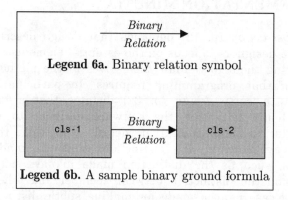

Legend 6a. Binary relation symbol

Legend 6b. A sample binary ground formula

Binary relation symbols model a range of simple behavioural and structural relations between classes and/or methods. There is no limit to which relations can be modelled using Codecharts, except that such relations are *decidable* (§2.2). Below we present what our experience has shown to be the most common relations and explain the precise interpretation of each.

---

[5]In §6.7 we refine this definition to account for subtyping.

Inherit **Relation**

The binary relation symbol *Inherit* models all kinds of inheritance relations, such as those indicated by the keywords `extends` and `implements` in Java. For instance, the two inheritance relations indicated by the Java declaration

class Vector **extends** AbstractList **implements** List ...

are modelled in Codechart 19 by the formulas *Inherit*(`vector,abstractList`) and *Inherit* (`vector,list`), respectively.

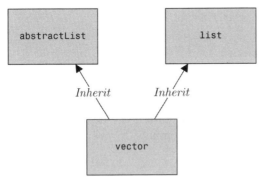

Codechart 19. Class Vector extends class AbstractList and implements interface List

Member **Relation**

Member is a binary relation symbol which stands for the relation between one class and the class of its member(s). For example, class `java.lang.Package` contains a field of type `URL`:

public class Package { ...
  private URL sealBase; ...
}

The formula *Member*(`package,url`) in Codechart 20 models this relation.

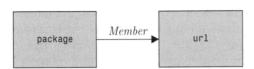

Codechart 20. Class Package contains a member ("field") of type URL

Note that the formula *Member*(`package,url`) in Codechart 20 asserts a relation between `Package` and `URL` without mentioning the name of the field (`sealBase`) or how many fields of type `URL` exist in class `Package`. This is not an accident but an application of the principle of abstraction in early design (p. 32). For example, class `Package` has several members of type `String`, all of which are modelled using the formula *Member*(`package, string`) in Codechart 21:

```
public class Package {
   …
   private String pkgName;
   private String SpecTitle;
   …
}
```

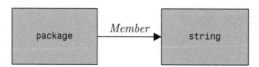

Codechart 21.   Class `Package` contains several members of type `String`

Nonetheless, if a case can be made for modelling the number of members of a specific type, then dedicated relation symbols for representing it can be introduced.[6]

Aggregate **Relation**

We may wish to model that a class has, or is, a collection of some sort. Precisely what constitutes a collection depends on the programming language in question. In Java we take collections to be arrays or an instance of a class that implements the `java.util.Collection` interface. The binary relation symbol *Aggregate* specifies this relation between the container and the aggregate (or aggregated) classes.

Consider, for example, the relation between the classes `Container` and `Component` in package `java.awt`

```
public class Container …
   Component component[] …
```

modelled using the formula *Aggregate*(`container, component`) in Codechart 22.

In Java 1.4, "collection" classes are themselves aggregates of class `Object`. Therefore, we take all implementations of `Collection` to be in the relation *Aggregate* with class `Object`. For example, the formula *Aggregate*(`linkedList, object`) in Codechart 22 models the relation between the class `LinkedList` and `Object` in Java 1.4.

The case is somewhat different with Java 1.5, where collection classes are generic. *Aggregate* can is used to model instances of generic collections. For example, class `CheckedKeySet` in package `java.lang` has an aggregate of type set of strings

---

[6]For example, ternary relations such as *Member*(`package, string, 3`) or *Member*(`package, string, "pkgName"`) can be introduced.

private class CheckedKeySet…
   private set<String> s;

modelled using the formula *Aggregate*(checkedKeySet,string) in Codechart 22.

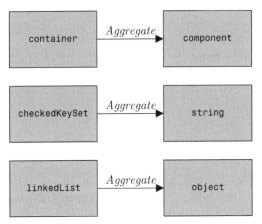

Codechart 22. Class Container has a member of type array of Component; class CheckedKeySet has a member of type set of String; and LinkedList implements the Collection interface

Call **Relation**

The binary relation symbol *Call* represents the (static) function invocation relation which exists between a calling method and the called method. The requirement of automated verifiability (p. 28) demands that it ignores any consideration to the actual binding of the call in runtime, to the order of method invocations, and to the conditions under which it is being invoked. For example, consider the method Test.main depicted in Program 3, which prints a message to the standard output. The object System.out is an instance of class PrintStream. Therefore the relation between the methods Test.main and the method print of System.out can be modelled as depicted in Codechart 23 with the formula

$$Call(\text{main} \otimes \text{test}, \text{print} \otimes \text{printStream})$$

Program 3. Method Test.main

```
public class Test {
  public static void main(String args[]) {
    if (…) {…
      System.out.print("Insufficient arguments");
      … }

  …
```

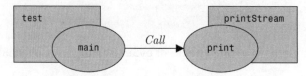

Codechart 23. Test.main contains a call to PrintStream.print

Note that Codechart 23 abstracts away information about the flow control of method Test.main. The actual location of the call may appear anywhere in the body of the method, possibly nested inside a conditional, a loop, or any other execution block.

Forward Relation

Certain categories of method calls are of special interest. Specifically we are interested in specifying that the calling method forwards its own formal arguments to another method with the exact same signature (name and argument types). This is commonly referred to [Craig 2000] as a *forwarding* relation, modelled in Codecharts using the *Forward* relation symbol.

Consider, for example, the relation between the method mark in class LineNumberReader and the method it overrides given in program 4.

Program 4. Method LineNumberReader.mark

```
public class LineNumberReader extends BufferedReader { …
    public void mark(int readAheadLimit) { …
        super.mark(readAheadLimit); …
    }
…
```

Note that method LineNumberReader.mark forwards the call to a method by the exact same name and argument types (signature) and that it also passes its formal argument to that method. Therefore, the relation between the two methods is modelled using the *Forward* relation symbol depicted in Codechart 24. The formula in Codechart 24 can also be represented symbolically as follows:

$$Forward(\,\textsf{mark} \otimes \textsf{lineNumberReader}, \textsf{mark} \otimes \textsf{bufferedReader})$$

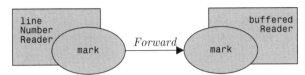

Codechart 24.   Method `LineNumberReader.mark` contains a call which forwards its formal arguments to `BufferedReader.mark`

Return **Relation**

The binary relation symbol *Return* represents the relation between a method that contains a `return` statement and the static type of the object that is being returned. For example, the body of the method `ArrayListItr.next()` contains a statement returning an object of type `Object`. Hence the relation between `ArrayListItr.next()` and `Object` can be modelled using the binary relation symbol *Return*, as demonstrated in Codechart 25.

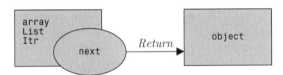

Codechart 25.   Method `ArrayListItr.next` returns objects of type `Object`

Since each method may contain any number of `return` statements, a Codechart may contain any number of formulas with the *Return* relation symbol, all of which originate from only one method.

Create **and** *Throw* **Relations**

The relation symbol *Create* represents the relation between a method and the type of object that is created by some statement in that method. Like *Call* and *Forward*, *Create* is a binary relation symbol that does not convey any information about the conditions under which the new object will be created. If necessary, these may be represented using other symbols. For example, the method in Program 5 contains a statement which creates an array of characters (in java: an instance of type `char[]`). The relation between the method `String.toLowerCase` and the type `char[]` is modelled in Codechart 26 by the formula

$$Create(\textsf{toLowerCase} \otimes \textsf{string},\textsf{char[]})$$

Program 5. Excerpts from `String.toLowerCase`

```java
public class String {
    ...
    public String toLowerCase(Locale) {
        ...
        if (...) { ... }
        else {
            ...
            for (...) {
                ...
                if (...) {
                    ...
                    char[] result2 = new char[result.length + mapLen - 1];
    ...
```

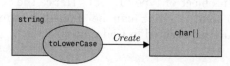

Codechart 26. `String.toLowerCase` contains an expression which creates an array of characters

Observe that Codechart 26 abstracts away the conditions under which the **new** statement will be executed because these can only be determined dynamically.

The relation *Create* may be used to model different kinds of Java statements whose execution leads to the creation of objects. For example, Program 6 contains a method whose execution may lead to the creation of an instance of the class `NullPointerException` in the process of throwing an exception.

Program 6. More Excerpts from `String.toLowerCase`

```java
public class String {
    ...
    public String toLowerCase(Locale) {
        if (...)
            throw new NullPointerException();
    ...
```

The relation between method `String.toLowerCase(Locale)` and class `NullPointerException` can also be modelled using the *Create* relation symbol, as demonstrated in Codechart 27. Note that Codechart 27 abstracts away the circumstances under which an instance of `NullPointerException` is created.

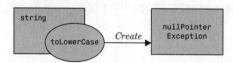

Codechart 27. Method `String.toLowerCase` contains an expression which creates an instance of `NullPointerException`

As an alternative to Codechart 27, the same program can be modelled using a *Call* relation between the method throwing the exception and the constructor of the exception class, as demonstrated in Codechart 28.

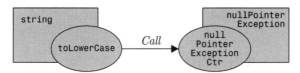

Codechart 28. `String.toLowerCase` contains an expression which calls the constructor of `NullPointerException`

The signature of the constructor of class `NullPointerException` is called `nullPointerExceptionCtr` and not simply `nullPointerException`. The reason is because the constant `nullPointerException` cannot be interpreted both as a class and as a signature. We can resolve this issue by defining the interpretation of the signature constant `nullPointerExceptionCtor` as follows:

$$\mathcal{I}(\text{nullPointerExceptionCtor}) = \underline{\text{nullPointerException()}}$$

As yet another alternative to Codechart 27 and Codechart 28, we may introduce a dedicated relation symbol for modelling the relation between methods and the exceptions they (*may*) throw, as demonstrated in Codechart 29.

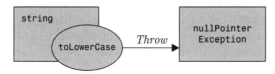

Codechart 29. Method `String.toLowerCase` contains an expression which may throw instances of class `NullPointerException`

Produce **Relations**

The binary relation symbol *Produce* represents a special kind of a *Create* relation in which the created object is returned by the method which created it. *Produce* is therefore useful for modelling the relation between "factory methods" and the type of objects they create.[7] For example, the method `LinkedList.newItr()` is a factory method which creates and returns instances of class `LinkedListItr`. The relation between this method and its product is therefore modelled in Codechart 30 and symbolically represented by the formula

$$\textit{Produce}(\text{newItr} \otimes \text{linkedList}, \text{linkedListItr})$$

---

[7]See, for example, the Factory Method (p. 149) and Iterator (p. 145) patterns.

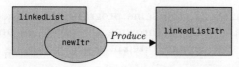

Codechart 30. Method `LinkedList.newItr` contains an expression which produces (creates and returns) an instance of `LinkedListItr`

6.6 MODELLING INDIRECT RELATIONS

Binary relation symbols can be generalized using *transitive relation symbols*, which specify possibly indirect relations. Precisely put, a *binary ground formula* can also have the form

$$BinaryRelation^+(\, t_1, t_2)$$

where *BinaryRelation⁺* is a **transitive binary relation symbol** (Legend 7) and t_1 and t_2 are *0*-dimensional terms. It specifies that the pair of entities represented by t_1 and t_2 is in the **transitive closure** (Definition III) of relation *BinaryRelation*.

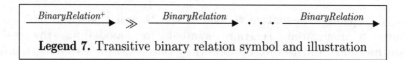

Legend 7. Transitive binary relation symbol and illustration

Transitive relations offer a powerful abstraction mechanism useful in modelling a range of notions of "indirectness", such as indirect inheritance and indirect method call. For example, the question of whether `LinkedList` directly or indirectly implements (or inherits from) `Collection` is an implementation detail which the software designer may wish to abstract away. Instead, we choose to specify that class `LinkedList` (Program 1, p. 47) implements the interface `Collection` *possibly indirectly*, modelled using the transitive binary relation symbol *Inherit⁺*, as demonstrated in Codechart 31 and symbolically represented by the formula

$$Inherit^+(\, \texttt{linkedList}, \texttt{collection})$$

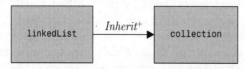

Codechart 31. Class `LinkedList` inherits indirectly from interface `Collection`

Precisely put, Codechart 31 specifies that:

- `LinkedList` inherits directly from `Collection`, or

- LinkedList inherits from some class *Super* and *Super* inherits directly from Collection, or
- LinkedList inherits from some class *Super*, *Super* inherits from some other class *Super2*, and *Super2* inherits directly from Collection, or

...

Transitive relations are also useful in modelling indirect method calls. For example, the transitive relation symbol *Forward⁺* can be used to model possibly indirect *Forward* relation between two methods. For example, the method HashMap.clone() in Program 7 does not call method object.clone() directly, but rather indirectly through Abstract Map.clone(). Since AbstractMap.clone() does little but forward the call to its superclass, it may be abstracted away. Instead we model the relation between HashMap.clone() and Object.clone()using the transitive relation symbol *Forward⁺*, as demonstrated in Codechart 32.

Program 7. Method clone in Three Classes

```
class Object { ...
  public Object clone() { ...

class AbstractMap ...
  public Object clone() { ...
    super.clone(); ...

class HashMap extends AbstractMap ...
  public Object clone() { ...
    super.clone(); ...
```

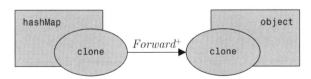

Codechart 32. Method HashMap.clone indirectly forwards the call to Object.clone

Precisely put, Codechart 32 specifies that:

- HashMap.clone() contains a statement which forwards the call to Object.clone(), or
- HashMap.clone() contains a statement which forwards the call to some m and m contains a statement which forwards the call to Object.clone(), or
- HashMap.clone()contains a statement which forwards the call to some m, m contains a statement which forwards the call to some m_2, and m_2 contains a statement which forwards the call to Object.clone(), or

...

In another example, consider the quote from the first edition of the *Java Language Specification*, depicted in Table 10.

Table 10. Excerpts from *The Java Language Specification*

A file input stream obtains input bytes from a file in a file system.

...

public class FileInputStream ... {

    public int read(byte [] b)

        throws IOException, NullPointerException;

...

Bytes for this operation are read from the actual file with which this file input stream is connected. ...

Source: Gosling et al. [1996]

The snippet in Table 10 intends to tell us that calling `FileInputStream.read` may *directly or indirectly* lead to creating instances of two exception classes. But using Java as a means for articulating this statement is clearly unsatisfying. This snippet is not, strictly speaking, a Java program, nor is it supposed to be. The reason that the authors resort to using Java is because of the absence of an adequate design description language. However, in Codecharts, the very same piece of information can be modelled precisely using the transitive closure of the binary relation *Call*, as demonstrated in Codechart 33.

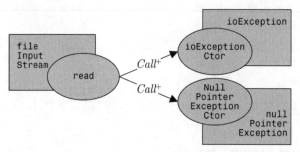

Codechart 33. Method `FileInputStream.read` contains an expression which calls (possibly indirectly) the constructors of two (exception) classes

6.7 * SUBTYPING

All class-based programming languages accommodate for some notion of subtyping with which every object-oriented programmer is familiar. In programming languages such as Java and C++, inheritance implies subtyping and hence is prevalent in all programs. Therefore our design description languages must also follow suit. To this end we amend our formal definition of the truth conditions for ground formulas (§6.5) as follows: A **binary ground formula** of the form

$$BinaryRelation(\,t_1, t_2)$$

specifies that:

- the pair of entities represented by t_1 and t_2 is in the relation _BinaryRelation_, or
- the entity represented by t_1 is in the relation _BinaryRelation_ with some other entity x that inherits from the entity represented by t_2, or
- the entity represented by t_2 is in the relation _BinaryRelation_ with some other entity y such that (the entity represented by) t_1 inherits from it.[8]

Let us illustrate the motivation to subtyping using an example borrowed from the Enterprise JavaBeans application (EJB) framework. The technical literature on EJB requires the "bean" class to hold a "field" (or "data member") of type `EJBContext`. This requirement can be specified using Codechart 34.

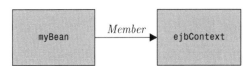

Codechart 34.   Class `MyBean` (or a supertype thereof) defines a member ("field") of class `EJBContext` (or subtypes thereof)

The meaning of Codechart 34 should be evident to any programmer. However, in practical applications they would soon discover that class `EJBContext` must be adapted by extending it with class `MyEJBContext`, namely a subtype of `EJBContex`. As a consequence, class `MyBean` is implemented in a slightly different way from what appears to be specified in Codechart 34: Instead of a member of type `EJBContext`, it has a member of type `MyEJBContext`, as demonstrated in Program 8.

Program 8.   Sample Enterprise JavaBeans Application

```
class MyEJBContext extends EJBContext … // Adapt EJBContext

class MyBean { …
   protected MyEJBContext context; …
}
```

Does Program 8 _satisfy_ Codechart 34? While most programmers will be happy to accept that is does, the narrow interpretation of ground formulas

---

[8]Naturally, subtyping is only relevant to formulas where at least one of its arguments are class terms. In other words, subtyping is only relevant to relations such as _Inherit_, _Member_, _Aggregate_, _Create_, and _Produce_. It has no effect on other relations such as _Call_ and _Forward_.

quoted in §6.5 does not allow it. In this case class `MyBean` in Program 8 does not contain a member of type `EJBContext` but of a subtype thereof.

A similar situation arises if class `MyBean` inherits the member `context` rather than defines it, as demonstrated in Program 9. Clearly, moving the member one class up the hierarchy has no effect on the remainder of the program, and Codechart 34 can be equally said to be satisfied by such an implementation.

These examples demonstrate that a narrow interpretation of Codechart 34 is too restrictive and therefore inadequate. A member need not be *exactly* of the type specified; subtypes should be admitted as valid implementations. More generally, narrow interpretations of ground binary formulas are inappropriate and violate the intent of the subtyping abstraction mechanism that class-based programming languages provide. Subtyping was therefore admitted into Codecharts.

Subtyping is useful in a range of situations. Consider, for example, Codechart 35.

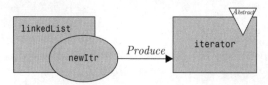

Codechart 35. `LinkedList.newItr` produces instances of (some implementation of) the `Iterator` interface

What exactly does Codechart 36 specify? Without subtyping, it appears to indicate that the method `LinkedList.newItr` produces instances of the `Iterator` interface. But that is impossible since Java interfaces cannot be instantiated. Subtyping allows us to understand Codechart 35 correctly: that `LinkedList.newItr` produces instances of *subtypes of* `Iterator`.

Subtyping is indispensable and it is relevant for any binary relation symbol that is used for modelling classes. Consider, for example, the *Aggregate* relation symbol used in modelling the relation between class `Window` (of package `java.awt`) and the aggregation of `Component` objects, modelled in Codechart 36. Without subtyping, Codechart 36 specifies that class `Window` contains some collection of instances of class `Component`. But with subtyping, Codechart 36 also allows the possibility that class Window is implemented to have an array of type `Pushbutton`, a subtype of `Component`, for example.

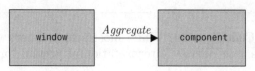

Codechart 36. Class `Window` contains an aggregate of (some subtype of) `Component`

Observe that, as a consequence of *subtyping*, formulas with the binary relation symbol *Inherit* are in effect synonymous with formulas with the transitive binary relation symbol *Inherit⁺*. Thus, for example, the two formulas in Codechart 37 are equivalent. However, we shall use the symbol *Inherit⁺* at times to specify explicitly that inheritance relations may be indirect.

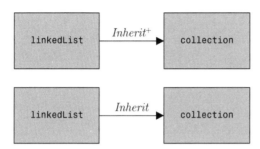

Codechart 37. Class `LinkedList` inherits (possibly indirectly) from interface `Collection`

Chapter 7

Modelling Large Programs

The Feynman–Tufte Principle: A visual display of data should be simple enough to fit on the side of a van.

—Shermer, 2005

Chapter 6 was concerned with modelling individual classes and methods, their properties, and relations between them. This chapter focuses on modelling programs that are too large to be modelled in this manner. As the size of programs increases, so grows the need for *abstraction* and *scalability* (p. 12). This chapter focuses on the challenge of providing abstraction mechanisms that are sufficiently potent, expressive, and informative for modelling large programs without cluttering our diagrams with too many symbols. The symbols introduced in this chapter, listed in Legend 8 on page 72, are tailored to meet this challenge.

A *1-dimensional class constant* may represent any (finite, nonempty) set of classes. For example, as the most radical abstraction of package `java.util`, the entire set of classes and interfaces in this package can be modelled using one *1*-dimensional class constant, as depicted in Codechart 38. When modelling any program it is imperative to use an appropriate level of abstraction. Codechart 38a, for example, is too abstract if the problem was to model Java collections and their respective iterators, but it does serve as a good starting point for (semi) automated design recovery tools [Gasparis 2009]. Therefore we demonstrate below how same package can be modelled at different levels of abstraction, starting from the most detailed Codechart and progressively abstracting it.

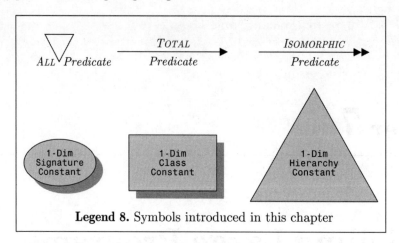

Legend 8. Symbols introduced in this chapter

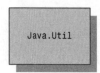

Codechart 38a. Package java.util modelled using a *1*-dimensional class constant

Program 1 (p. 47) defined two concrete collection classes from package java.util and their interfaces, modelled in Codechart 9 (p. 48). Let us now consider six more classes from the same package, listed in Program 10.

Program 10. More Extracts from java.util

```
class TreeSet                        class TreeSetItr
    implements Collection { …            implements Iterator { …
    public Iterator newItr() { …         public Object next() { …
        // produce a (new) instance          // iterate over a TreeSet
        // of TreeSetItr                      // return Object
```
```
class HashSet                        class HashSetItr
    implements Collection { …            implements Iterator { …
    public Iterator newItr() { …         public Object next() { …
        // produce a (new) instance          // iterate over a HashSet
        // of HashSetItr                      // return Object
```
```
class ArrayList                      class ArrayListItr
    implements Collection { …            implements Iterator { …
    public Iterator newItr() { …         public Object next() { …
        // produce a (new) instance          // iterate over an ArrayList
        // of ArrayListItr                    // return Object
```

Note: Again, identifiers were altered for the purposes of this demonstration.

Program 10 depicts 3 additional concrete collection classes (TreeSet, HashSet, and ArrayList) as well as 3 additional concrete iterator classes (TreeSetItr, HashSetItr, and ArrayListItr). Each such concrete collection is associated with exactly one concrete iterator, respectively. Together with the 4 classes in Program 1, these 10 classes consist of four pairs of concrete collection/iterator. In other words, each concrete iterator offers a means of iteration over objects of the respective concrete collection class.

Let us turn to examine the relations between these 10 classes. Observe that each concrete collection overrides the method newItr() with a method that produces instances of the respective concrete iterator class. For example, the method LinkedList.newItr() produces instances of class LinkedListItr and the method ArrayList.newItr() produces instances of class ArrayListItr. Similarly, observe that each concrete iterator class inherits from the interface Iterator and overrides the method Iterator.next() such that it returns an instance of class Object (or a subtype thereof). Codechart 38b models the combination of the classes and methods in Programs 1 and 10 and the relations amongst them.

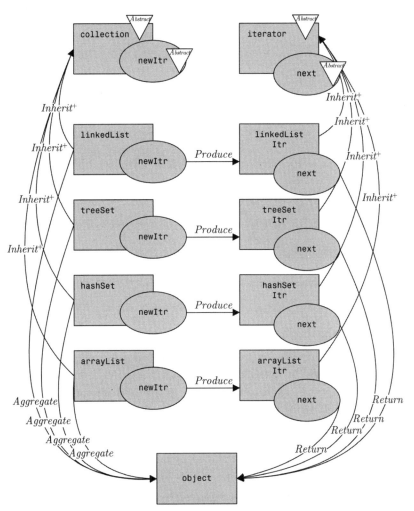

Codechart 38b. Some classes in package java.util modelled using *0*-dimensional terms. Clearly, modelling individual elements of the program does not scale

Codechart 38b is quite verbose, demonstrating the inadequacy of modelling individual entities in larger programs. Actual programs contain many more classes and methods, the modelling of which becomes increasingly difficult using the *0*-dimensional constants. However, *1*-dimensional constants can help us solve this problem. For example, compare Codechart 38b with Codechart 38c, which demonstrates how to model the same program using some of the abstraction mechanisms in Codecharts. Note that *1*-dimensional class constants (shadowed rectangles) represent sets of classes and the *ISOMORPHIC* and *TOTAL* predicates (double- and single-headed arrows, respectively) represent total and isomorphic relations between sets.

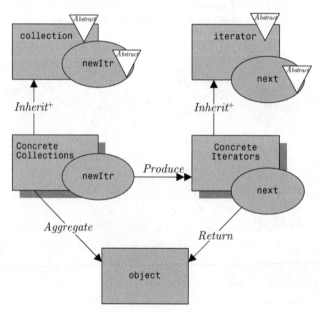

Codechart 38c.   Some classes in package `java.util` modelled using *0*- and *1*-dimensional class constants

Compare Codechart 38b with Codechart 38c and observe the following:

- Four constants each representing an individual concrete collection were replaced by `ConcreteCollections`.
- Four constants each representing an individual concrete iterator were replaced by `ConcreteIterators`.
- Four *Produce* edges were replaced by one (double-headed arrow) *Produce* edge.
- Four *Return* edges were replaced by one.
- Four *Inherit⁺* edges on each side of the chart were replaced by one.
- Four *Aggregate* edges were replaced by one.

Next, consider Codechart 38d (designated JavaUtil), which constitutes the next step in the abstraction of `java.util`, modelling the classes in this package using *1*-dimensional hierarchy constants.

Compare Codechart 38c with Codechart 38d and observe the following.

- `ConcreteCollections` and `collection` were replaced by `CollectionsHrc`.
- `ConcreteIterators` and `iterator` were replaced by `IteratorsHrc`.

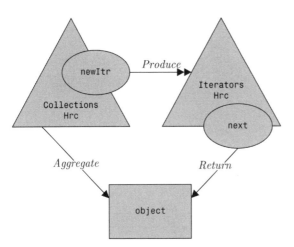

Codechart 38d. Some classes in package `java.util` modelled using *1*-dimensional hierarchy constants

The four Codecharts used in this example (Codecharts 38a–38d) demonstrate four levels of abstraction in modelling the same package. But *1-dimensional constants*, which model sets, and *predicates*, which model correlations between sets, can be used to model the program at *any* level. The remainder of this chapter is dedicated to the precise meaning of each one of these symbols.

7.1 MODELLING SETS OF CLASSES

When modelling larger programs, it is often useful to abstract a particular set of classes with one symbol. Likewise, *1*-dimensional class constants can be used to model any collection of classes, including packages, libraries, namespaces, subsystems, subprograms, components, connectors, ports, and almost any other design abstraction.

Precisely put, a *1*-**dimensional class constant** (Legend 9) is a term which represents a specific, finite, non empty set of classes and/or static types.

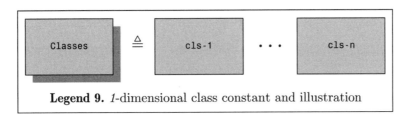

Legend 9. *1*-dimensional class constant and illustration

For example, the four individual classes modelled in Codechart 39a using four *0*-dimensional class constants can be modelled in Codechart 39b using one *1*-dimensional class constant ConcreteCollections.

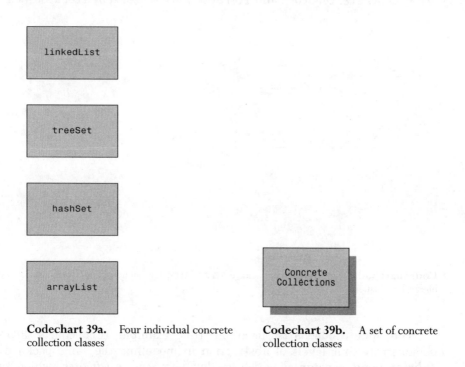

Codechart 39a. Four individual concrete collection classes

Codechart 39b. A set of concrete collection classes

The meaning of ConcreteCollections is obvious from Codechart 39. But if more explicit means are needed for spelling out precisely the set of classes which ConcreteCollections stands for, it can be done using the interpretation function notation, as demonstrated below:

$$\mathcal{I}(\texttt{ConcreteCollections})$$
$$= \{\mathcal{I}(\texttt{linkedList}), \mathcal{I}(\texttt{treeSet}), \mathcal{I}(\texttt{hashSet}), \mathcal{I}(\texttt{arrayList})\}$$

Note however that the interpretation function notation is optional and need only be used if necessary. For example, this is required for the purposes of design verification (Chapter 15) and the use of an automated verification tool (§15.4).

The package structure of many large class libraries contains valuable information about the structure and organization of the library. This useful information can be conveyed simply by modelling each package using one *1*-dimensional class constant. For example, Codecharts 40a and 40b demonstrate two ways in which the core packages of Java 6.0 SDK can be modelled.

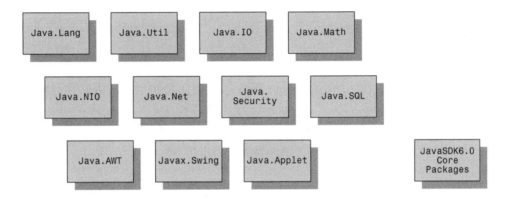

Codechart 40a. The set of classes in each core packages of Java 6.0 SDK can be modelled using *1*-dimensional class constants

Codechart 40b. The entire set of classes in all the core packages can also be modelled using one *1*-dimensional class constant

Codechart 40 does not model the hierarchical nesting of the sub packages of Java 6.0 SDK, which describes the hierarchical modular structure of the class library, not the many correlations that exist between classes in each package. These can be modelled using the abstraction mechanisms to be presented further in this chapter. In particular, Codechart 43 (p. 81) depicts inheritance relations between packages in Java 6.0 SDK, and Codechart 101 (p. 163) depicts the hierarchical structure between packages and sub packages in the Java 6.0 SDK.

7.2 MODELLING TOTAL RELATIONS BETWEEN SETS

Relations between sets of entities can be modelled using the predicate symbol *TOTAL*. Precisely put, a *TOTAL* **predicate formula** (Legend 10b), symbolically transcribed as

$$TOTAL(\ BinaryRelation, Domain, Range)$$

specifies that each element of the set *Domain* is in the relation *BinaryRelation* with some element of the set *Range*.[1]

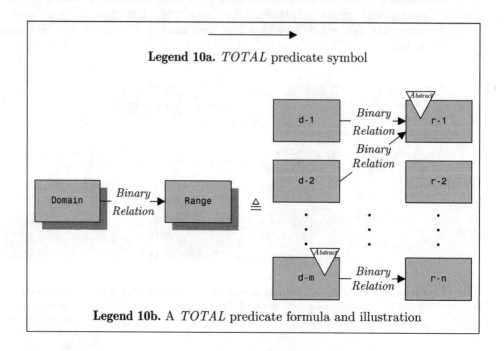

Legend 10a. *TOTAL* predicate symbol

Legend 10b. A *TOTAL* predicate formula and illustration

For example, observe that each concrete collection class (LinkedList, TreeSet, HashSet, and ArrayList) inherits from Collection, as modelled in Codechart 41a. If we model the set of concrete collection classes using the *1*-dimensional class constant ConcreteCollections, then the *TOTAL* predicate symbol can be used to model the inheritance relation between each member of the set of concrete collection classes and the interface Collection, as demonstrated in Codechart 41b. The *TOTAL* predicate formula in Codechart 41b can also be transcribed as follows:

$$TOTAL(\,Inherit^+,\texttt{ConcreteCollections},\texttt{collection})$$

Note that *TOTAL* predicate formulas are visually indistinguishable from ground formulas. By the principle of *minimality* (§3.7), we reuse the same symbol because no ambiguity may arise. More precisely, the truth conditions of a *TOTAL* predicate formula with binary relation symbol *Relation* are identical to the truth conditions for a binary ground formula with the same relation symbol and arguments. For example, the formula

$$TOTAL(\,Inherit,\texttt{linkedList},\texttt{collection})$$

is semantically equivalent to the formula *Inherit*(linkedList, collection).

---

[1]The precise and complete definition is offered in Definition XII; see also the discussion in §8.4.

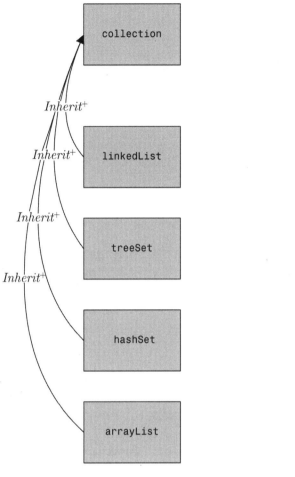

Codechart 41a. Each of four individual classes inherits from Collection

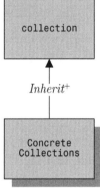

Codechart 41b. Each class in the set ConcreteCollections inherits from Collection

Let us illustrate the use of *TOTAL* predicates with another example. Note that each one of the concrete collection classes in java.util holds an "aggregate" of class Object.[2] Therefore, we can model the relation between the concrete collection classes (ConcreteCollections) and class Object using the *TOTAL* predicate formula, depicted in Codechart 42b.

---

[2]Subtyping (§6.7) allows also subtypes of Object here.

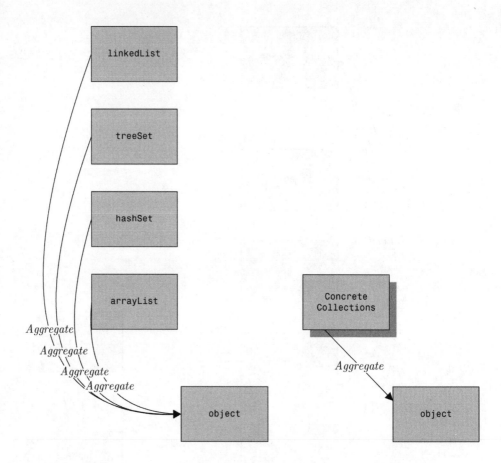

Codechart 42a.   Each of four individual classes is an aggregate of instances of (subtypes of) Object

Codechart 42b.   Each class in **ConcreteCollections** is an aggregate of instances of (subtypes of) Object

TOTAL predicate formulas can be used to model the relations between two sets of classes. For example, all the classes in package java.util inherit from class Object in package java.lang. This relation can therefore be modelled using a *TOTAL* predicate formula between the packages, as demonstrated in Codechart 43, representing the statement "every class on the set **Java.Util** inherits from some class in **Java.Lang**". Since the same applies to classes in all of the core subpackages of Java 6.0 SDK, the combination of statements specifying all these predicate formulas can be combined in one Codechart, as demonstrated in Codechart 43.

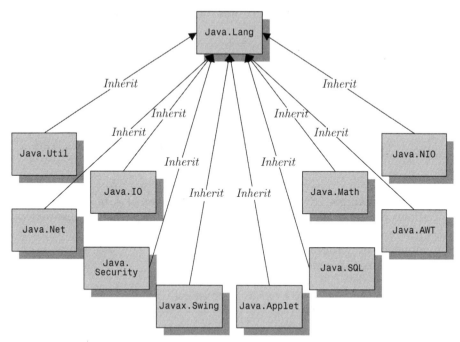

Codechart 43. Inheritance in the core packages of Java 6.0 SDK

7.3 MODELLING SETS OF METHODS (CLANS)

Dynamic binding (§3.1) is a powerful abstraction mechanism fundamental to class-based programming languages. It allows programmers to defer the decision of which variation of a method needs to be called. A precondition for forming a set of dynamically binding methods (one of which may be dynamically bound to each method invocation) is that all methods share the same signature—namely the method name and argument types.[3] For this reason we can use one signature constant to model sets of dynamically bound methods, to which we refer as a *clan*.

Precisely put, the superimposition of a *0*-dimensional signature constant sig over a *1*-dimensional class constant Classes is a *1*-dimensional **superimposition term** is symbolically transcribed as

$$\text{sig} \otimes \text{Classes}$$

It represents that set of methods that are each a member of (or inherited by) a class in Classes and have the signature sig. In other words,

---

[3]Since return types are not part of the signature, Java's covariance of return types is covered by our description. Sadly, it excludes more sophisticated mechanisms of covariance and contravariance in method argument types such as those supported by the Eiffel programming language.

$$\mathcal{I}(\,\mathsf{sig} \otimes \mathsf{Classes}) = \{\,\mathcal{I}(\,\mathsf{sig} \otimes \mathsf{cls}_i)\,,\ldots\mathcal{I}(\,\mathsf{sig} \otimes \mathsf{cls}_n)\,\}$$

where $\mathsf{cls}_i,\ldots\mathsf{cls}_n$ stand for all the classes in $\mathsf{Classes}$. We call such a set of methods a **clan in a set of classes**, or simply a **clan** (Legend 11).

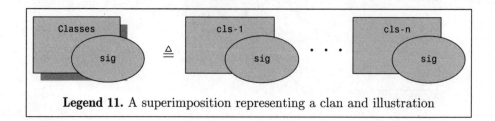

Legend 11. A superimposition representing a clan and illustration

For example, dynamic binding in Version 1.4 of package $\mathsf{java.util}$ allows clients to use a collection and its iterator without knowing exactly how either has been implemented. The method $\mathsf{AbstractSet.removeAll}$, depicted in Program 11, demonstrates how iterators are used without committing to a concrete collection or iterator.

Program 11.   The Calls for $\mathsf{this.remove}$ and $\mathsf{i.next}$ Are Dynamically Bound

```
public boolean removeAll(Collection c) {
    for (Iterator i = c.iterator(); i.hasNext(); )
        this.remove(i.next());    …
```

Which method is actually invoked by the call to $\mathsf{i.next()}$? If i is an instance of class $\mathsf{TreeSetItr}$, then method $\mathsf{TreeSetItr.next()}$ is called. And if i happens to be an instance of class $\mathsf{ArrayListItr}$, then $\mathsf{ArrayListItr.next()}$ is called. This set of dynamically bound methods can therefore be described as follows:

- Each method is a member of (or inherited by) a class in $\mathsf{ConcreteCollections}$.
- All methods share the same signature, $\mathsf{next()}$.

Therefore it forms a clan which can be modelled using the *1*-dimensional superimposition term $\mathsf{next} \otimes \mathsf{ConcreteIterators}$, depicted in Codechart 44b.

Should we wish to, we may spell out the interpretation of $\mathsf{ConcreteIterators}$ as follows:

$\mathcal{I}(\,\mathsf{ConcreteIterators})$

$= \{\mathcal{I}(\,\mathsf{linkedListItr})\,,\mathcal{I}(\,\mathsf{treeSetItr})\,,\mathcal{I}(\,\mathsf{hashSetItr})\,,\mathcal{I}(\,\mathsf{arrayListItr})\}$

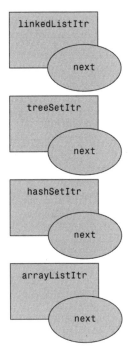

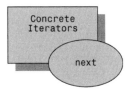

Codechart 44a. Four individual methods with same signature

Codechart 44b. A *clan* in a set of classes

7.4 *MODELLING ISOMORPHIC RELATIONS

Large programs often contain many pairs of classes and methods: Factory methods are paired with products, collections are paired with iterators, and graphic classes are paired with their renderings. The ISOMORPHIC predicate captures such pair wise relations between two sets, namely a 1 : 1 and onto relation (also known as a *bijective relation*), promoting abstraction and scaling.

Precisely put, an ISOMORPHIC **predicate formula** (Legend 12b), symbolically transcribed as

$$ISOMORPHIC(\ BinaryRelation, Domain, Range)$$

specifies that *BinaryRelation* pairs each element in the *Domain* with exactly one element of *Range*.[4]

---

[4] The precise and complete definition is offered in Definition XIII; see also the discussion in §8.5.

Legend 12a. *ISOMORPHIC* predicate symbol

Legend 12b. *ISOMORPHIC* predicate formula and illustration

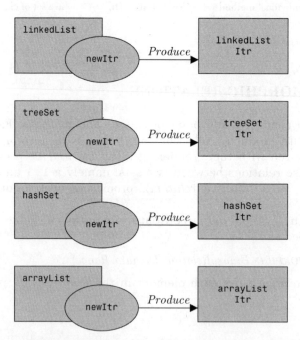

Codechart 45a. Four individual methods produce instances of four individual classes

For example, each one of the concrete collection classes depicted in Codechart 45a defines a method with signature newItr which produces instances of exactly one concrete iterator class. Therefore, the relation *Produce* pairs each factory method in the clan `newItr⊗ConcreteCollections` with a concrete iterator. This isomorphism is modelled in Codechart 45b by the double-arrow edge marked *Produce*.

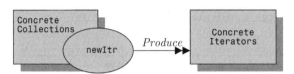

Codechart 45b. Each method in the clan `newItr⊗ConcreteCollections` produces instances of a unique class in `ConcreteIterators`

The *ISOMORPHIC* predicate formula in Codechart 45b can also be symbolically transcribed as follows:

ISOMORPHIC(*Produce*, `newItr⊗ConcreteCollections`, `ConcreteIterators`)

Note the advantage of using *ISOMORPHIC* over the *TOTAL* predicate: *ISOMORPHIC* tells us not only that each concrete iterator produces instances of some concrete iterator but also that there are as many concrete iterators as there are concrete collections. The *ISOMORPHIC* predicate therefore conveys more information than *TOTAL*.

7.5 MODELLING SETS OF METHODS (TRIBES)

When modelling a large number of methods, it is also useful to cluster together methods that do *not* share the same signature. We refer to such a set as a *tribe*. Modelling *tribes* requires the representation of a set of signatures.

Precisely put, a *1*-**dimensional signature constant** (Legend 13) is a term that stands for a specific (finite and non empty), set of method signatures.

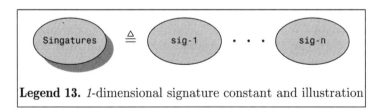

Legend 13. *1*-dimensional signature constant and illustration

One-dimensional signatures are used in modelling methods with different signatures: The superimposition of a *1*-dimensional signature constant `Signatures` on a *0*-dimensional class constant `cls` is also a *1*-**dimensional superimposition term**, symbolically transcribed as

`Signatures⊗cls`

It represents that set of methods which consists of the members of (or inherited by) class cls with a signature in the set represented by Signatures, that is,

$$\mathcal{I}(\text{Signatures} \otimes \text{cls}) = \{\mathcal{I}(\text{sig}_1 \otimes \text{cls}), \ldots \mathcal{I}(\text{sig}_n \otimes \text{cls})\}$$

where $\text{sig}_1, \ldots \text{sig}_n$ stand for the signatures in Signatures. We call such a set of methods a **tribe in a class**, or simply a **tribe** (Legend 14).

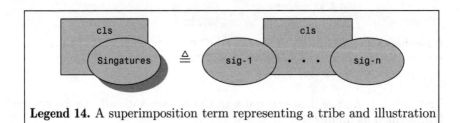

Legend 14. A superimposition term representing a tribe and illustration

Consider, for example, three of the methods of class BufferedReader in package java.io, depicted in Program 12.

Program 12. Three Methods in Class java.io.BufferedReader

```
public class BufferedReader …
    public int read() …
    public void mark(int) …
    public void reset() …
}
```

The methods in Program 12 can be characterised as follows:

- Each method has a distinct signature.
- Each method is a member of class BufferedReader.

The set of methods in Program 12 is therefore a *tribe* in class BufferedReader. They can be modelled individually, as demonstrated in Codechart 46a. More abstractly, we may use the *1*-dimensional signature constant BufferOps to model the set of their signatures, which if superimposed over bufferedReader models the entire tribe, as demonstrated in Codechart 46b.

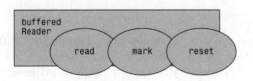

Codechart 46a. Three individual methods in BufferedReader

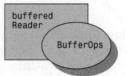

Codechart 46b. A tribe in BufferedReader

As was the case with other constants, the set of signatures that a
1-dimensional constant stands for can be spelled out using the interpretation
function notation. For example, the set of signatures that BufferOps stands
for is made explicit in the following equation:

$$\mathcal{I}(\,\texttt{BufferOps}\,) = \{\,\mathcal{I}(\,\texttt{read}\,), \mathcal{I}(\,\texttt{mark}\,), \mathcal{I}(\,\texttt{reset}\,)\,\}$$

Consider also the problem of modelling three of the methods in the class
LineNumberReader, which extends class BufferedReader (p. 86), depicted
in Program 13. Each method in LineNumberReader overrides a method in
its superclass with the same signature. Since the methods in class
LineNumberReader have the same three signatures represented by
BufferOps, it is a tribe that can also be modelled using BufferOps, as
demonstrated in Code chart 47b.

Program 13.   Three Methods in Class java.io.LineNumberReader

```
public class LineNumberReader extends BufferedReader { …
   public int read() {…
      super.read(); …
   }
   public void mark(int readAheadLimit) {…
      super.mark(readAheadLimit); …
   }
   public void reset(){…
      super.reset(); …
   }
   …
}
```

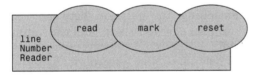

Codechart 47a.   Three individual methods in
LineNumberReader

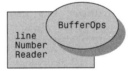

Codechart 47b.   A tribe in
LineNumberReader

Consider now the fact that each method in class LineNumberReader also
forwards the call to the method it overrides. In other words, the *Forward*
relation between the methods in LineNumberReader and the methods in
BufferedReader is an isomorphic relation. It can be modelled using three
individual *Forward* relation symbols, as demonstrated in Codechart 48a, but it
can also be modelled using the *ISOMORPHIC* predicate symbol, as
demonstrated in Codechart 48b.

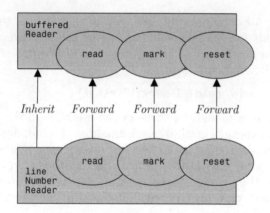 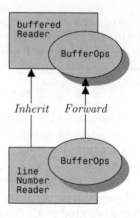

Codechart 48a. Each of three individual methods in `LineNumberReader` forwards the call to the method it overrides in `BufferedReader`

Codechart 48b. Each method in the tribe **BufferOps** ⊗ **lineNumberReader** forwards the call to the method it overrides in `BufferedReader`

Observe that the *ISOMORPHIC* predicate in Codechart 48b ensures that each method in class `LineNumberReader` matches with exactly one method in class `BufferedReader`. But does it also specify that each one be matched with the correct method? In other words, does Codechart 48b require that `LineNumberReader.read()` calls `BufferedReader.read()` and not any other method? The answer is Yes, by virtue of the *Forward* relation (see §6.5), which can only exist between methods with the same signature.

The symbols described in this chapter offer powerful abstraction mechanisms. Consequently, Codecharts can be very parsimonious. Consider, for example, the problem of modelling the relation between the set of methods in the class `Container` in package `java.awt` and the methods they override, depicted in Codechart 49b.

This illustrates the economy of expression gained by using predicate symbols and *1*-dimensional constants. We return to the problem of modelling classes `Container` and `Component` in our discussion in the Composite pattern (§11.1).

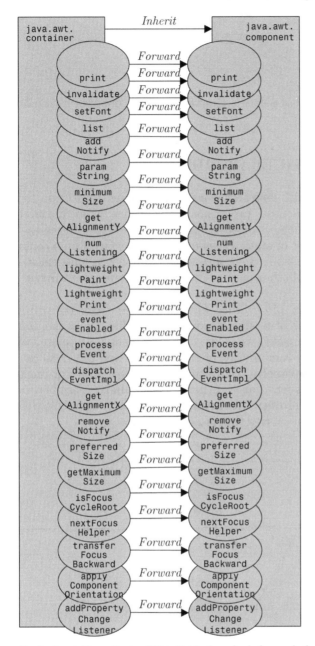

Codechart 49a. Each of 23 individual methods forwards the call to the method it overrides

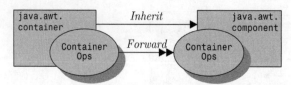

Codechart 49b. Each method in the tribe **ContainerOps**⊗ **container** forwards the call to the method it overrides

7.6 MODELLING CLASS HIERARCHIES

Inheritance is a powerful abstraction mechanism used by all non trivial and well-designed object-oriented programs. Inheritance class hierarchies are therefore ubiquitous in object-oriented programs and class libraries. In some programs, the entire set of static types (classes, interfaces, etc.) constitutes a single such hierarchy, as one class serves as a "universal base class", namely the class from which all other classes in the implementation inherit (directly or indirectly).

What exactly is an *inheritance hierarchy*? We focus our attention to hierarchies that consist of a single "root" class. That is, by an *inheritance hierarchy* (in short, *hierarchy*) we refer to a set of classes associated via single inheritance (in Java any combination of implements and extends relations).

Precisely put, a **hierarchy** (Definition IV) is a set of two or more classes that contain one class such that all other classes inherit (possibly indirectly) therefrom. A *1*-**dimensional hierarchy constant** (Legend 15) is a term which stands for a set of classes that is also a *hierarchy*.

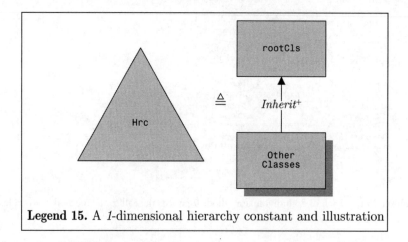

Legend 15. A *1*-dimensional hierarchy constant and illustration

Hierarchy constants offer us a powerful abstraction mechanism. For example, the combination of the interface Collection from package java.util with the four concrete collections that implement it, modelled in Codechart 50a, constitutes a hierarchy, modelled using the *1*-dimensional hierarchy constant CollectionsHrc in Codechart 50c.

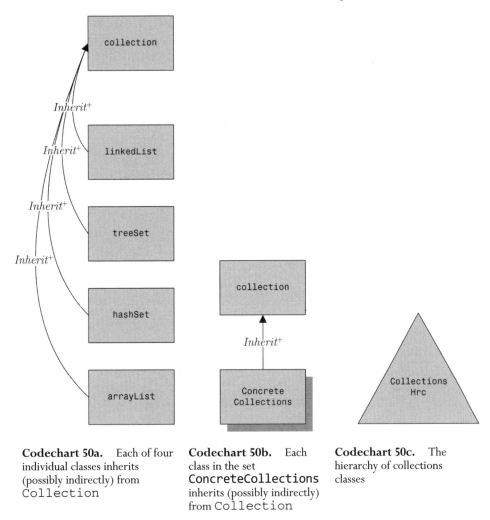

Codechart 50a. Each of four individual classes inherits (possibly indirectly) from `Collection`

Codechart 50b. Each class in the set `ConcreteCollections` inherits (possibly indirectly) from `Collection`

Codechart 50c. The hierarchy of collections classes

Should we wish to spell the set of classes that `CollectionsHrc` stands for, we may use the usual interpretation function notation, for example,

$$\mathcal{I}(\mathsf{CollectionsHrc})$$
$$= \{\mathcal{I}(\mathsf{collection}), \mathcal{I}(\mathsf{linkedList}), \mathcal{I}(\mathsf{treeSet}), \mathcal{I}(\mathsf{hashSet}), \mathcal{I}(\mathsf{arrayList})\}$$

By definition, a hierarchy is also a set of classes, and a *1*-dimensional hierarchy constant can be used in the same ways as a *1*-dimensional class constant, such as in predicate formulas. For example, consider the set of classes modelled by the `CollectionsHrc` hierarchy constant (Codechart 50). Since `Collection` is a subtype of `Object`, and since all the other classes in `CollectionsHrc` implement `Collection`, then the relation between the `CollectionsHrc` hierarchy and `Object` can be modelled using the *TOTAL* predicate formula

$$\mathit{TOTAL}(\mathit{Inherit^+}, \mathsf{CollectionsHrc}, \mathsf{object})$$

depicted in Codechart 51b. But this Codechart can be further abstracted, since the combination of all collection classes with class Object can too be modelled using a hierarchy constant, as demonstrated in Codechart 51c.

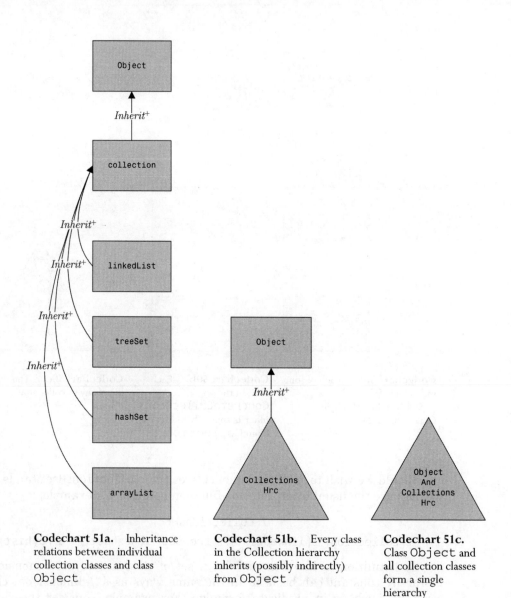

Codechart 51a. Inheritance relations between individual collection classes and class Object

Codechart 51b. Every class in the Collection hierarchy inherits (possibly indirectly) from Object

Codechart 51c. Class Object and all collection classes form a single hierarchy

Hierarchy constants offer a surprisingly useful abstraction mechanism. For example, since any class (and interface) in the Java™ or Smalltalk-80 programming languages inherits (possibly indirectly) from class `Object`, the entire set of classes and interfaces in any program written in these languages can be modelled by a single *1*-dimensional hierarchy constant, as demonstrated in Codechart 52.

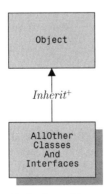

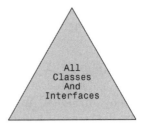

Codechart 52a. Any (fixed) set of classes/interfaces in Java or Smalltalk modelled using *0*- and *1*-dimensional class constants

Codechart 52b. Any (fixed) set of classes/interfaces in Java or Smalltalk modelled using a *1*-dimensional hierarchy constant

7.7 MODELLING METHODS IN HIERARCHIES

Section 7.3 introduced *clans* as sets of methods that share one signature. The examples we have encountered were clans in a set of classes. But in object-oriented programming, dynamic binding also requires that these classes form a *hierarchy*. Clans in hierarchies need therefore be modelled using hierarchy constants. They are modelled in the most obvious way, namely by superimposing a signature constant over a hierarchy constant.

Precisely put, the superimposition of a *0*-dimensional signature constant `sig` on a *1*-dimensional hierarchy constant `Hrc` is a *1*-**dimensional superimposition term**, symbolically transcribed as

$$sig \otimes Hrc$$

It is a term that represents that set of methods with signature `sig` which are members of (or inherited by) the classes in `Hrc`, that is,

$$\mathcal{I}(sig \otimes Hrc) = \{\mathcal{I}(sig \otimes cls_1), \dots \mathcal{I}(sig \otimes cls_n)\}$$

where $cls_1, \dots cls_n$ stand for the classes in `Hrc`. We refer to this kind of sets of methods as a **clan in a hierarchy** (Legend 16), otherwise simply as a **clan**.

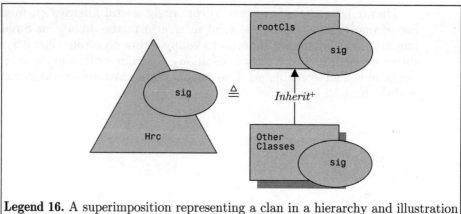

Legend 16. A superimposition representing a clan in a hierarchy and illustration

For example, the interface List is inherited by four classes in package java.util, depicted in Codechart 53a. Together these five classes constitute a hierarchy, modelled in Codechart 53b using the *1*-dimensional hierarchy constant **ListsHrc**. Each class in this hierarchy defines a method with the signature Add(Object), which can be represented using the *0*-dimensional signature constant **add**. The set of methods that override List.add(Object) is therefore a clan in **ListsHrc**, which may be modelled using the superimposition term **add⊗ListsHrc**, as demonstrated in Codechart 53b.

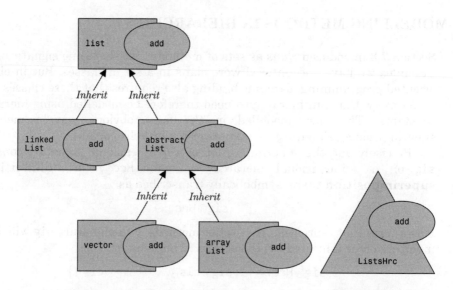

Codechart 53a. Five individual methods in the List classes modelled using *0*-dimensional terms

Codechart 53b. A set of dynamically bound methods modelled as a clan in hierarchy **ListsHrc**

The relations between clans and other methods or classes can also be modelled using the *TOTAL* and the *ISOMOPRHIC* predicate symbols. For example, consider the set of methods with signature next defined in the set of iterator classes in java.util, modelled in Codechart 54a. Since the set of iterator classes constitutes a hierarchy, the set of methods therein with signature next can be modelled using the superimposition term next⊗IteratorsHrc. The relation between this clan and class Object can therefore be modelled using a *TOTAL* predicate formula, as demonstrated in Codechart 54b.

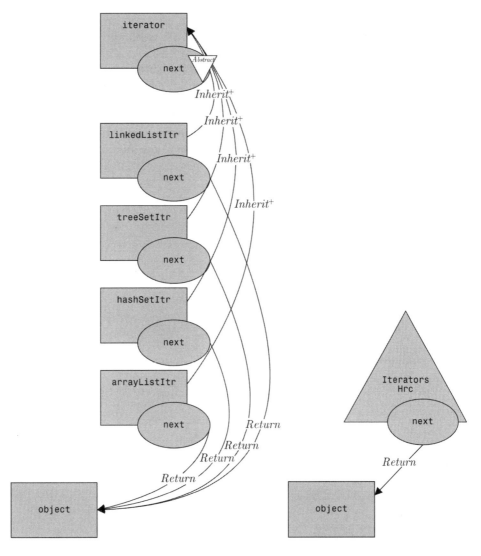

Codechart 54a. Five individual methods, all non abstract versions of which return instances of (subtypes of) Object

Codechart 54b. Each non abstract method in next⊗IteratorsHrc returns instances of (subtypes of) Object

It is important to add that *TOTAL* predicate formulas impose no constraints on abstract methods in their domain (Definition XII). For example, the formula

$$TOTAL(\ Return, \text{next} \otimes \text{IteratorsHrc}, \text{object})$$

in Codechart 54b requires only the concrete methods in next⊗IteratorsHrc to return instances of class Object. It requires nothing from the abstract method Iterator.next(). This exception was made because abstract methods have no body and may not contain any return statements.

A clan in a hierarchy may also be part of an *ISOMORPHIC* predicate formula. Consider, for example, the set of methods with signature newItr defined in the set of collection classes in java.util, depicted in Codechart 55a. Since this set of collection classes constitutes a hierarchy, represented by CollectionsHrc in Codechart 55b, its set of methods with signature newItr is a clan in CollectionsHrc, represented by newItr⊗CollectionsHrc. Since each method produces instances of exactly one class, the relation between this clan and the set of concrete iterators can be modelled using the *ISOMORPHIC* predicate formula, depicted in Codechart 55b.

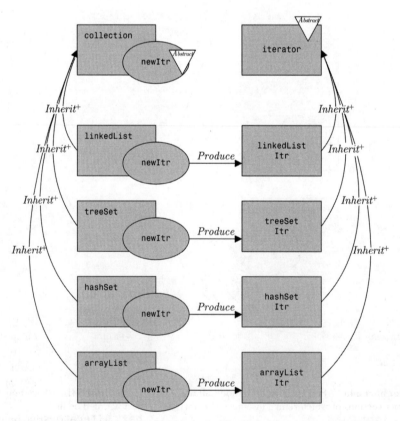

Codechart 55a. Five individual methods, all nonabstract versions of which produce instances of a unique iterator class

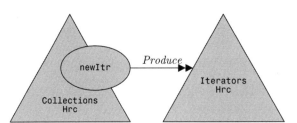

Codechart 55b. Each nonabstract method in newItr⊗CollectionsHrc produces instances of a unique nonabstract class in IteratorsHrc

7.8 MODELLING PROPERTIES OF SETS

If all elements of a set share a property, then this property can be modelled in the obvious way, namely by placing the respective unary relation symbol over the constant representing said set. In such cases the visual token used for representing unary relations (Legend 5) is referred to as the *ALL* predicate symbol.

Precisely put, an *ALL* **predicate formula** (Legend 17b), symbolically transcribed as

$$ALL(\ UnaryRelation, Domain)$$

specifies that all the elements of *Domain* are in the relation *UnaryRelation*.

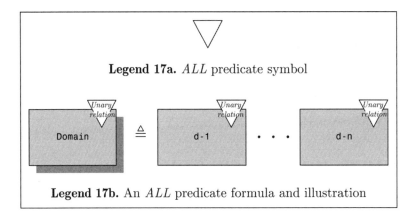

Legend 17a. *ALL* predicate symbol

Legend 17b. An *ALL* predicate formula and illustration

For example, abstract class AbstractList inherits from the interface List, which in turn inherits from the interface Collection, modelled in Codechart 56a. This set of three classes constitutes a hierarchy (with Collection as its root), so it can be modelled using the AbstractListHrc hierarchy constant, depicted in Codechart 56b. And since each one of these classes is abstract (or an interface), they can be modelled by the *ALL* predicate formula

$$ALL(\ Abstract, \text{AbstractListsHrc})$$

depicted in Codechart 56b

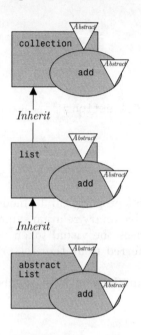

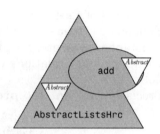

Codechart 56a. Three individual abstract classes and methods

Codechart 56b. A hierarchy of abstract classes and a clan of abstract methods

Similarly, each class in **AbstractListHrc** defines an abstract method with the signature **add**. Therefore, every method in the clan modelled by the superimposition **add**⊗**AbstractListHrc** is abstract. This property can be modelled using the *ALL* predicate formula

$$ALL(\textit{Abstract}, \textbf{add}{\otimes}\textbf{AbstractListsHrc})$$

also depicted in Codechart 56b.

7.9 * CASE STUDY: TOTAL VERSUS ISOMORPHIC

What exactly is the difference between the *TOTAL* and *ISOMORPHIC* predicates? The answer can be illustrated using a simple example taken from package java.lang, excerpts of which appear in Program 14.

Program 14. Extracts from java.lang

```
class Integer … implements Comparable { …
   int value; …
}
```
```
class Float … implements Comparable { …
   float value; …
}
```

Program 14 is modelled in Codechart 57. Let us now attempt to abstract Codechart 57. To do so we may introduce three *1*-dimensional class constants. To be precise, we may spell out the interpretation of each one of these constants:

$$\mathcal{I}(\texttt{TypeInterfaces}) = \{\mathcal{I}(\texttt{observer}), \mathcal{I}(\texttt{comparable})\}$$

$$\mathcal{I}(\texttt{NumberClassTypes}) = \{\mathcal{I}(\texttt{Integer}), \mathcal{I}(\texttt{Float})\}$$

$$\mathcal{I}(\texttt{NumberPrimitiveTypes}) = \{\mathcal{I}(\texttt{int}), \mathcal{I}(\texttt{float})\}$$

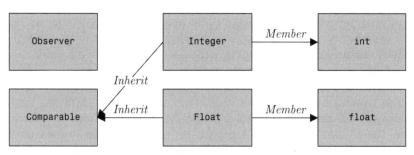

Codechart 57.   Program 14 modelled using binary relation symbols

Let us examine whether the *TOTAL* and *ISOMORPHIC* predicate symbols can be used to model the relations between these constants. Consider, for example, Codechart 58, in which both predicate symbols are used. Which one of these Codecharts is correct?

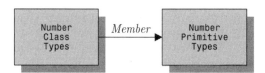

Codechart 58a.   Correct modelling of Program 14 using the *TOTAL* predicate symbol

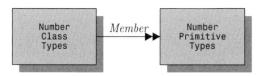

Codechart 58b.   Correct modelling of Program 14 using the *ISOMORPHIC* predicate symbol

As it happens, both Codechart 58a and Codechart 58b model Program 14 correctly. Let us see why: The formula

$$TOTAL(\textit{Member}, \texttt{NumberClassTypes}, \texttt{NumberPrimitiveTypes})$$

in Codechart 58a models this program correctly, because each number type (Integer and Float) holds a member of *some* primitive type (int or float). The formula

$$ISOMORPHIC(\ Member, \texttt{NumberClassTypes}, \texttt{NumberPrimitiveTypes})$$

in Codechart 58b also models Program 14 correctly because each number type (Integer and Float) holds a member of a *distinct* primitive type (int and float, respectively).

But while both Codecharts are correct, one of them (which uses the *ISOMORPHIC* predicate symbol) tells us more about the program. That is, Codechart 58b states that each number class has a member of *exactly one* primitive type, whereas Codechart 58a only tells us that each number class has a member of *some* primitive type. This demonstrates that relations that are isomorphic are also total. In other words, a double-headed arrow can *always* be replaced by a single-headed arrow.[5] Replacing an *ISOMORPHIC* symbol with a *TOTAL* symbol is therefore a step of abstraction.

The reverse however is not true. That is, a *TOTAL* predicate symbol may not always be replaced by an *ISOMORPHIC* symbol. Consider, for example, using these two predicate symbols in modelling the relations between NumberClassTypes and TypeInterfaces in Program 14, modelled in Codechart 59. Which one (or maybe both) of these charts is correct?

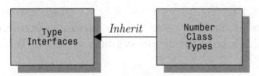

Codechart 59a.   Correct modelling of Program 14 using the *TOTAL* predicate symbol

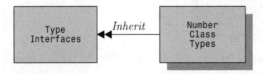

Codechart 59b.   Incorrect modelling of Program 14 using the *ISOMORPHIC* predicate symbol

Only one of the formulas in Codechart 59 models Program 14 correctly. Let us see why: The formula

$$TOTAL(\ Inherit, \texttt{NumberClassTypes}, \texttt{TypeInterfaces})$$

(Codechart 58a) models Program 14 correctly because each number type (Integer and Float) inherits from *some* interface type (Comparable). However, the formula

$$ISOMORPHIC(\ Inherit, \texttt{NumberClassTypes}, \texttt{TypeInterfaces})$$

---

[5]This operation is called "abstraction viz. predicate weakening"; see p. 204.

(Codechart 58b) does *not* model Program 14 correctly because no number class inherits from class Observer.

7.10 CASE STUDY: JDOM

Let us demonstrate the use of the symbols introduced in this chapter in modelling the JDOM class library. JDOM is an open-source Java class library which offers means of reading, writing, and manipulating files encoded in the eXtensible Markup Language (XML). Instances of two hierarchies of classes in JDOM can be used to create a tree structure which represents the contents of the XML file. These hierarchies are referred to as the Parent and the Content class hierarchies, modelled in this case study.

Three of the classes in the Parent hierarchy along with class Content are modelled in Codechart 60. At the root of this hierarchy is the interface Parent, from which the classes Document and Element inherit. These classes provide the basis for the JDOM tree data structure. Also modelled in Codechart 60 is the abstract method Parent.getContent(int), which is overridden by the concrete classes in this hierarchy. Each version of this method returns an instance of class Content which represents the actual value of each particular node in the tree.

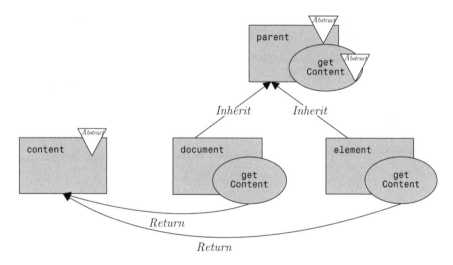

Codechart 60a.   The JDOM Parent hierarchy modelled using *0*-dimensional terms

These individual classes, methods, and relations can be abstracted as demonstrated in Codechart 60b: Since Parent, Document, and Element constitute a *hierarchy*, they can be modelled using a *1*-dimensional hierarchy constant ParentHrc. The set of methods with the signature getContent is a *clan in hierarchy* ParentHrc; hence it can be modelled by superimposing getContent over the hierarchy constant. Finally, the relation between this clan and class `Content` can now be modelled using a *TOTAL* predicate formula, also depicted in Codechart 60b.

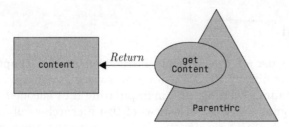

Codechart 60b. The JDOM Parent hierarchy modelled using a *1*-dimensional hierarchy constant

The `Content` class we have encountered in Codechart 60 is at the root of a hierarchy of seven classes, modelled in Codechart 61a. The hierarchy of Content classes can also be modelled more abstractly using a *1*-dimensional hierarchy constant, as demonstrated in Codechart 61b.

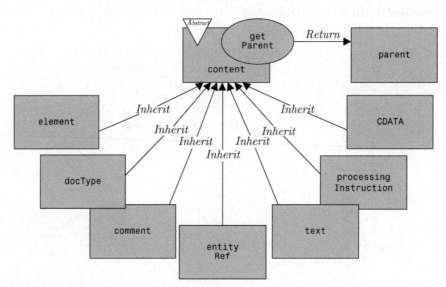

Codechart 61a. The JDOM Content hierarchy modelled using *0*-dimensional terms

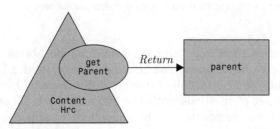

Codechart 61b. The JDOM Content hierarchy modelled using a *1*-dimensional hierarchy constant

Note that only the root of this hierarchy (class `Content`) defines a method with the signature `getParent()`. Since the method `Content.getParent()` is not overridden anywhere, the superimposition term **getParent**⊗**ContentHrc** in Codechart 61b stands for a clan with only one method: `Content.getParent()`. What use can a clan of one method be? Codechart 61b illustrates the answer to this question: abstraction. The set of (one) method modelled by the superimposition term **getParent**⊗**ContentHrc** conveys the fact that the method `getParent()` can be called with instances of any class in the Content hierarchy.

At the next step of abstraction, let us model the two hierarchies using the hierarchy constants **ContentHrc** and **ParentHrc**. Note that the *0*-dimensional class constants **Parent** (Codechart 60) and **Content** (Codechart 61) have disappeared, so no individual classes are modelled. Yet the *TOTAL* predicates with the *Return* relation symbol persist. What does Codechart 62 specify?

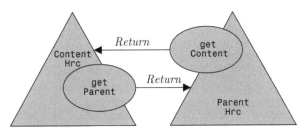

Codechart 62.   The JDOM Parent and Content hierarchies modelled using hierarchy constants

The formula

$$TOTAL(\,Return, \textbf{getParent} \otimes \textsf{ContentHrc}, \textsf{ParentHrc})$$

in Codechart 62 specifies that each one of the methods with signature `getParent()` in the Content hierarchy returns an instance of *some* class in the Parent hierarchy.

Symmetrically, the formula

$$TOTAL(\,Return, \textbf{getContent} \otimes \textsf{ParentHrc}, \textsf{ContentHrc})$$

in Codechart 62 specifies that each one of the methods with signature `getContent()` in the Parent hierarchy returns an instance of *some* class in the Content hierarchy.

7.11   CASE STUDY: JAVA 3D

Java 3D [https://java3d.dev.java.net] is a platform-independent class library supporting the representation, manipulation, and graphic rendering of three-dimensional geometrical objects in "virtual worlds" for use by applications such as games and simulated reality.[6] Since the API of version 1.5.2 of the

---

[6]The analysis reported here is based on [Maniati 2008]. As in other chapters, some of the details of Java 3D have been adapted for the purposes of this presentation.

Java 3D class library (henceforth: Java 3D) is very large and complex, the purpose of this case study is not to document it in full but merely to demonstrate how Codecharts can be used as roadmaps to the structural aspects of a large class library.

Java 3D data structures (graphs) are created to specify *three*-dimensional geometrical objects (such as cones and boxes) populating a simulated "universe", to move these objects about, and to specify some visual properties (such as illumination, fog, and shades). In common with many class libraries, services in Java 3D are offered through a well-defined interface, the library's API, designed to shield client applications from the complexity of the library's internal workings. Given the breadth and complexity of the problem domain, it is not surprising that even the library's API is rather large, consisting of over a thousand classes and inner classes. Hence any visualization of the API in terms of individual classes and methods—a fraction of which is depicted in Figure 7-1—is ineffective, thereby reiterating the concern for abstraction and scaling.

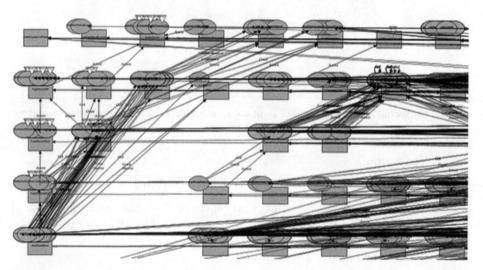

Figure 7-1.   Few of the individual classes and methods in Java 3D (adapted from [Maniati 2008], screenshot produced by the Design Navigator)

The *three*-dimensional objects that Java 3D applications create populate a virtual world that is called a "scene". Such objects and their principal visual properties are primarily represented using instances of classes that are organized in three hierarchies, depicted in Codecharts 63 and 64. Classes in the SceneGraphObjectHrc hierarchy (containing 156 classes) are intimately linked with classes organized in two other class hierarchies: SceneGraph ObjectStateHrc (containing 97 classes) and SceneGraphObjectRetainedHrc (containing 111 classes). This section is dedicated to Codecharts illustrating some of the correlations between classes in these three hierarchies.

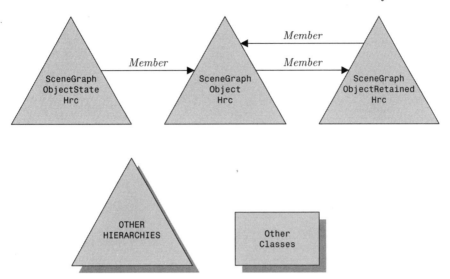

Codechart 63. Some hierarchies in Java 3D

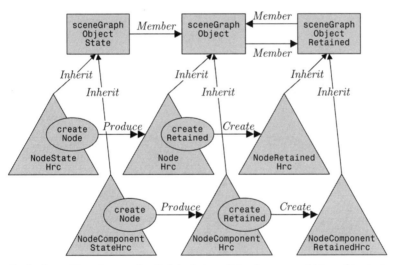

Codechart 64. A more detailed depiction of the three central hierarchies in Java 3D

"Nodes" in a scene graph are the objects that represent a *three*-dimensional virtual world. These objects are instances of subclasses of class Node, which inherits from the root class SceneGraphObject. A roadmap to this part of Java 3D is depicted in Codechart 65. It specifies that internal nodes in the scene graph are instances of subclasses of class Group, such as the *three*-dimensional objects (e.g., Sphere, Box, and Cylinder). A separate sub hierarchy of Node are the Leaf classes, instances of which are leaves in a scene graph, whose role is to determine the positioning and orienting of a view in the virtual world (e.g., Light and Fog).

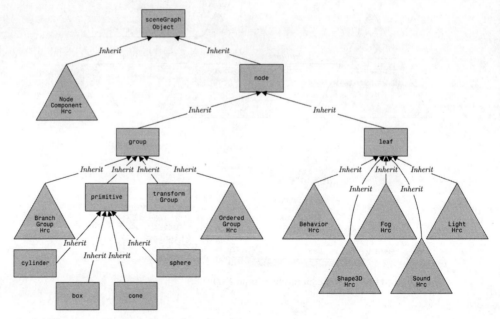

Codechart 65. The Node hierarchy in Java 3D

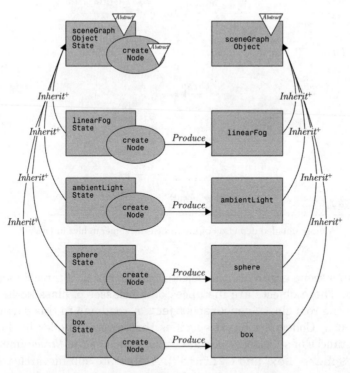

Codechart 66a. Four of the 90 concrete methods with the signature `createNode()` in the `SceneGraphObjectStateHrc` hierarchy and their respective products in the `SceneGraphObjectHrc` hierarchy

Classes in the SceneGraphObjectStateHrc hierarchy are responsible for reading from and writing into a persistent, linear representation of the scene graph data structure. Towards this end, this hierarchy effectively replicates the SceneGraphObjectHrc hierarchy, the relation between which is modelled in Codechart 66.

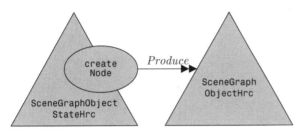

Codechart 66b. Each of the 90 concrete methods with the signature createNode() in the SceneGraphObjectStateHrc hierarchy produces instances of a unique class in the SceneGraphObjectHrc hierarchy

Codechart 66 specifies that the abstract root class SceneGraphObject State defines a member of type SceneGraphObject, which holds an instance of the respective class. For example, each instance of class linearFogState holds an instance of class LinearFog, whereas each instance of class SphereState holds an instance of class Sphere. In addition, each subclass in the SceneGraphObjectStateHrc hierarchy defines a factory method, called createNode(), which is responsible for producing an instance of the respective class from the SceneGraphObjectState hierarchy. For example, the method linearFogState.createNode() creates and returns an instance of class LinearFog, whereas SphereState.create Node()creates and returns an instance of class Sphere. This suggests that Codechart 66 depicts an instance of the Factory Method design pattern (to which §11.3 is dedicated).

A similar symmetry exists between the SceneGraphObjectHrc and the SceneGraphObjectRetained hierarchy, depicted in Codechart 67. The Codechart demonstrates that even the inheritance hierarchy structure is replicated in every detail in large parts of the hierarchy. In addition, each one of the classes in the former is responsible for creating an instance of the respective class in the latter, whereas each one of the classes in the latter is responsible for rendering instance of the respective class in the former. Furthermore, the mirroring is reinforced by a set of methods that change properties (whose names begin with set) and another set of methods that retrieve properties (whose names begin with get).

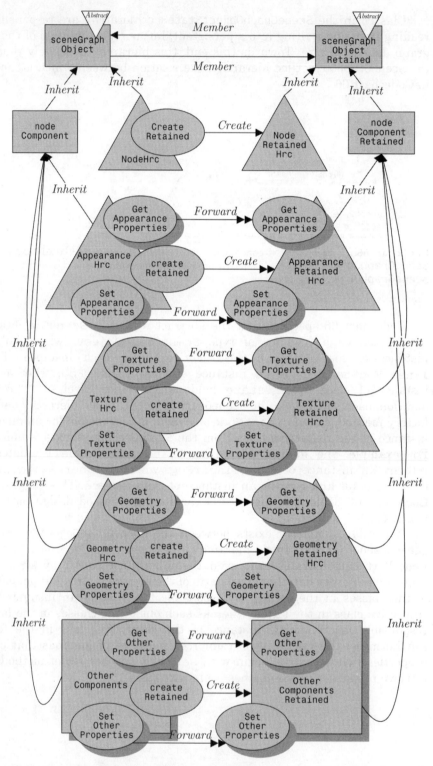

Codechart 67. Classes in the SceneGraphObjectHrc hierarchy mirror those in the SceneGraphObjectRetainedHrc hierarchy

Chapter 8

* Modelling Industry-Scale Programs

In Chapter 2 we discussed the need for powerful abstraction mechanisms that represent useful information about the design of our programs without clutter. And in Chapter 2 we were introduced to *1*-dimensional constants, which are powerful abstraction mechanisms for modelling large programs. But are *1*-dimensional constants enough to model industry-scale programs? Can a diagram that models such a system still "fit on the side of a van"? At first glance it appears that the *1*-dimensional constants should be enough because each may stand for sets of *any* number of classes or methods. However, in very large (industry-scale) programs, there can be hundreds of such sets, and the representation of each may very well clutter our diagrams. The scale of such systems therefore compels us to consider an even more abstract representation, one which stands for sets of sets, to which we refer as *entities of dimension 2*. Keeping true to our principle of elegance (p. 17), we only need introduce one new symbol to this end (Legend 18 on page 110). Indeed, correlations between sets of sets of classes and methods can be found not only in industry-scale programs but also in design patterns such as the Abstract Factory (§11.4) and the Visitor (Appendix I).

Let us demonstrate this using an example from package `java.util` in Java's SDK. Codechart 68a models five of the inheritance class hierarchies in the package. Each hierarchy is modelled using a *1*-dimensional hierarchy constant.

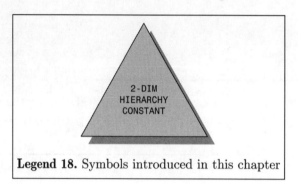

Legend 18. Symbols introduced in this chapter

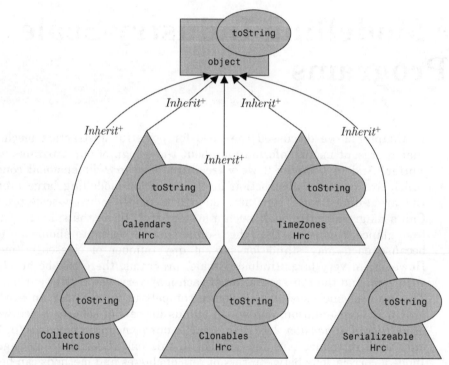

Codechart 68a. Some hierarchies in Java SDK modelled using *1*-dimensional hierarchy constants

Does Codechart 68a satisfy the Feynman–Tufte Principle? Just about. However, Java's SDK contains many more class hierarchies which are not depicted in Codechart 68a: exception classes, input–output facility classes, and security classes, to name but a few. Evidently modelling each hierarchy in the Java SDK library using *1*-dimensional hierarchy constants will lead to a cluttered chart, casting doubt on the scalability of Codecharts. Can these hierarchies be modelled in a more abstract manner without losing too much information about the structure of this class library?

One solution is to use a *1*-dimensional class constant for modelling all the classes that extend `Object`. But this solution is of little use because it merely conveys the trivial fact that there are many classes that inherit from class `Object`.[1] Can there be a more informative means of modelling the library? Alternatively, consider using a *2-dimensional hierarchy constant* for modelling the set of SDK hierarchies, such as `JAVA-SDK-HIERARCHIES` depicted in Codechart 68b. Fortunately, all we need to model a set of hierarchies is to extend our language with one additional symbol, that of a *2*-dimensional hierarchy constant (Legend 18). As can be seen in Codechart 68b, the combination of a *2*-dimensional hierarchy constant with the existing signature constants can be used to model sets of sets of dynamically bound methods. We shall continue to use the same predicate and relation symbols in the normal way.

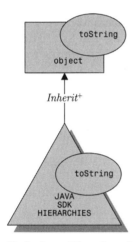

Codechart 68b. Some hierarchies in Java SDK modelled using a *2*-dimensional hierarchy constant

Compare Codechart 68b with Codechart 68a and observe the following:

- All the hierarchy constants were replaced with `JAVA-SDK-HIERARCHIES`.
- All occurrences of `toString` were replaced by one.
- All *Inherit* edges were replaced by one.

The remainder of this chapter is dedicated to demonstrating how *2*-dimensional hierarchy constants are used.

8.1 MODELLING SETS OF HIERARCHIES

When modelling large programs, it is useful to represent a set of class hierarchies with one symbol. A **2-dimensional hierarchy constant** (Legend 19) is a term that represents a specific set of *hierarchies* (§7.6).

---

[1]Note that interfaces such as `Cloneable` and `Serializeable` are subtypes of `Object`. Java subtyping is modelled using the binary relation symbol *Inherit*.

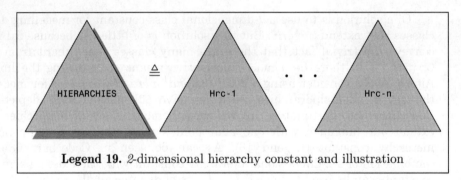

Legend 19. *2*-dimensional hierarchy constant and illustration

Two-dimensional hierarchy constants are useful in modelling a wide range of large applications. One example is the Java SDK library given at the introduction to this chapter. As another example, consider the set of classes in `java.util` that inherit from `Collection`. Each one of these classes inherits (possibly indirectly) from the interfaces `List` and `Set`. Therefore, the set of collection classes can be broken into two class hierarchies modelled in Codechart 69a using the `ListsHrc` and `SetsHrc` *1*-dimensional hierarchy constants. Alternatively, these two hierarchies can be modelled using the *2*-dimensional hierarchy constant `COLLECTION-HRCS`, as demonstrated in Codechart 69b.

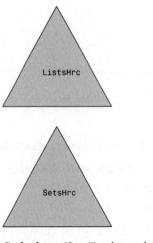

Codechart 69a. Two hierarchies in `java.util`

Codechart 69b. A set of hierarchies in `java.util`

8.2 MODELLING SETS OF SETS OF METHODS (CLANS)

Sets of sets of methods are modelled using *2*-dimensional terms using the superimposition mechanism in a manner similar in principle to modelling sets of methods. In particular, we may use a *0*-dimensional signature constant to specify that all the methods in all the sets share one signature.

Precisely put, the superimposition of a *0*-dimensional signature constant `sig` over a *2*-dimensional hierarchy constant `HIERARCHIES` is called a **2-dimensional superimposition term**, symbolically transcribed as

$$\texttt{sig} \otimes \texttt{HIERARCHIES}$$

It represents that set of sets of methods with signature `sig` that are members of (or inherited by) the classes in each hierarchy in `HIERARCHIES`. In other words,

$$\mathcal{I}(\texttt{sig} \otimes \texttt{HIERARCHIES}) = \{\mathcal{I}(\texttt{sig} \otimes \texttt{Hrc}_1), \dots \mathcal{I}(\texttt{sig} \otimes \texttt{Hrc}_n)\}$$

where $\texttt{Hrc}_1, \dots \texttt{Hrc}_n$ stand for the hierarchies in `HIERARCHIES`. Since such a set of sets of methods is also a set of *clans* (§7.3), and since it is deemed a natural extension to a *clan*, we refer to it as a **clan of clans** (Legend 20).

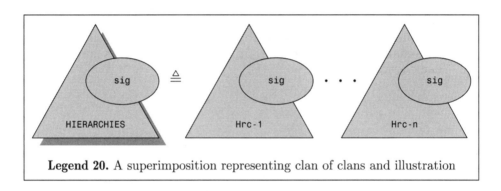

Legend 20. A superimposition representing clan of clans and illustration

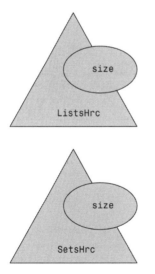

Codechart 70a. Two clans in two hierarchies

Codechart 70b. A clan of clans in a set of hierarchies

Clans of clans are abundant in large software libraries. For example, there is a clan of methods with the signature `size()` in each one of the hierarchy of collection classes in `java.util`. Specifically, the (abstract) methods which override `Collection.size()` in the interfaces `List` and `Set` are each in turn overridden by methods in the classes which implement each interface. These clans are modelled in Codechart 70a using two superimposition terms, **size**⊗**ListsHrc** and **size**⊗ SetsHrc. Alternatively, since this set of clans constitutes a clan of clans in **COLLECTION-HRCS**, it can be modelled using the superimpositions of the signature constant **sig** over the set of hierarchies in **COLLECTION-HRCS**, as demonstrated in Codechart 70b.

In another example, consider modelling the set of `toString()` methods that are members of (or inherited by) classes in the Java SDK. This set of methods may be divided into several clans, each in a different hierarchy, and modelled using *1*-dimensional superimposition terms as demonstrated in Codechart 71a. Alternatively, it can be modelled as a clan of clans as demonstrated in Codechart 71b.

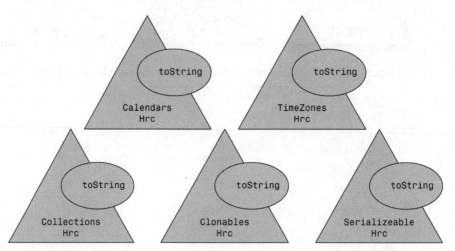

Codechart 71a.   Five clans in five hierarchies in Java SDK

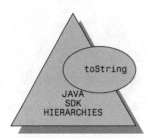

Codechart 71b.   A clan of clans in Java SDK

8.3 MODELLING SETS OF SETS OF METHODS (TRIBES)

When modelling industry-scale programs, we may wish to represent collectively not only a clan of clans but also other sets of clans. In particular, we may wish to cluster together clans which do not share a unique signature. For example, there can be several clans in the same hierarchy, each of which is associated with a distinct signature. These are modelled collectively by superimposing the representation of the set of signatures (a *1*-dimensional signature constant) over the representation of the hierarchy (a *1*-dimensional class or hierarchy constant).

Precisely put, the superimposition of a *1*-dimensional signature constant `Signatures` over a *1*-dimensional class constant `Classes` is a *2*-**dimensional superimposition term**, symbolically transcribed as

$$\mathtt{Signatures} \otimes \mathtt{Classes}$$

which represents that set of clans in `Classes` such that each clan has a signature in `Signatures`. In other words,

$$\mathcal{I}(\mathtt{Signatures} \otimes \mathtt{Classes}) = \{\mathcal{I}(\mathtt{sig}_1 \otimes \mathtt{Classes}), \ldots \mathcal{I}(\mathtt{sig}_n \otimes \mathtt{Classes})\}$$

where $\mathtt{sig}_1, \ldots \mathtt{sig}_n$ stand for the signatures in `Signatures`. Since such a set of sets of methods is a natural extension to the notion of a *tribe* (§7.5), we refer to it as a **tribe of clans** (Legend 21a). The superimposition of a *1*-dimensional signature constant over a *1*-dimensional hierarchy is similarly defined (Legend 21b).

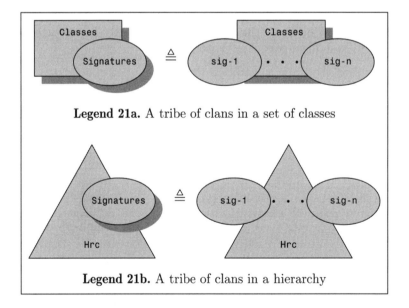

Legend 21a. A tribe of clans in a set of classes

Legend 21b. A tribe of clans in a hierarchy

Tribes of clans can be illustrated using a small example from Java's HTTP servlets. To simplify matters, let us begin with the problem of modelling a single servlet, called `WebAppServlet`, which consists of four methods modelled in Codechart 72a. Since these are a *tribe* in `WebAppServlet`, they may also be modelled using the superimposition term `ServletOps⊗webAppServlet`, depicted in Codechart 72b.

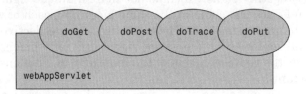

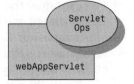

Codechart 72a. Four individual methods in class `WebAppServlet`

Codechart 72b. A tribe in `WebAppServlet`

Consider now the problem of modelling not one but many HTTP servlets and the four methods defined in each servlet. Each such class must override the same four methods that `WebAppServlet` defines. We may start by introducing a *1*-dimensional class constant `ManyServlets`, depicted in Codechart 73. Introducing this constant allows us to model all the servlet methods by superimposing each one of the four signature constants over `ManyServlets`, as demonstrated in Codechart 73a. This Codechart therefore depicts four clans in `ManyServlets`: `doGet⊗ManyServlets`, `doPost⊗Many Servlets`, `doTrace⊗ManyServlets`, and `doPut⊗ManyServlets`.

Alternatively, since each set of methods is a clan in `ManyServlets`, this set of clans constitutes a tribe of clans in `ManyServlets`. Therefore it can be modelled by superimposing the *1*-dimensional signature `ServletOps` over `ManyServlets`, as demonstrated in Codechart 73b.

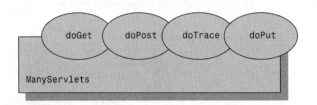

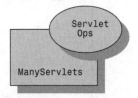

Codechart 73a. Four clans in `ManyServlets`

Codechart 73b. A tribe of clans in `ManyServlets`

A tribe of clans in a hierarchy is modelled in a similar manner to a tribe of clans in a set of classes. For example, consider the `ListsHrc` hierarchy modelled in Codechart 53 (p. 94). Each class in this hierarchy defines (or inherits) methods that override the methods in class `List`, including `List.add(Object)`, `List.size()`, and `List.clear()`. Therefore, the set of methods with the signature add(Object) is a clan in ListsHrc, and so are the sets of methods with the signatures size() and clear(). These three clans may be modelled separately using three superimposition terms, as demonstrated in Codechart 74a. Note that if the three signatures are abstracted using a 1-dimensional signature constant ListOps, then all three clans can jointly be modelled as a *tribe of clans* using the term ListOps⊗ListsHrc, as demonstrated in Codechart 74b.

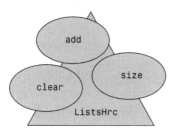

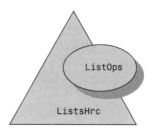

Codechart 74a.   Three clans in the List hierarchy

Codechart 74b.   A tribe of clans in the List hierarchy

We need not always cluster together all the methods under one symbol. Consider, for example, the seven clans in the JDomFactoriesHrc hierarchy modelled in Codechart 75a. The set of clans whose signature is of the form element... create instances of class Element, whereas the set of clans whose signature is of the form docType... create instances of class DocType. It is therefore sensible to model the first set of clans as one tribe of clans and the

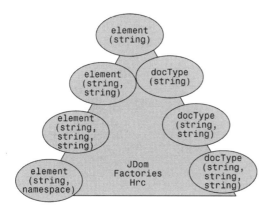

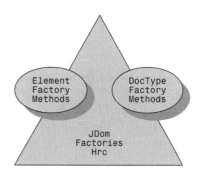

Codechart 75a.   Seven clans in JDOM's Factory hierarchy

Codechart 75b.   Two tribes of clans in JDOM's Factory hierarchy second set of clans as another, as demonstrated in Codechart 75b. To do so we introduce two separate *1*-dimensional signature constants: `ElementFactory Methods` and `DocTypeFactoryMethods`.

8.4 MODELLING TOTAL RELATIONS REVISITED

Correlations between the *2*-dimensional entities are modelled using the same predicate symbols introduced in the previous chapter with the obvious meaning. In particular, our definition for total predicates extends naturally for higher dimensions. That is, a *TOTAL* predicate symbol between terms modelling sets of sets of entities specifies a mapping of *each* element in the domain with *some* element in the range.

Precisely put, the formula

$$TOTAL(\ BinaryRelation, Domain, Range)$$

where *Domain* and *Range* are *2-dimensional terms* specifies that each set *D* in the set represented by *Domain* [2] there exists some set *R* in the set represented by *Range* such that the following formula holds[3]:

$$TOTAL(\ BinaryRelation, D, R)$$

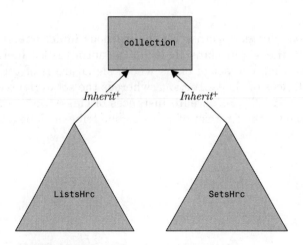 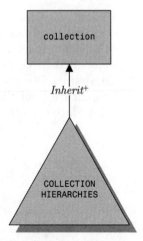

Codechart 76a. Every class in `ListsHrc` and `SetsHrc` inherits (possibly indirectly) from `Collection`

Codechart 76b. Every class in one of the hierarchies in **COLLECTION-HIERARCHIES** inherits (possibly indirectly) from `Collection`

[2] Except for abstract methods, see Definition XII.
[3] Where by convention we assume $\mathcal{I}(D) = \underline{D}$ and $\mathcal{I}(R) = \underline{R}$

For example, consider the set of collection hierarchies modelled in Codechart 69. From this example we know that the abstract and concrete List and Set collection classes can be organized into two hierarchies, modelled in Codechart 76a by ListsHrc and SetsHrc. We also know that all these classes inherit (possibly indirectly) from Collection. The relations between all the classes in ListsHrc and SetsHrc and class Collection are total relations and therefore can be modelled using the *TOTAL* predicate formulas depicted in Codechart 76a. Alternatively, the two *1*-dimensional hierarchy constants can be replaced with a *2*-dimensional hierarchy constant COLLECTION-HRCS, as demonstrated In Codechart 76b.

The predicate formulas in Codechart 76b can be symbolically transcribed as follows:

$$TOTAL(\mathit{Inherit^+}, \mathtt{ListsHrc}, \mathtt{collection})$$

$$TOTAL(\mathit{Inherit^+}, \mathtt{SetsHrc}, \mathtt{collection})$$

Note that the *TOTAL* predicate formula Codechart 76b serves the same role as it does in modelling relations between sets. That is, the formula

$$TOTAL(\mathit{Inherit^+}, \mathtt{COLLECTION\text{-}HIERARCHIES}, \mathtt{collection})$$

specifies that every hierarchy in COLLECTION-HRCS inherits from class Collection, which in turn means that each class in each hierarchy in COLLECTION-HIERARCHIES inherits from class Collection.

Let us consider another example for total relations between sets of sets. To do so, we return to the example of the JDOM factory methods in the JDomFactoriesHrc hierarchy (§7.10), in which we have encountered seven clans of factory methods in the JDomFactoriesHrc hierarchy. These clans were modelled using seven superimposition terms, modelled in Codechart 77a. Also modelled in this chart are seven *TOTAL* predicate formulas that model the *Produce* relation between each clan and class Element or DocType. Alternatively, we may represent these seven clans using two tribes of clans: The first, modelled using the superimposition term ElementFactory Methods⊗JDomFactoriesHrc, stands for the set of clans that produce instances of class Element, whereas the second, modelled using the term DocTypeFactoryMethods⊗JDomFactoriesHrc, stands for the clans that produce instances of DocType, as demonstrated in Codechart 77b.

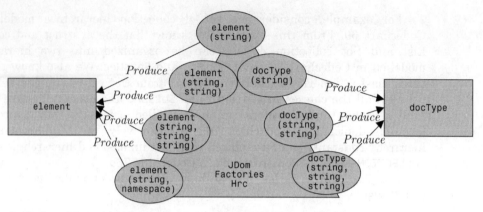

Codechart 77a.   Each method in four clans produces instances of Element, and each method in three other clans produces instances of DocType

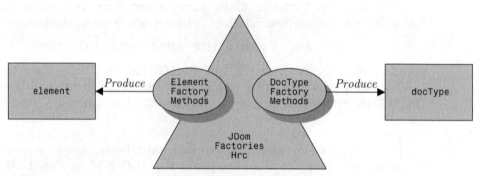

Codechart 77b.   Each method in one tribe of clans produces instances of Element, and each method in a different tribe of clans produces instances of DocType

8.5   MODELLING ISOMORPHIC RELATIONS REVISITED

The definition of the *ISOMORPHIC* predicate symbol provided in §7.4 extends naturally to represent a pair wise relation between elements of sets. Precisely put, an *ISOMORPHIC* **predicate formula**, symbolically transcribed as

$$ISOMORHIC(\ BinaryRelation, Domain, Range)$$

where *Domain* and *Range* are 2-dimensional terms, specifes that each set D in *Domain* matches with exactly one set R in *Range* such that the formula[4]

$$ISOMORPHIC(\ BinaryRelation, D, R)$$

holds. In other words, the isomorphism extends to the sets in *Domain* and *Range*, as illustrated in Figure 8-1.

---

[4]Where by convention we assume $\mathcal{I}(\mathsf{D}) = \underline{\mathsf{D}}$ and $\mathcal{I}(\mathsf{R}) = \underline{\mathsf{R}}$.

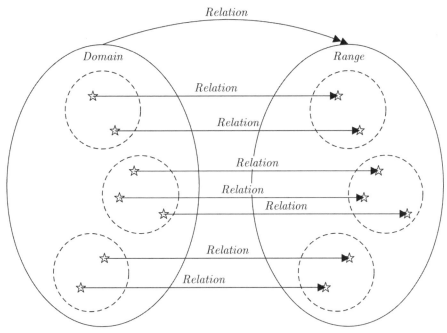

Figure 8-1. Illustration: an isomorphic relation between 2-dimensional entities

To demonstrate the use of the *ISOMORPHIC* predicate formulas with sets of sets, consider, for example, the portable widget factory application [Gamma et al. 1995, p. 87]. We present this example below in a bottom-up fashion: We begin with modelling the details of simple relations between individual classes and methods and conclude with the problem of modelling sets of sets.

The portable widget factory is an application that operates across different operating systems, each using a different native user interface. Each one of the operating systems implements a set of graphical user interface tokens called *widgets*: windows, scroll bars, push buttons, radio buttons, check boxes, and so on. Libraries providing such sets of graphical user interfaces and desktop environments are called *window managers*. These include, amongst many, Motif, which was used in a range of UNIX operating systems, and Presentation Manager, which is associated with IBM's OS/2 operating system. Many other window managers are in existence (which further justifies the introduction a level of abstraction between them and their clients), but for the sake of simplicity of this example we restrict it to the former two.

For example, the class `MotifWindow` encapsulates the notion of a "window" in Motif: It implements the operations that windows generally support using the functions in Motif and UNIX services, such as maximize, minimize, and move. In contrast, class `PMWindow` implements the same operations using the functions in Presentation Manager and the OS/2's services. Similarly, class `MotifScrollBar` provides scrollbar functionality to Motif, whereas class `PMScrollBar` provides similar functionality to Presentation Manager. These four widget classes are depicted in Codechart 78.

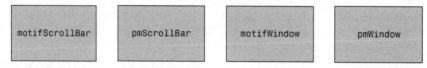

Codechart 78.   Scrollbar and window classes for two kinds of window managers

Each set of widgets (all window classes for example) can be abstracted into a *hierarchy* by introducing an abstract root class standing for the abstract widget (an abstract window class). Abstract widgets define an interface for the functionality that is common to concrete widgets of that category. For example, the abstract window class is a superclass of `MotifWindow` and of `PMWindow`. It defines the operations for maximize, minimize, move, and so on, that are implemented by methods in `MotifWindow` and in `PMWindow`. Together these three classes constitute a hierarchy of window classes which allows the users to operate on any window using dynamic binding, as demonstrated in Program 15. Note that no specific operating system is mentioned in Program 15. This step of abstraction therefore offers programmers the opportunity to write *polymorphic* code.

Program 15.   Sample Use of Abstract Class Window

```
class client {
  public void windowClient(Window aWindow) {...
    anyWindow.minimize();
    ...
    anyWindow.maximize();
    ...
  }
...
```

In a similar way, all scrollbar classes can be abstracted using one abstract class called `ScrollBar`, which defines the interface that is common to all scrollbar classes. Codechart 79 models the abstract and concrete widget classes in this application.

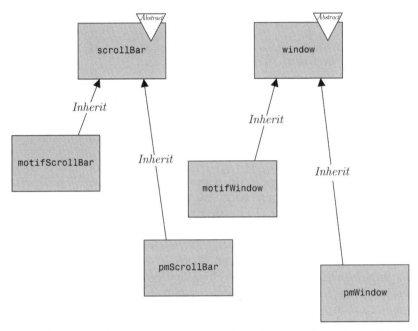

Codechart 79. Abstract and concrete scrollbar and window classes for two kinds of window managers

Introducing an abstract class for each category of widgets is useful because it allows applications to use widgets without extensive commitment to any particular window manager. This is true with only one exception: the creation of widgets. For example, when an instance of the window class need be created, the constructor of either class `MotifWindow` or class `PMWindow` needs to be called. This forces the clients of our widget classes to break the principle of abstraction and start introducing references to particular operating systems, as demonstrated in Program 16. Such a programming style, referred to as *monomorphic* (as opposed to *polymorphic*), poses a problem when programs evolve. A system implemented in this manner will be "brittle": Any change to the number and type of window managers—a change that is very likely to occur with the development of new operating systems—will break the program and render it invalid. For instance, introducing support for the Windows Vista window manager means that all monomorphic statements such as the above `switch` statement will "break". This conflicts with the need for *changeability* (Chapter 1).

Program 16. Sample Use of Abstract Class Window

```
class client {
  public void windowCreator() {
    …
    // A new window is needed, create one the old-fashioned way:
    Window newWindow;

    switch (kind_of_window_manager) {
        case MOTIF                  : newWindow = new MotifWindow();
        case PRESENTATION_MANAGER   : newWindow = new PMWindow();
        … // and so forth for each window manager
    }  …
  }…
```

Fortunately, a polymorphic alternative to Program 16 is possible. It involves the use of a set of "factory methods" in "widget factories": classes that provide a polymorphic mechanism of creating new widgets. For example, instead of using a switch statement, a client using a widget factory will be able to create a window by writing the commands such as those demonstrated in Program 17. By this solution, the only part of the portable widget factory that will be monomorphic is where the global widget factory (aWidgetFactory in Program 17) is generated, as demonstrated in Program 18. For example, if aWidgetFactory is an instance of class MotifWidgetFactory, then executing the statement aWidgetFactory.CreateWindow() will dynamically bind to MotifWidgetFactory.CreateWindow(), which produces instances of class MotifWindow. The set of CreateWindow() is therefore a set of factory methods: a clan which jointly offers a dynamically bound set of methods for creating the window class that is most appropriate to each window manager.

Program 17. Sample Use of an Abstract Widget Factory for Creating a Window

```
// Use a widget factory to create the CORRECT window
Window aWindow = aWidgetFactory.CreateWindow();

// Call will generate an instance of either MotifWindow or
PMWindow
```

Program 18. The Only Monomorphic Code Necessary for a Widget Factory

```
switch (operating_system) {
  case MOTIF                  : aWidgetFactory = new MotifWidgetFactory();
  case PRESENTATION_MANAGER   : aWidgetFactory = new PMWidgetFactory();
}
```

The resulting sets of widget classes, factory classes, and factory methods constitute a widget factory, modelled in Codechart 80a.

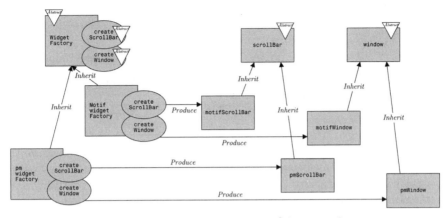

Codechart 80a. The Widget Factory modelled using *0*-dimensional terms

Consider now the problem of modelling individual classes and methods in the widget factory. Codechart 80a fits on the side of a van merely because it is a simplistic example, considering only two window managers and two kinds of widgets. But actual software systems normally contend with many more window managers (arising from the need to write portable applications that can be used across different operating systems) and widgets, such as radio buttons, push buttons, check boxes, and dialog boxes. Modelling an entire widget factory would be unwieldy.

As a first step of abstraction, consider modelling the hierarchy of windows, the hierarchy of scrollbars, and the hierarchy of factory classes using a *1*-dimensional hierarchy constant, as demonstrated in Codechart 80b. Note that the *Produce* relations in Codechart 80b are isomorphic, meaning that each factory method in `createWindow⊗WidgetFactories` produces instance of a distinct (concrete) window, and each factory method in `createScrollBar⊗WidgetFactories` produces instances of a distinct nonabstract scrollbar.

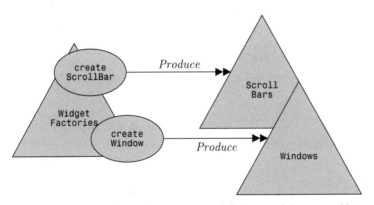

Codechart 80b. The Widget Factory modelled using *1*-dimensional hierarchies

If necessary, the interpretation of these hierarchy constants can be spelled out as follows:

$$\mathcal{I}(\text{Windows}) = \{\underline{\text{window}}, \underline{\text{motifWindow}}, \underline{\text{pMWindow}}\}$$

$$\mathcal{I}(\text{ScrollBars}) = \{\underline{\text{scrollBar}}, \underline{\text{motifScrollBar}}, \underline{\text{pMScrollBar}}\}$$

$$\mathcal{I}(\text{WidgetFactories}) = \{\underline{\text{widgetFactory}}, \underline{\text{motifWidgetFactory}},$$
$$\underline{\text{pMWidgetFactory}}\}$$

But our abstraction need not stop with Codechart 80b. Observe that each *Produce* formula associates exactly one clan in **WidgetFactories** with exactly one widget hierarchy. In other words, the *Produce* relation is also an isomorphism between the set of clans in **WidgetFactories** and the set of widget hierarchies. This gives us the opportunity to further abstract Codechart 80b without losing too much information by modelling *2*-dimensional methods and class hierarchies with the Isomorphic predicate between them. Specifically, we may introduce the *1*-dimensional signature constant **FactoryMethods** to stand for the set of signatures of all the factory methods and the *2*-dimensional hierarchy constant **WIDGETS** to stand for the set of widget hierarchies, as demonstrated in Codechart 80c. Codechart 80c demonstrates the economy of expression that *2*-dimensional terms and *ISOMORPHIC* predicate symbols provide. It illustrates that, where regularities such as isomorphic relations are found, abstraction need not introduce ambiguity or lose too much of the information. Indeed, Codechart 80c does not specify what kinds of widgets exist, but it does specify that for each kind of widget a corresponding set of factory methods exists in the application. Often, this is all that a software designer may wish to specify about the program.

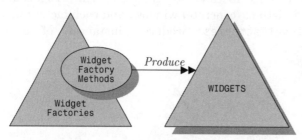

Codechart 80c.   The Widget Factory modelled using *1*- and *2*-dimensional hierarchies

In §15.3 we prove that the widget factory is an implementation of the Abstract Factory design pattern.

Chapter 9

Modelling Design Motifs

The previous chapters were concerned with the problem of modelling specific programs and class libraries, small and big. This chapter is concerned with a different problem: that of modelling design motifs such as design patterns and application frameworks. Below we examine the requirements posed by the principle of *genericity* (§3.6). We discuss *design motifs* and try and understand why modelling them poses a different set of problems to those encountered so far. This discussion will motivate the introduction of *variables* into our design description language.

We take a **design motif** to be a blueprint or a template, an abstraction that can be implemented in (at least in principle) an unbounded number of ways—the word "pattern" comes to mind except that this term has become rather specialized (see §10.2). Design motifs are *not* programs; they are abstractions of programs. For example, the Widget Factory (§8.5) is said to *implement* the Abstract Factory design pattern, but there is an unbounded number of other possible implementations of the same pattern. Therefore, we think of design patterns such as the Abstract Factory as design motifs.

How should design motifs be modelled? The constants introduced in the previous chapters represent specific parts of specific programs: classes, methods, and sets thereof. Design motifs are not any part of any specific programs. Therefore the problem of modelling design motifs is fundamentally different from the problem of modelling programs. Unfortunately, this distinction is lost on most informal modelling notations. But in Codecharts, design motifs and in particular design patterns receive special attention, a commitment to which we refer as the principle of *genericity* (§3.6). In fact, modelling design patterns is important enough to compromise our commitment to the *minimality* principle (§3.7) and justify the introduction of variables, a whole new set of symbols designed for the very purpose of modelling design motifs.

We introduce the subject of modelling design motifs using Java Remote Method Invocation (RMI) as an example. The RMI documentation states that [Sun 1999]:

> *A remote interface must at least extend, either directly or indirectly, the interface java.rmi.Remote*

Let us attempt to model this statement using one of the constants encountered so far. For example, let us use *0*-dimensional class constants (§6.1) for this purpose, as demonstrated in Codechart 81.

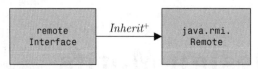

Codechart 81.   Elements in an implementation of Java RMI

In Codechart 81, "a remote interface" is represented using the `remoteInterface` constant. However, constants have specific interpretations. What may the interpretation of `remoteInterface` be? Perhaps to a (Java) class called `RemoteInterface`?

$$\mathcal{I}(\,\texttt{remoteInterface}) = \underline{\texttt{remoteInterface}}$$

Of course, doing so is absurd: Surely forcing every remote interface class to be called `RemoteInterface` is unnecessarily restrictive. For example, making such a commitment means that we cannot have more than one remote interface in any given package. Clearly, *a* remote interface is not a name of a class but a place holder for *any* remote interface. A *hypothetical* remote interface should not be confused with a *particular implementation* of a remote interface. Using a constant in this case would therefore be a mistake.

If there exists more than one implementation of it then perhaps a remote interface should be represented as a *1*-dimensional class constant, say, `RemoteInterfaces`, which stands for all classes implementing it. Or perhaps `RemoteInterfaces` should be understood as the set of all *hypothetical* classes and static types. Unfortunately, neither of these solutions are appropriate because the set which constitutes "the entire *category* of implementations" is rather ill-defined: It must change each time we implement it. It is also misleading because some programs have no remote interfaces, but that should not affect the specification of Java RMI. In conclusion, constants will not do. What is required is therefore an altogether different mechanism of abstraction.

This motivates the introduction of *variables* into our design description language. For example, let us use a *0*-dimensional class variable to model any remote interface, as demonstrated in Codechart 82.

Codechart 82. Elements in the generic Java RMI design motif

The change here is subtle but important: While the constant `remoteInterface` stands for a fixed, specific class, the variable *remoteInterface* stands for a *hypothetical* class. Variables such as *remoteInterface* have no specific interpretations. Instead, *remoteInterface* is used in Codechart 82 as a placeholder for the purpose of specifying constraints on the hypothetical class. Specifically, Codechart 82 requires this hypothetical remote interface class to inherit (possibly indirectly) from class `java.rmi.Remote`. It poses no other restrictions on this class. For this reason, Codechart 82 captures and conveys Java RMI much better than Codechart 81.

Variables, as distinguished from *constants*, are commonplace in many programming and specification languages. For example, the variable `timeout` in Program 19 represents a location in the computer's memory which holds the numerical value that was passed as an argument to the method `Object.wait` in each invocation thereof during the execution of the program. It is a variable because the value it holds may be different each time the method is invoked. In contrast, the digit 0 in Program 19 is called a constant because it represents a fixed numerical value which is used to represent the integer *0*.

Program 19. Variables and Constants in Java

```
class Object { …
   public void wait(long timeout, int nanos) {
      if (timeout < 0) {
…
```

Variables are also prevalent in all areas of mathematics. Algebraic variables serve as placeholders too. For example, x is a variable, and *2* and *5* are constants in the equation

$$2x^2 + x - 3$$

We say that x ranges over the set of values that it may take, such as the set of real numbers or the set of composite numbers.

Variables and constants are also commonplace in mathematical logic. Consider, for example, the following formula in the predicate logic:

$$\forall x \bullet \mathit{Orbits}(x, \mathsf{TheSun}) \Rightarrow \mathit{Galaxy}(x, \mathsf{TheMilkyWay})$$

It specifies that *any* entity (represented by the variable x) that orbits *the* sun (represented by the constant TheSun) is also part of *the* Milky Way galaxy (TheMilkyWay). While the constants TheSun and TheMilkyWay stand for the fixed, specific astronomical objects, x is a variable that ranges over all astronomical objects.

The notion of a *variable* in the language of Codecharts is not very different. Variables do not have any specific interpretation as constants do. Instead, variables serve as placeholders that range over specific parts of the program (classes, methods, and sets thereof, depending on the type of variable). Variables allow us to represent generic participants of a design pattern without making unnecessary commitments. Therefore, variables offer the level of abstraction that is necessary for modelling design motifs. The set of variables is given in Legend 22.

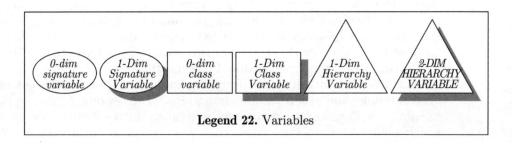

Legend 22. Variables

Note that each variable in Legend 22 mirrors one of the constants (introduced in the previous chapters): Each variable corresponds to a constant of the same type and dimension. For example, the variables *remoteInterface* in Codechart 82 and *composite* and *component* in Codechart 83 are each a *0*-dimensional class variable. Each stands for a *hypothetical* class.

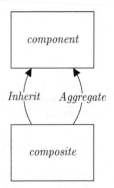

Codechart 83. The *composite* class inherits from and contains an aggregate of the *component* class

Codechart 83 models a design motif[1]: a pattern of inheritance and aggregation relations between two classes. Codechart 83 can be implemented by many different programs. For example, Program 20 contains two separate implementations of the design motif modelled in Codechart 83.

---

[1]Compare Codechart 83 with the recursive composite pattern (§11.1).

Program 20. Two Sample Implementations of Codechart 83

```
package java.awt;

public class Container extends Component { …
    Component component[] = new Component[0];
…
```
```
Package sample;

public class Folder extends File {
    Set<File> contents;
…
```

We say that the variable *composite* represents the Composite participant in the design motif modelled in Codechart 83. And while neither class `Container` nor class `Folder` in Program 20 is "the" interpretation of *composite*, each one of these classes *can* be assigned to the interpretation of *composite*. In Chapter 15 we show that we can *verify* that package `java.awt`, as alluded to in Program 20, indeed implements codechart 83 by creating an *assignment* mapping *composite* to class `Container`.

Chapter 10

Modelling Application Frameworks

Object-oriented application frameworks [Fayad & Schmidt 1997] (henceforth, application frameworks) are most typically semicomplete applications that offer a quick and easy means of generating an application. One example is the Microsoft Foundation Classes, an application framework that can be used to develop graphical user interface–based applications for the Microsoft Windows operating systems. Enterprise JavaBeans™ is also an application framework which "defines an architecture for the development and deployment of transactional, distributed object applications-based, server-side software components" [jGuru 2000]. Many other application frameworks exist in the public domain and in the commercial market. Let us illustrate the most relevant aspects of application frameworks in terms of the small Java RMI example modelled in the previous chapter.

Applications created using an application framework consist of two distinct parts:

1. Prefabricated (fixed) classes, which were distributed as part of the application framework (e.g., class `java.rmi.Remote`)

2. User-defined classes, which were implemented by the framework's clients who customized it to their needs (e.g., a remote interface)

Most application frameworks impose very specific constraints on the user-defined classes and their interactions with the prefabricated classes. Therefore, they are commonly accompanied by detailed examples and lengthy descriptions of these constraints.

For example, in the Java's RMI example discussed in the previous section, a remote interface is a user-defined class which must "extend, either directly or indirectly, the interface `java.rmi.Remote`" [Sun 1999], a prefabricated class. This interaction is modelled in Codechart 82 using a constant (`java.rmi.Remote`) for the prefabricated class and a variable (*remoteInterface*) for the user defined class. Adhering to this convention allows Codecharts to capture precisely the distinction between the prefabricated and user-defined classes. In the absence of variables, a situation from which popular modelling notations suffer, the technical literature documenting the application framework is forced to resort to modelling specific examples. Examples, however, can confuse the reader because it is not at all clear which parts of the example must be replicated and which are merely there to demonstrate a point.

Let us illustrate this problem with a description of some of the simplest aspects of the Enterprise JavaBeans framework, quoted in Table 11.

Table 11. Descriptions of Enterprise JavaBeans™

The home interface extends the …`javax.ejb.EJBHome` interface.

Remote interfaces are subclassed from the `javax.ejb.EJBObject` interface.

Source: Monson-Haefel [2001].

This description is accompanied by a specific example which is modelled in the class diagram in Figure 10-1.

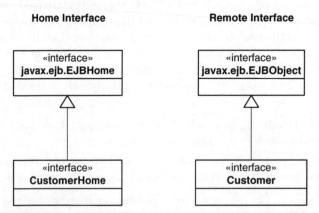

Figure 10-1. Enterprise JavaBeans™ elements (Table 11) modelled in UML (Glossary: p. 233, adapted from [Monson-Haefel 2001]). Classes `Customer` and `CustomerInterface` are sample implementations of "home interface" and "remote interface"

Compare Figure 10-1 with Codechart 84 as specifications of EJB.

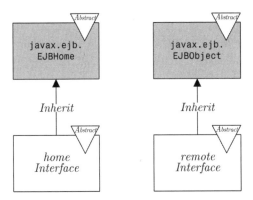

Codechart 84. Enterprise JavaBeans™ as described in Table 11. Variables (empty shapes) represent user-defined (yet to be implemented) entities whereas constants (filled shapes) represent prefabricated (fully implemented) entities

What is the difference between Codechart 84 and Figure 10-1? Aside from the superficial differences, Figure 10-1 fails to convey the difference between class `Customer`, which is not part of the framework, and class `javax.ejb.EJBObject`, which is. Class `Customer` is merely an instance of the "home interface". Codechart 84, however, conveys the fact that the home interface class needs to be implemented by the user and that it needs to extend class `javax.ejb.EJBObject`, which is already implemented by the application framework.

10.1 CASE STUDY: ENTERPRISE JAVABEANS

Let us expand the example of Enterprise JavaBeans (EJB) given in the previous section. Consider the following additional quotes from the documentation of EJB delivered by Monson-Haefel [2001]:

- Every bean [class] obtains an `EJBContext` object, which is a reference to the container [class].
- The home interface extends the ...`javax.ejb.EJBHome` interface.
- A home [interface] may have many `create()` methods, ... , each of which must have corresponding `ejbCreate()` and `ejbPostCreate()` methods in the bean class. The number and datatype of the arguments of each `create()` are left up to the bean developer, but the return type must be the remote interface datatype.
- When a `create()` method is invoked on the home interface, the container delegates the invocation to the corresponding `ejbCreate()` and `ejbPostCreate()` methods on the bean class.
- An implementation for the bean's home interface ("home implementation") is generated by the container.

- Remote interfaces are subclassed from the `javax.ejb.EJBObject` interface. ... For every remote interface there is an implementation class, a business object that actually implements the business methods defined in the remote interface. This is the bean class.

These statements are modelled in Codechart 85.

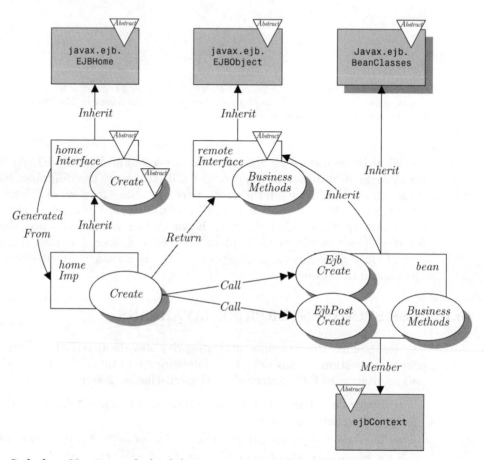

Codechart 85. Bean and related classes in Enterprise JavaBeans™

10.2 CASE STUDY: JUNIT

We present here a second case study of application frameworks which focuses on the popular Java testing framework JUnit. Consider the following requirements, paraphrased from the JUnit documentation (JUnit JavaDoc for version 4.5) for a test case:

- Implement a subclass of `TestCase`, which is a subclass of class `Assert` and implements interface `Test`.
- Define instance variables that store the state of the fixture.
- Initialize the fixture state by overriding `setUp()`.

- Cleanup after a test by overriding `tearDown()`.
- Implement one method for each test to be executed, the results of which should be verified with assertion methods from the `Assert` class.
- Override `runTest()` so that it calls each desired test method.

These statements are modelled in Codechart 86.

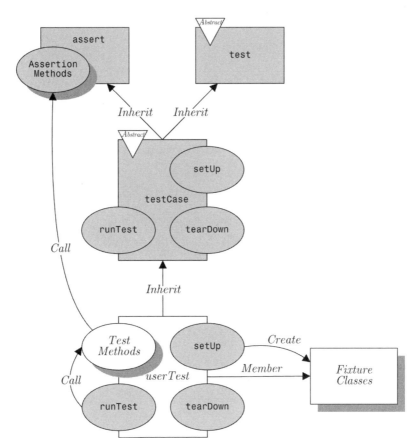

Codechart 86.   JUnit test cases

Chapter 11

Modelling Design Patterns

Design patterns [Schmidt et al. 1996] are the most widely recognized kind of design motifs. Given the central role that they play in object-oriented design, we pay special attention to the problem of modelling design patterns, in particular design patterns from the catalogue called *Design Patterns: Elements of Reusable Object-Oriented Software* [Gamma et al. 1995].

The design patterns catalogue offers a useful vocabulary of design motifs (a "pattern language"). Patterns such as Factory Method, Observer, Iterator, Proxy, and Visitor capture software design practices that are immediately recognized by any veteran programmer. Many software designers report having to come up with a solution similar to one of those advocated in this catalogue through years of trial and error. The catalogue seeks to spare novice programmers from repeating these mistakes. A pattern in each chapter of the catalogue carefully describes a set of generic forces and advocates a solution that addressed the concerns of good design practices. Each pattern is illustrated using clear examples drawn from open-source and widely cited programs in C++ and Smalltalk. Today, this is one of the most popular textbooks in software design. Its success can be attributed, we believe, to its conceptual contribution to the level of abstraction in which the object-oriented software designer operates. Better mechanisms of abstractions offer one of the most effective methods of addressing the problem of *complexity* (Chapter 1).

In the following sections, we discuss case studies in modelling design patterns from the Gamma et al. [1995] catalogue. We briefly examine how each design motif is informally described using class diagrams and natural language and then suggest how it can be precisely modelled in LePUS3. Whenever appropriate, we expand on the relations between patterns and programs. Other patterns from the Gamma et al. [1995] catalogue are also modelled in the Gang of Four Companion (Appendix I).

11.1 CASE STUDY: THE COMPOSITE PATTERN

The Composite design pattern, also known as the Recursive Composite, offers a simple solution to the problem of programming objects which recursively contain compositions of other objects in tree-like structures. The informal description of the Composite pattern is summarized in Table 12, and the class diagram "modelling" its structure in UML is depicted in Figure 11-1.

Table 12. Informal Description of the Composite Pattern

> **Intent**: Compose objects into tree structures to represent part–whole hierarchies.
>
> **Applicability**: Use the Composite pattern when you want clients to be able to ignore the difference between compositions of objects and individual objects.
>
> **Participants**
>
> - Component: Declares the interface for objects in the composition and implements default behaviour for the interface common to all classes.
> - Leaf: Represents leaf objects (namely objects that have no children) in the composition. Also defines behaviour for primitive objects in the composition.
> - Composite: Defines behaviour for components having children, stores child components, and implements child-related operations in the Component interface.
>
> **Collaborations**: Clients use the Component class to interact with objects in the composite structure. If the recipient is a leaf, then the request is handled directly.
> If the recipient is a Composite, then it usually forwards requests to its child components, possibly performing additional operations before and/or after forwarding.

Source: Adapted from Gamma et al. [1995].

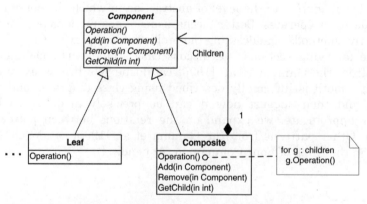

Figure 11-1. UML Class diagram of the structure of the Composite pattern (adapted from [Gamma et al. 1995] by conversion from the OMT notation)

We illustrate the Composite pattern using the Abstract Windowing Toolkit (AWT) class library (package `java.awt` in Java's Software Development Toolkit) as an example. Class `Component` is the abstract root class for all graphical representations designed for screen display and user interaction, offering an interface for all common operations on such objects. A particular kind of a component is implemented using class `Container`, instances of which are components that can contain (recursively) other components. Class `Container` can therefore be described generically as the "composite" participant in this design motif. Other kinds of "components" in `java.awt` are classes `Canvas`, `ScrollBar`, and `Button`. Since instances of these classes are not composite objects—they do not contain other components in the tree structure of component objects—they can be described generically as "leaves" (as in leaves in the tree object in Figure 11-2). Whenever a `Container` method is invoked, it often forwards the call to the respective method in each one of the contained objects. Figure 11-2 illustrates a small collection of `Container` and leaf class objects from `java.awt` and how they handle such method calls. These classes and the relations between them are modelled in Codechart 87a.

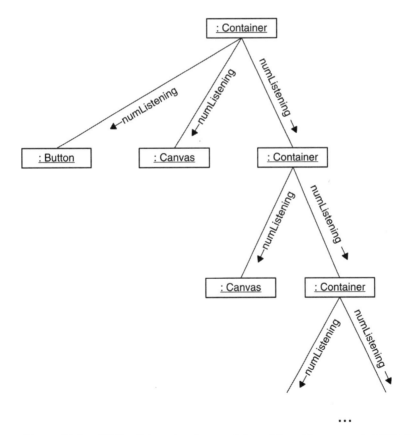

Figure 11-2.   UML collaboration diagram (adapted from [Gamma et al. 1995]) illustrating the recursive structure of the subclasses of `java.awt.Component` (Glossary: p.233)

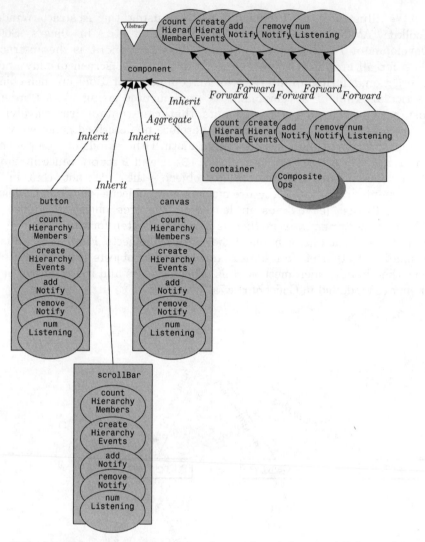

Codechart 87a.   Class Component and some of its subclasses modelled using *0*-dimensional terms

The constant CompositeOps in Codechart 87a stands for the set of signatures of those methods that manage the collection of objects that each Container holds, such as Container.add(Component) and Container. remove(Component).

Note that the method Container.addNotify(), depicted in Program 21, forwards the call to Component.addNotify(), the method it overrides. It demonstrates the relation between methods in implementations of the composite and the methods in the component participants. Codechart 87a models four other methods in class Container which follow the example of addNotify(), each forwarding the call to its superclass counterpart.

Program 21. Sample Method in a *composite* Participant of the Composite Pattern

```
package java.awt;

class Container extends Component { …
  Component component[] … ;
  public void addNotify() { …
    for (int i = 0 ; i < ncomponents ; i++) {
      component[i].addNotify();
    } …
```

At the first step of abstraction, we introduce the *1*-dimensional signature constant `ComponentOps` to represent the set of signatures of `Component` methods which forward the call to their superclass counterparts. Since the *Forward* relation pairs each method in the set of methods in class container with its superclass counterpart, it can be modelled using the isomorphic predicate formula depicted in Codechart 87b.

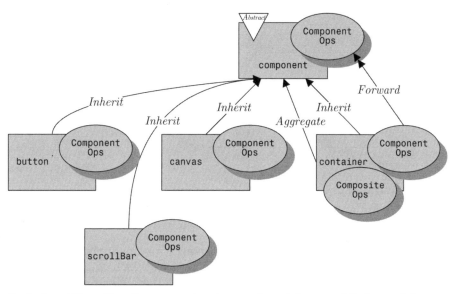

Codechart 87b. Class `Component` and some of its subclasses modelled using *1*-dimensional signature constants

At the final step of abstraction, depicted in Codechart 87c, we introduce the *1*-dimensional class constant `Leaves` to represent all of the leaf classes (`Canvas`, `ScrollBar`, and `Button`). Note that the superimposition term `ComponentOps⊗Leaves` in Codechart 87c stands for a *tribe of clans* (set of sets of methods). In §15.4 we show how the Two-Tier Programming Toolkit can be used to prove that package `java.awt` implements (or *satisfies*) Codechart 87c.

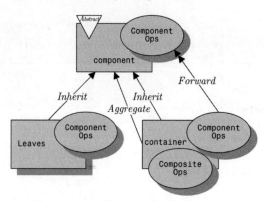

Codechart 87c. Class Component and some of its subclasses modelled using *1*-dimensional class constants

This concludes our example from package java.awt. The Composite design pattern, modelled in Codechart 88, generalizes each element in the description given so far:

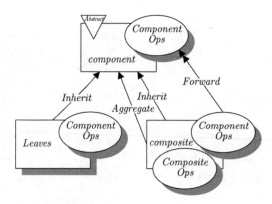

Codechart 88. Composite pattern

- *Component* stands for that abstract component class (class java.awt. Component in the AWT example), which declares the interface *ComponentOps* (numListeners(), countHierarchyMembers(), ...) for all classes in the components hierarchy. Each method in *ComponentOps⊗ component* implements the default behaviour for the interface common to all the component hierarchy classes.

- *Composite* stands for the composite class (java.awt.Container), which inherits from *component* and defines a kind of component which aggregates ("children") components. Methods in *ComponentOps⊗ composite* forward the call to the respective methods in the aggregated components via the *component* interface

- *Leaves* stands for the set of leaf classes (Button, Canvas, ScrollBar), each of which inherits from *component* and may override *ComponentOps* with behaviour that is more appropriate.

What, precisely, is the relation between the Codecharts JavaAWT (Codechart 87c) and Composite (Codechart 88)? Clearly the Codecharts are very similar: Each one of the constant terms in JavaAWT has a parallel variable term in Composite and the formulas in JavaAWT are preserved by this substitution. This affinity suggests that the program modelled in JavaAWT *implements* the pattern modelled in Codechart 88. Chapter 15, dedicated to *verification*, offers a precise definition to the *implements* relation (Definition XVIII). It allows us to prove our intuition that package `java.awt` indeed *implements* the Composite pattern (Proposition 4, p. 186).

11.2 CASE STUDY: THE ITERATOR PATTERN

The Iterator pattern offers a simple solution to the problem of iterating over the elements of a collection of objects. The problem arises from the complexity of concrete data structures (in Java: collections or aggregates), such as linked lists, sorted lists, and hash maps. Each data structure is unique in the manner by which it organises its elements. Unless encapsulated by a uniform interface, even the simplest iteration operations (such as get first element, get next element, and so on) may require intimate knowledge of implementation detail. This not only complicates the task of their clients but also creates a dependency between the client and the implementation detail of each data structure, violating the basic principles of good design: abstraction and information hiding. The Iterator pattern hides this complexity and removes this dependency: A programmer can iterate over a data structure knowing neither how it is implemented nor what kind of data structure it is. This mechanism of abstraction ensures not only that the iteration is easy but also that changing the data structure used by the implementation will not break any code. The informal description of the pattern in summarized in Table 13, and the class diagram "modelling" its structure in UML is depicted in Figure 11-3.

Table 13. Informal Description of the Iterator Pattern

Intent: Provide access to the elements of an aggregate object sequentially without exposing its underlying representation.

Applicability: Use the Iterator pattern to provide a uniform interface for traversing different aggregate structures (that is, to support polymorphic iteration).

Participants

- Iterator: defines an interface for accessing and traversing elements.
- ConcreteIterator: implements the Iterator interface and keeps track of the current position in the traversal of the aggregate.
- Aggregate: defines an interface for creating an Iterator object.
- ConcreteAggregate: implements the Iterator creation interface to return an instance of the proper ConcreteIterator.

Collaborations: A ConcreteIterator keeps track of the current object in the aggregate and can compute the succeeding object in the traversal.

Source: Adapted from Gamma et al. [1995]

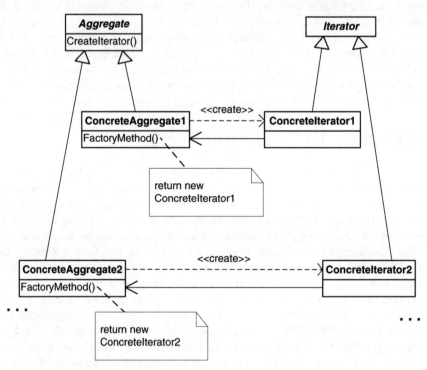

Figure 11-3. UML Class diagram of the structure of the Iterator pattern (adapted from [Gamma et al. 1995] by conversion from the OMT notation)

Let us illustrate the iterator pattern using the example from Chapter 7 of package `java.util` in Java's standard Software Development Kit. Each data structure in this package, called "concrete collection", is accompanied by an iterator class which hides the complexity of iteration operations behind a uniform interface. For example, class `LinkedList` is a concrete collection that is accompanied by class `LinkedListItr`. To iterate over an instance of `LinkedList`, all that is required is an instance of `LinkedListItr`. Codechart 89a models four such concrete collections and their respective concrete iterator classes.

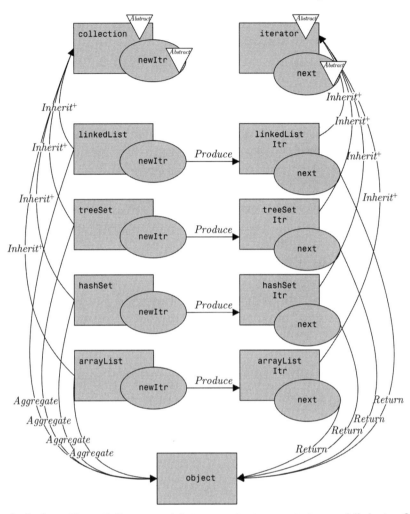

Codechart 89a.   Collections and their respective iterators in Java modelled using *0*-dimensional terms

Collection offers a uniform interface to all concrete collections whereas Iterator offers a uniform interface to all concrete iterators. Together, these interfaces allow clients to iterate over a collection without being exposed to its implementation, as demonstrated in Program 11 (p. 82).

Codechart 89b demonstrates how Codechart 89a can be further abstracted using hierarchy constants.

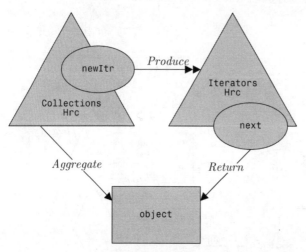

Codechart 89b. Collections and their respective iterators in Java modelled using *1*-dimensional terms

Using constants, Codechart JavaUtil (Codechart 89b) models only the set of collection and iterator classes in Java's SDK. It does not model the pattern of relations between collection and iterators. The Iterator pattern can be obtained by generalizing JavaUtil, as demonstrated in Codechart 90.

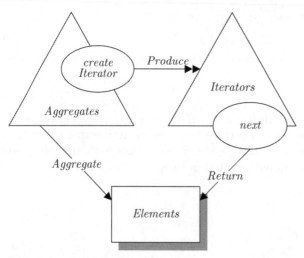

Codechart 90. Iterator pattern

Iterator (Codechart 90) specifies the following:

- Each concrete aggregate class a_n in *Aggregates*
  1. aggregates instances of some class e_m in *Elements* and
  2. implements a factory method with signature *createIterator* (i.e., *createIterator* $\otimes a_n$) which produces instances of the respective concrete iterator class i_n in *Iterators*.

- Each nonabstract method with signature *next* in concrete iterator i_n (*next* $\otimes i_n$) iterates over the collection of instances of a_n, returning an instance of e_m.

Note that Iterator (Codechart 90) can be obtained by replacing each constant in JavaUtil (Codechart 89b) with a variable of the same type and dimension.[1] This suggests that package `java.util` indeed *implements* the Iterator pattern. In Proposition 3 (p. 186) we formally prove this claim.

11.3 CASE STUDY: THE FACTORY METHOD PATTERN

Most class-based programming languages require the programmer to specify explicitly the class of each new object created as well as the specific constructor that should be called. This leads to the unfortunate dependency between the client code and the class to be instantiated, an implementation detail that may be undesirable. (See discussion of this problem and its solutions in §8.5.) The Factory Method pattern solves the problem by abstracting the means by which objects are produced. The informal description of the Factory Method pattern is summarized in Table 14, and the class diagram modelling its structure in UML is depicted in Figure 11-4.

Table 14. Informal Description of the Factory Method Pattern

Intent: Define an interface for creating an object but let subclasses decide which class to instantiate. Factory Method lets a class defer instantiation to subclasses.

Applicability: Use the Factory Method pattern when classes delegate responsibility to one of several helper subclasses, and you want to localize the knowledge of which helper subclass is the delegate.

Participants

- Product: defines the interface of objects the factory method creates.
- ConcreteProduct: implements the Product interface.
- Creator: declares the factory method, which returns an object of type Product.
- ConcreteCreator: overrides the factory method to return an instance of a ConcreteProduct.

Collaborations: Creator relies on its subclasses to define the factory method so that it returns an instance of the appropriate ConcreteProduct.

Sources: Adapted from Gamma et al. [1995].

[1]With the exception of the 1-dimensional variable *Elements*, which stands for a set of `element` classes rather than one.

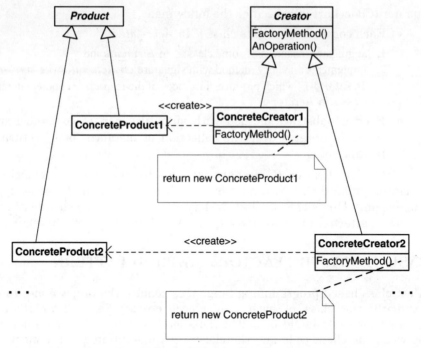

Figure 11-4. UML Class diagram of the structure of the Factory Method pattern (adapted from [Gamma et al. 1995] by conversion from the OMT notation)

Let us illustrate the solution offered by the Factory Method design pattern using the same set of classes in java.util discussed earlier. Codechart 91a lists four factory methods in this set of classes:

- LinkedList.newItr() produces instances of LinkedListItr
- TreeSet.newItr() produces instances of TreeSetItr
- HashSet.newItr() produces instances of HashSetItr
- ArrayList.newItr() produces instances of ArrayListItr

Clustered together, as in Codechart 91b, factory methods dynamically bind using a "polymorphic factory": a *hierarchy* (§7.6) of factory classes, each of which defines a dynamically bound factory method. The set of concrete and abstract collection classes designated CollectionsHrc is such a polymorphic factory, and the superimposition term newIter⊗CollectionsHrc represents the set of dynamically bound factory methods.

A similar correlation exists between subclasses of class Permission and subclasses of PermissionCollection in package java.security (Java SDK), seven of which are modelled in Codechart 92a. The factory methods have the signature newPermissionCollection(). For example, the method newPermissionCollection() in class FilePermission produces instances of class FilePermissionCollection, and the method with the same signature in class BasicPermission produces instances of class BasicPermissionCollection.

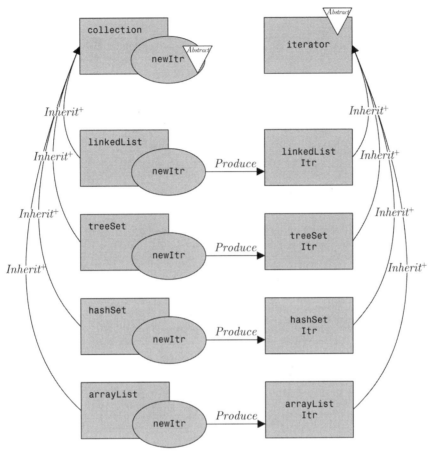

Codechart 91a. Factory methods and their products in `java.util` modelled using *0*-dimensional terms

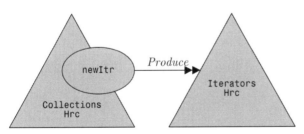

Codechart 91b. Factory methods and their products in `java.util` modelled using *1*-dimensional hierarchy constants

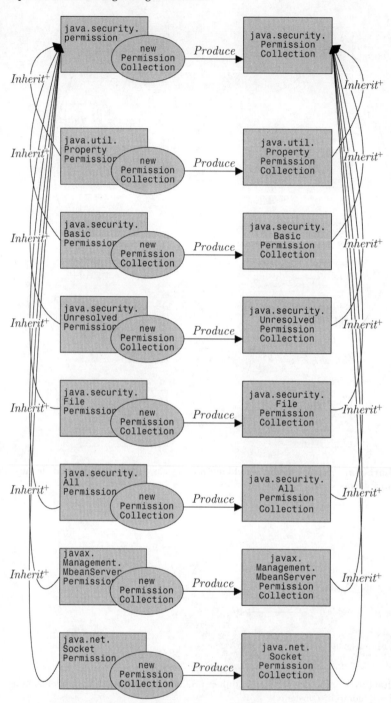

Codechart 92a. Factory methods and their products in `java.security` modelled using *0*-dimensional terms

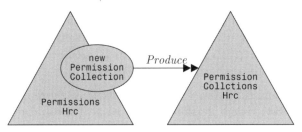

Codechart 92b. Factory methods and their products in `java.security` modelled using *1*-dimensional hierarchy constants

Another very similar correlation between a polymorphic factory, factory methods, and a hierarchy of product classes appears also in the Java 3D API (§7.11), depicted in Codechart 93.

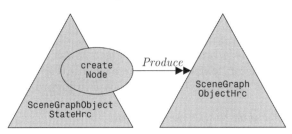

Codechart 93. Factory methods and their products in Java 3D modelled in *0-* and *1*-dimensional terms

The Factory Method design pattern, modelled in Codechart 94, is essentially a generalization of these two examples.

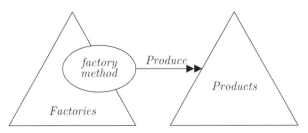

Codechart 94. Factory Method pattern

The terms in FactoryMethod (Codechart 94) reflect the division of labor between the participants in the informal description of the Factory Method pattern (Table 14):

- *Products* encapsulates the abstract and concrete products.
- *Factories* encapsulates the abstract and concrete creator classes, which defines the set of factory methods.

- The clan modelled by the term *factoryMethod⊗ Factories* stands for the set of factory methods: Each concrete factory class f_n in *Factories* implements a method *factoryMethod⊗f_n* which produces instances of the respective concrete product class p_n in *Products*.

Note that FactoryMethod (Codechart 94) can be obtained by replacing each constant in Codechart 91b with a variable of the same type and dimension. This suggests that package `java.util` indeed also *implements* the Factory Method pattern. In Proposition 12 (p. 210) we formally prove this claim.

Note also that FactoryMethod is a subset of the terms and formulas in Iterator (Codechart 90). This suggests that the Factory Method design pattern is an abstraction or a generalization of the Iterator pattern. In Chapter 18 we formulate this intuition and prove it in Proposition 5 (p. 203).

11.4   * CASE STUDY: THE ABSTRACT FACTORY PATTERN

Section 8.5 is dedicated to a discussion of the Widget Factory, an example borrowed from the Gang of Four catalogue [Gamma et al. 1995]. The Factory Method design pattern is a generalization of the Widget Factory. The informal description of the Abstract Factory pattern in summarized in Table 15, and the class diagram modelling its structure in UML is depicted in Figure 11.5.

Table 15.   Informal Description of the Abstract Factory Pattern

---

Intent: Provide an interface for creating families of related or dependent objects without specifying their concrete classes.

Applicability

Use the Abstract Factory pattern when:

- A system should be independent of how its products are created, composed, and represented.
- A system should be configured with one of multiple families of products.
- A family of related product objects is designed to be used together.

Participants

- AbstractFactory: declares an interface for operations that create abstract product objects.
- ConcreteFactory: implements the operations to create concrete product objects.
- AbstractProduct: declares an interface for a type of product object.
- ConcreteProduct: defines a product object to be created by the corresponding concrete factory and implements the AbstractProduct interface.

Collaborations: AbstractFactory defers creation of product objects to its ConcreteFactory subclass.

Source: Adapted from Gamma et al. [1995].

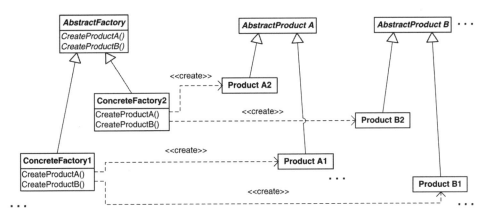

Figure 11-5. UML Class diagram of the structure of the Abstract Factory pattern (adapted from [Gamma et al. 1995] by conversion from the OMT notation)

To recap the example in §8.5, the Widget Factory described how the factory methods for creating various widgets (scrollbars and windows) can be organized into a hierarchy of factory classes. The example modelled in Codechart 95 therefore consisted of three sets of participants:

- A set of widget hierarchies (WIDGETS), including a hierarchy of window classes and a hierarchy of scrollbar classes
- A hierarchy of factory classes (WidgetFactories) which define the set of factory method clans
- A set of factory method clans (WidgetFactoryMethods⊗Widget Factories), each of which is responsible for producing instances of classes in one widget hierarchy.

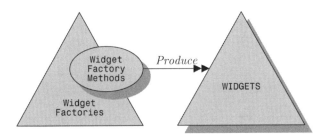

Codechart 95. A widget factory (§8.5)

The Abstract Factory pattern is largely a generalization of the Widget Factory. It concerns large and complex applications which make use of many factory methods (§11.3) for producing instances of multiple "product" hierarchies. In the general case, the number of product hierarchies is immaterial, but each product hierarchy is always paired with exactly one clan of factory methods, a relation modelled using the Isomorphic predicate formula depicted in Codechart 96.

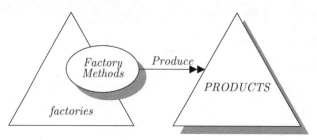

Codechart 96.   Abstract Factory pattern

Compare AbstractFactory (Codechart 96) with WidgetFactory (Codechart 95) and observe the similarity between them. This similarity suggests that the Widget Factory program *implements* the Abstract Factory design pattern. In Proposition 10 (p. 208) we prove that this is indeed the case.

Note also the similarity between the Factory Method (§11.3) and the Abstract Factory patterns, modelled side by side in Codechart 97. This similarity is evident in their informal descriptions. But the similarity between the Codecharts modelling the two patterns is striking: It is emphasized by the fact that the only difference between them is (essentially) in the dimension of two variables.

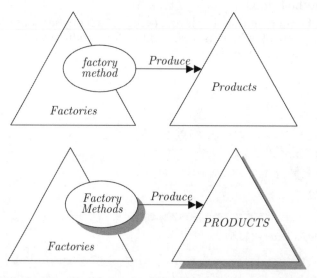

Codechart 97.   Factory Method (top) vs. Abstract Factory (bottom) patterns

This similarity suggests that the Abstract Factory is an *abstraction* of the Factory Method. Indeed, in Chapter 18 we formulate the intuitive notion of Abstraction, namely, exponentiation, and prove the claim that, indeed, the Abstract Factory is an *abstraction* of the Factory Method, a relation formally represented by the semantic entailment notation ⊨ as in the expression

$$\text{FactoryMethod} \vDash \text{AbstractFactory}$$

(Proposition 10, p. 208).

In the second part of this book we also prove that the Factory Method is an *abstraction* of the Iterator pattern (Proposition 5) and that the *abstraction* relation is transitive (Corollary 1, p. 201). This leads us to conclude that the Abstract Factory is an *abstraction* of the Iterator pattern, written

$$\text{Iterator} \vDash \text{AbstractFactory}$$

(Proposition 13, p. 211).

11.5 * CONCLUDING REMARKS

Why is it so important to model design patterns, and do we focus on modelling the so-called Gang of Four catalogue [Gamma et al. 1995]? The answer to this question is in the historical background to patterns.

Software patterns were inspired by the work on architectural patterns by Christopher Alexander [1996]. Alexander's patterns encoded solutions to problems that occupied many architects. The solutions encoded were in common practice across a wide range of domains. Each pattern was encoded in that most cases consisted of the following:

- A description of a problem
- A constellation of constraints in the context in which the solution must be found
- A recipe for a solution
- Examples

Patterns offered a new language for architects: a common vocabulary of methods and recipes. And collections of related patterns came to be known as a "pattern language". With time, these *pattern languages* became a powerful medium of communication between architects. Examples accompanying each pattern served not only to illustrate the abstract ideas but also helped to turn each pattern into effective textbook examples. Alexander's patterns came to be widely known for their contribution to the theory and the practice of architecture.

During the late 1980s, Alexander's patterns were imported into software design by skilled and experienced programmers[2] who shared the view on the "software's chronic crisis" (Chapter 1) and in particular were frustrated with the lack of powerful mechanisms of abstraction in software design. Arising from their experience with designing and implementing programs in object-oriented languages such as Smalltalk, the earliest pattern catalogues focused

---

[2]Most prominently by Ward Cunningham and Kent Beck, who then formed the Hillside Group.

on the design of programs in particular categories of applications such as graphical user interfaces and data processing applications. Some catalogues addressed the problems which arise from using specific programming languages, such as garbage collection in C++ [Coplien 1991]. Others focused on solutions in a particular architectural style such as distributed architectures [Schmidt et al. 2000]. The most influential set of patterns appeared in a catalogue by Gamma, et al. [1995], a group that came to be known[3] as the Gang of Four.

The Gang of Four catalogue's success served both the theory and practice of object-oriented design. The patterns described struck a chord with many experienced object-oriented programmers, designers, and architects who, like the members of the Hillside Group, were dissatisfied with the traditional language of software design. Focused on algorithms and data structures, traditional programming curricula suited imperative (or procedural) programming languages and were ill suited to the object-oriented technology that emerged during the 1990s. In contrast, the rich vocabulary that the Gang of Four catalogue offered was much better suited to object-oriented programming in languages such as Smalltalk, C++, Java, and C#, which emerged as the dominant programming languages in the era of Web programming. And the catalogue's impact on the industry was enhanced by the success of the Java programming language, much of which was heavily influenced by the catalogue.

Becoming immediately recognizable, the vocabulary of design patterns was integrated into programming environments, documentation systems, and to a lesser degree even the Unified Modelling Language. This vocabulary became the *lingua franca* of software design: the de facto standard language of describing, documenting, communicating, and codifying the design in the literature about a wide range of industrial software applications.

This is the motivation to our focus on design patterns. But our treatment raises a number of objections. A common criticism of formal languages that attempt to model design patterns is that specifications in these languages at most capture only the design motif, not the entire pattern. For example, they fail to model the problem that it attempts to solve and the constraints in the context of the offered solution. This criticism applies also to Codecharts. Indeed, as a design description language, Codecharts are suitable for codifying solutions, not problems.

Beyond this, the vocabulary that pattern languages created (Factory Methods, Iterators, Proxies, Composites, etc.) mainly constitutes references to the design motif that each pattern advocates as a solution. When programmers say "I've used the Factory Method here", they refer to the Factory Method's design motif. And the standard practice in the modelling community is that the term "pattern" is shorthand for a design motif. We have therefore merely followed the normal practice.

---

[3]Despite its political ring, this term was apparently adopted for no reason other than the group of authors counting four members.

Chapter 12

Modelling Early Design Revisited

Variables, introduced in §7.11, can be used not only for modelling design motifs but also for representing "undetermined" or unknown parts of the program. This chapter demonstrates how variables can be used during the early stages of design for the purpose of modelling programs that are yet to be developed.

Experienced software designers are well aware of the fact that premature commitment to implementation detail is detrimental to the remaining phases in the program's life cycle [Stroustrup 2000, Ch. 23]. The principle of abstraction in early design (p. 32) therefore dictates that constraints on the implementation should be introduced as late as possible. A design description language used for representing program blueprints must therefore offer us a means to articulate requirements without making premature commitments to implementation detail. For example, it should allow the designer to indicate the existence of classes or methods that satisfy specific requirements but whose remaining details are yet to be determined.

For example, rather than making a commitment to a particular class, a software designer may wish to specify that *there exists* some class that defines a method which overrides the abstract method `Stack.push` and which returns instances of (subclasses of) `Stack`. S/he does *not* wish to make any further commitments: for example, which class should implement this method, how many levels of inheritance separate it from class `Stack`, and so forth. How can this be articulated with Codecharts? The answer is offered in Codechart 98. The class variable *some* in Codechart 98 represents "some class" that extends class `Stack`. Superimposed by the signature constant **push**, the class variable *some* requires the class to define a method with this

Codecharts: Roadmaps and Blueprints for Object-Oriented Programs, by Amnon H. Eden
Copyright © 2011 John Wiley & Sons, Inc.

signature, and the *Return* ground formula requires that same method also returns instances of class Stack.

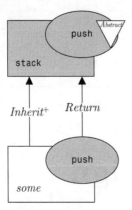

Codechart 98. Stack.push is overridden by a method that returns an instance of a subtype of Stack

Observe that the method in class *some* is modelled here using a superimposition of a constant (**push**) over a variable (*some*). This combination stands for a method whose signature is predetermined but the class containing it is not.

Next, let us also consider modelling the requirement that there exists *some* undetermined method in class Math which creates an instance of class random, as demonstrated in Codechart 99. Observe that the roles of constants and variables in this example are symmetrical to those in Codechart 98 except that in Codechart 99 the class is fixed using a constant and the signature remains undetermined using a variable.

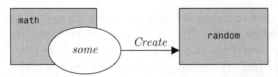

Codechart 99. Some method in class Math creates random numbers

Chapter **13**

* Advanced Modelling Techniques

In this chapter we demonstrate how Codecharts can be used in ways that do not conform to the narrow definition of our design description language. In §13.1 we discuss deriving various visual dialects of Codecharts using ad hoc edge styles. And in §13.2 we discuss a possible extension to the language of Codecharts that supporting the notion of information hiding.

13.1 AD HOC SYMBOLS

Clutter in Codecharts is possible despite the many abstraction mechanisms provided in previous chapters. Clutter is unfortunate: Program roadmaps should at all times convey as clear a picture as possible. Additional techniques for avoiding clutter and promote program visualization should therefore also be considered. Ad hoc edge styles are one option.

Ad hoc visual symbols can be used to reduce clutter when the same relation symbol recurs many times in a Codechart or when we wish to set some relation symbol apart from all others. In particular, ad hoc edge styles that may be considered include different arrowheads and various dashed styles *àla* UML. In such cases, a glossary of the ad hoc symbols must be supplied.

For example, in modelling the relation between classes and their metaclasses in Smalltalk-80 we can substitute the binary relation symbols *Inherit* and *InstanceOf* with specific symbols, as demonstrated in Codechart 100. Arguably, the result is clean enough to warrant enriching the visual language with new symbols.

Codecharts: Roadmaps and Blueprints for Object-Oriented Programs, by Amnon H. Eden
Copyright © 2011 John Wiley & Sons, Inc.

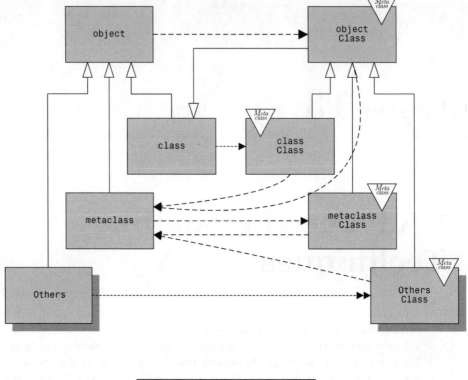

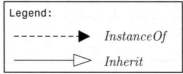

Codechart 100.   Metaclasses in Smalltalk-80

Indeed, Codechart 100 nicely visualizes the seemingly complex relations between classes and their metaclasses in Smalltalk-80; to summarize the spirit of these relations:

1. All classes inherit (possibly indirectly) from class `Object`.
2. All metaclasses inherit (possibly indirectly) from class `Class`.
3. Each class `X` is an instance of a metaclass called `Xclass`.[1]
4. All metaclasses are instances of class `Metaclass`.

Ad hoc edge styles in such spirit were adopted in the first version of LePUS [Eden 2000] for each relation recurring in object-oriented design models, including *Inherit, Member, Members, Call,* and *Forward.* However, there are several clear disadvantages to such an approach: While different edge styles

---

[1]The predicate formula *ISOMORPHIC*(*InstanceOf,* `Others`, `OthersClasses`) is indicated by the double arrowhead connecting the respective terms in Codechart 100.

may reduce clutter, they also make Codecharts cryptic and more difficult to follow. In other words, the answer to the elegance question (p. 17) posed in Chapter 1 is that the 15 visual tokens are enough and it is very difficult to justify a larger number.

Physical units of modularity such as packages, folders, and files can be modelled as sets of classes using *1*-dimensional class constants. Ad hoc edge styles can then be used to reduce the labelling of the recurring correlations between them. For example, Codechart 101 models the packages in version 6 of Java's Software Development Kit. The relations between the sets of classes in a package and its subpackages can be modelled using the relation *IsInSubpackageOfThePackageOf*. Shorter relation names, of course, are also possible, but clutter would be unavoidable unless an ad hoc style is used.

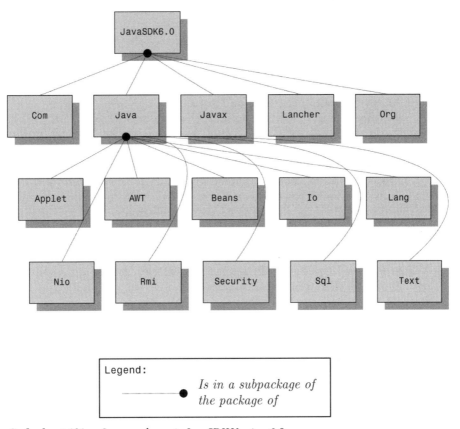

Codechart 101. Some packages in Java SDK Version 6.0

13.2 MODELLING INFORMATION HIDING

Information hiding (also called data abstraction) is one of the fundamental principles of object-oriented programming.[2] Mechanisms supporting information hiding are in place in all object-based (modular), object-oriented, and class-based programming languages. Essentially, it dictates that a class can be considered to be composed of two parts: Its public part constitutes its functionality as a service provider exposed via a public interface and its private part constitutes its implementation, a set of operations and data kept "hidden" from its clients. Commonly, keywords such as `public` and `private` enforce this division explicitly. This distinction reduces dependencies between modules, thereby promoting modularity and *changeability* (Chapter 1).

Unfortunately, information-hiding statements are *nonlocal* [Eden & Kazman 2003]. This means that verifying statements about information hiding requires us to consider the entire implementation. Consider, for example, method `RangeCheck(int)`, which is private to class `java.util.ArrayList`. A compiler enforces the requirement imposed by the keyword `private` by verifying that no method outside `ArrayList` calls it anywhere else in the program. This example demonstrates that introducing information hiding into Codecharts would have violated many of the desirable properties of the language. Nonlocal statements have therefore been excluded from our design description language. Nonetheless, we show below how such statements can be modelled in an extension to the language of Codecharts and how it affects our ability to model programs and patterns.

We model a generalized notion of information hiding, for which we add two "exclusivity" predicates to our language, *LEFT-EXCLUSIVE* and *RIGHT-EXCLUSIVE*. The exclusivity predicates specify that only entities of a particular set may be in a specific (binary) relation with entities of another set.

Precisely put, we say that the binary relation represented by *BinaryRelation* is **left exclusive** between the set represented by the term *Domain* and the term *Range* if and only if the following two conditions hold:

- The predicate formula $TOTAL(BinaryRelation, Domain, Range)$ holds (Definition XII).

- For any entity $\underline{x}$, if $BinaryRelation(\underline{x}, r)$ holds for some entity $\underline{r}$ in *Range,* then $\underline{x}$ must be in *Domain.*

This is specified using a *LEFTEXCLUSIVE* predicate formula (Legend 23), symbolically transcribed as

$$LEFTEXCLUSIVE(BinaryRelation, Domain, Range)$$

Similarly, a binary relation *BinaryRelation* is **right exclusive** between the sets represented by the term *Domain* and the term *Range* if and only if it satisfies the following two conditions:

- The predicate formula $TOTAL(BinaryRelation, Domain, Range)$ holds.

- For any entity $\underline{y}$, if $BinaryRelation(d, \underline{y})$ holds for some entity $\underline{d}$ in the set represented by *Domain,* then $\underline{y}$ must be in the set represented by *Range.*

---

[2]The term *encapsulation* is often confused with information hiding.

This is specified using a *RIGHTEXCLUSIVE* predicate formula (Legend 23), symbolically transcribed as

$$RIGHTEXCLUSIVE(\ BinaryRelation, Domain, Range)$$

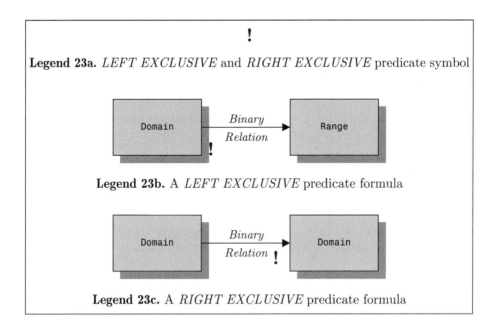

Legend 23a. *LEFT EXCLUSIVE* and *RIGHT EXCLUSIVE* predicate symbol

Legend 23b. A *LEFT EXCLUSIVE* predicate formula

Legend 23c. A *RIGHT EXCLUSIVE* predicate formula

For example, one of the interpretations of the Singleton pattern requires that the singleton class contains a method (usually called `getInstance()`) which returns the single instance of this class and that only this method may create instances of the singleton. This requirement can be articulated using the *LEFTEXCLUSIVE* predicate formula modelled in Codechart 102.

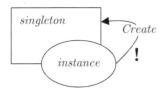

Codechart 102. Only the method with signature *instance* in the *singleton* class may create instances of class *singleton*

In another example, the Proxy design pattern requires that the proxy object controls access to the "real subject" object. This can mean a number of things, depending on the kind of proxy:

1. That instances of the proxy class hold, as members, instances of the real subject, and *only* they may do so. This statement can be specified using the *LEFTEXCLUSIVE* predicate formula modelled in Codechart 103.

Codechart 103. Only instances of *proxy* have members of type *realSubject*

2. Certain methods of the proxy class call methods of the real subject,[3] and *only* these methods may do so. This statement can be specified using the *LEFTEXCLUSIVE* predicate formula modelled in Codechart 104.

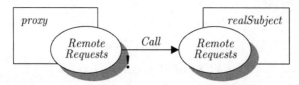

Codechart 104. Only methods of *proxy* may call methods of *realSubject*

[3]Normally, each method forwards the call to a method of the same the signature.

Part II

Theory

The design of computing systems can only properly succeed if it is well-grounded in theory, and ... the important concepts in a theory can only emerge through protracted exposure to application.

— Robin Milner

It has long been my personal view that the separation of practical and theoretical work is artificial and injurious. Much of the practical work done in computing, both in software and in hardware design, is unsound and clumsy because the people who do it have not any clear understanding of the fundamental design principles of their work. Most of the abstract mathematical and theoretical work is sterile because it has no point of contact with real computing.

— Christopher Strachey

This part offers a rigorous foundation for LePUS3, the language of Codecharts. We define precisely the relation between programs and specifications, and provide an answer to the *verification question*. We also describe Class-Z, an equivalent specification language to LePUS3. We conclude with the subject of reasoning on Codecharts.

Most formal statements provided in this chapter (propositions and lemmas) will include sketched "proofs", the simplest of which will be omitted. Formal definitions can be found in Appendix II.

NOTATIONAL CONVENTIONS

The following writing conventions are adopted throughout this chapter:

- If is shorthand for "if and only if"
- The notation $\{\underline{a},\underline{b}\}$ denotes a set with two elements $\underline{a}$ and $\underline{b}$.
- Given a set T, we use $\mathcal{P}(T)$ to denote the set of all subsets of T (the power set of T) and $\mathcal{P}^n(T)$ to denote $\mathcal{P}(\mathcal{P}^{n-1}(T))$, where $\mathcal{P}^0(T)$ is T.
- The notation $\uplus$ stands for the disjoint union.
- We reserve `typewriter` (courier new) typeface for source code, fixed-width `Monospace` typeface for constants, <u>`Monospace`</u> <u>`Underlined`</u> for entities, *Euclid Italics* for variables, and <u>*Underlined*</u> <u>*Euclid*</u> <u>*Italics*</u> for sets.
- Uppercase Greek letters, Φ, Ψ, Δ, ..., and large Euclid typeface (Iterator) are reserved for specifications, that is Codecharts and schemas.
- Unless otherwise specified, <u>*Relation*</u> is a finite set represented by the relation symbol *Relation* and the *interpretation* of `constant` is <u>`constant`</u>.

Chapter 14

Abstract Semantics

Meaning is what an explanation of meaning explains.

—Ludwig Wittgenstein

The principle of *automated verifiability* (§3.4) dictates that the *verification question* ("does program *p satisfy* specification Ψ?") must have an algorithmic answer, that is, that it can be answered by a computer program. It requires us to establish rigorously the relation between specifications and programs. We do so by offering a precise and appropriately abstract representation of object-oriented programs, an *abstract semantics*, which can then be fed into the verification algorithm. This chapter is concerned with such representations of programs.

Programs in object-oriented languages such as Java, C++, and C# are normally encoded and represented as text files. The collection of these files (along with some compilation information) is generally referred to as the *source code*. The source code is the ultimate specification of the program: It is the means by which programmers encode programs. The source code consists of the detailed set of instructions dictating how the target computer operates. By speaking of "the program" or "the implementation" we normally refer to the source code.

However, source code poses serious problems for design verification and reasoning. Source code is generally:

- Very large: consisting of many thousand (or millions) lines of code
- Decentralized: spanning hundreds of text files across a directory structure
- Complex and verbose: containing myriad implementation minutia, much of which is irrelevant for design

- Nonstandard: each programming language (and dialects thereof) adheres to a somewhat different set of syntactic and semantic rules

We conclude that the source code is not always an appropriate medium for reasoning about the program. In particular, to perform design verification, the source code must be simplified into a precise form of representation, one that allows us to abstract from it a representation that better serves our purposes. This is the role of the *abstract semantics*.

An *abstract semantics* is a simplified picture of a program. It can be thought of as a "database" of all the facts that may be relevant for the purpose of design verification. Since mathematical logic has been the medium in which we formalized the definitions so far, model theory is a natural framework for capturing abstract semantics.[1] Below we introduce *finite structures*, which offer us a simplification of programs; define *abstract semantics functions*, which map each program to a finite structure; and introduce the notion of *design models*, which enrich finite structure with higher dimensional (sets of) entities and an *interpretation function*. We conclude this chapter by revisiting our notion of *program modelling* and establish its meaning in precise terms.

14.1   FINITE STRUCTURES

Since Codecharts are *decidable* statements about classes and methods, *verification* in this context merely requires comparing specifications with the collection facts about the program that may potentially be relevant. *Finite structures* represent these facts. A finite structure is a simplification of a program—an *abstract semantics*—because it strips the source code from its complex grammatical structure. Instead, finite structures define a universe of primitive entities. Tools that generate finite structures, such as the Two-Tier Programming Toolkit (§15.4), use static analyzers to reverse engineer a representation of the finite structure from the source code in the form of a relational database listing the program elements ("entities") and their relationships.

Consider, for example, the short Java program in Program 22.

Program 22.   A Short Java Program

```
class AClass extends Object { void aMethod(int) {} }
```

We consider the following to be the basic elements of Program 22:

- Classes:[2] `AClass`, `Object`, and `int`
- Methods: `AClass.aMethod(int)`
- Signatures: `aMethod(int)`

---

[1]We use model theory only to the extent of checking program conformance; our models do not give meaning to the program.

[2]Which in LePUS3 include all static types, such as interfaces, primitive types, and array types in Java.

In the abstract semantics of Program 22 these elements are represented as **entities of dimension** *0* (Definition II):

- `Object` is a *class of dimension 0*
- `AClass` is a *class of dimension 0*
- `int` is a *class of dimension 0*
- `AClass.aMethod(int)` is a *method of dimension 0*
- `aMethod(int)` is a *signature of dimension 0*

The set of all entities of dimension *0* is known as the **universe**, and it is designated $\mathbb{U}_0$. For example, the universe of the abstract semantics of Program 22 is listed in the following equation:

$$\mathbb{U}_0 = \{\,\texttt{Object},\texttt{AClass},\texttt{int},\texttt{AClass.aMethod(int)}\,\}$$

In most class-based languages classes and methods are usually thought of as composite entities. For example, classes are thought of "containing" methods and fields, and methods are thought of as containing statements. Here we treat classes and methods as primitives, namely as atomic or indivisible entities. The association between classes and methods is represented using the *Member* binary relation (see below).

Relations (Definition II) are sets that represent the *decidable* properties of classes, methods, signatures, and the relations between them. We consider only two kinds of relations: *unary* and *binary relations*.

Unary relations are sets of entities of dimension *0*, which represent properties of entities, such as *Abstract* and *Class*. For example, in the finite structure representing Program 22 we have the following unary relations:

- *Class* $= \{\,\texttt{Object},\texttt{AClass},\texttt{int}\,\}$
  A relation that lists the types in the program
- *Method* $= \{\,\texttt{AClass.aMethod(int)}\,\}$
  A relation that lists the methods in the program
- *Signature* $= \{\,\texttt{aMethod(int)}\,\}$
  A relation that lists the method signatures in the program

Binary relations are sets containing pairs of entities of dimension *0*, which represent relations between entities. For example, in the finite structure representing Program 22 we have the following binary relations:

- *Inherit* $= \{\,\langle\texttt{AClass},\texttt{Object}\rangle\,\}$
  A relation containing one element, the pair $\langle\texttt{AClass},\texttt{Object}\rangle$, which indicates that class `AClass` inherits from class `Object`
- *Member* $= \{\,\langle\texttt{AClass},\texttt{AClass.aMethod(int)}\rangle\,\}$
  A relation containing only one pair, which indicates that the method `AClass.AMethod(int)` is a member of class `AClass`
- *SignatureOf* $= \{\,\langle\texttt{aMethod(int)},\texttt{AClass.aMethod(int)}\rangle\,\}$
  A relation containing only one pair, which indicates that the method `AClass.AMethod(int)` has the signature `aMethod(int)`

The set of all relations is designated $\mathbb{R}$. For example, the set $\mathbb{R}$ for the abstract semantics of Program 22 consists of the following relations:

$$\mathbb{R} = \{ \underline{Class}, \underline{Method}, \underline{Signature}, \underline{Inherit}, \underline{Member} \}$$

The entities and relations in the abstract semantics of a program are jointly referred to as a *finite structure*. Precisely put, a **finite structure** $\mathfrak{F}$ (Definition I) is a pair consisting of a universe $\mathbb{U}_0$ of entities of dimension 0 and a set of relations $\mathbb{R}$ over tuples of entities from $\mathbb{U}_0$:

$$\mathfrak{F} = \langle \mathbb{U}_0, \mathbb{R} \rangle$$

such that

$$\mathbb{U}_0 = \underline{Class} \uplus \underline{Method} \uplus \underline{Signature}$$

In formal writing, we adopt a writing convention to emphasize the distinction between symbols in the specification language (int), entities (<u>int</u>), and elements of the program (`int`). Symbols in the specification language act as representations of entities in the abstract semantics, which in turn act as abstractions of elements of the program. To this end, syntactic elements of the programming language (`int`) are printed in the `typewriter` typeface, constants (int) are printed in Monospace typeface, and entities (<u>int</u>) are printed in <u>Monospace</u> typeface. Note that constants are part of the specification language whereas entities are elements in the abstract semantics. For example, <u>int</u> is an entity in (the universe of a) finite structure, whereas int is a constant which represents the static type `int` and whose *interpretation* is taken to be the entity <u>int</u>.

Observe also the distinction between *relations* (<u>Inherit</u>) and *relation symbols* (*Inherit*). Both share an intuitive notion of representing "inheritance", except that the relation <u>Inherit</u> stands for a set of pairs, whereas the relation symbol *Inherit* is part of LePUS3, our design description language. The distinction between relation symbols and relations therefore parallels the distinction between constants and entities.

Let us now consider the finite structures representing a more complex program. Table 16 depicts the finite structure of Program 1 (p. 47), which consists of some excerpts from package `java.util` in Java's Software Development Kit.

Table 16. The Finite Structure Representing Program 1

Entities ($\mathbb{U}_0$):

<u>Object</u>, <u>Collection</u>, <u>List</u>, <u>LinkedList</u>, <u>Iterator</u>, <u>ListIterator</u>, <u>LinkedListItr</u>,
<u>Collection.newItr()</u>, <u>LinkedList.newItr()</u>, <u>Iterator.next()</u>,
<u>LinkedListItr.next()</u>, <u>newItr()</u>, <u>next()</u>

Table 16. (*Continued*)

Relations ($\mathbb{R}$):

Class = { Object, Collection, List, LinkedList, Iterator, ListIterator, LinkedListItr }

Method = { Collection.newItr(), LinkedList.newItr(), Iterator.next(),
    LinkedListItr.next() }

Signature = { newItr(), next() }

SignatureOf = { ⟨ newItr(), Collection.newItr() ⟩ , ⟨ newItr(), LinkedList.newItr() ⟩ ,
    ⟨ next(), Iterator.next() ⟩ , ⟨ next(), LinkedListItr.next() ⟩ }

Abstract = { Collection, List, Iterator, ListIterator,
    Collection.newItr(), Iterator.next() }

Inherit = { ⟨ LinkedList, List ⟩ , ⟨ List, Collection ⟩ , ⟨ Collection, Object ⟩ ,
    ⟨ LinkedListItr, ListIterator ⟩ , ⟨ ListIterator, Iterator ⟩ , ⟨ Iterator, Object ⟩ }

Member = { ⟨ Collection.newItr(), Collection ⟩ , ⟨ LinkedList.newItr(), LinkedList ⟩ ,
    ⟨ Iterator.next(), Iterator ⟩ , ⟨ LinkedListItr.next(), LinkedListItr ⟩ }

Aggregate = { ⟨ LinkedList, Object ⟩ }

Produce = { ⟨ LinkedList.newItr(), LinkedListItr ⟩ }

Note: For simplicity's sake we provide an abridged structure and omit the package prefix (java.util or java.lang) from all identifiers.

Table 16 demonstrates the role of signatures in the abstraction of programs. Although there are four methods in Program 1 (and four methods of dimension *0* in its finite structure, respectively), there are only two entities in *Signature*. The reason is because the methods Collection.newItr() and LinkedList.newItr() share the signature newItr() and because the methods Iterator.next() and LinkedListItr.next() share the signature next(). The relation between methods and their respective signatures is represented using the binary relation *SignatureOf*.

The relation *Member* represents the relation between a class and its members. Thus, for example, the pair ⟨Collection.newItr(), Collection⟩ indicates that the method Collection.newItr() is in the interface Collection, and the pair ⟨int, Integer⟩ indicates that there is a field of type int in class Integer.

Since in Java each method is a member of exactly one class, the relation *Member*, when restricted to methods, is a total functional relation. This, however, is not generally true for C++ programs, where global functions are not members of any class. In addition, for multiple-dispatch languages such as CLOS, methods of dimension *0* can be members of as many classes of dimension *0* as specified in the program.

Other relations such as *Abstract*, *Produce*, *Return*, *Create*, *Call*, and *Forward* indicate that the conditions set by the respective relation symbols described in Chapter 6 are met.

14.2 ABSTRACT SEMANTICS FUNCTIONS

How does a program written in a particular class-based language relate to a finite structure? To define the mapping from programs to finite structure, we introduce *abstract semantics functions*. Precisely put, let $\mathbb{L}$ designate the set of well-formed expressions (programs) in a particular programming language and $\mathfrak{F}^*$ designate the set of all possible *finite structures* (Definition I). An **abstract semantics function** $\mathcal{A}$ is a (total) functional relation which maps each element of $\mathbb{L}$ (a "program") into a respective finite structure, namely,

$$\mathcal{A} : \mathbb{L} \rightarrow \mathfrak{F}^*$$

For example, let $\mathrm{JAVA}1.4$ stand for the set of well-formed expressions (programs) in version 1.4 of the Java™ programming language [Gosling et al. 1996]. The abstract semantics function mapping each Java 1.4 program to a finite structure can thus be represented by the function

$$\mathcal{A}_{Java1.4} : \mathrm{JAVA}1.4 \rightarrow \mathfrak{F}^*$$

$\mathcal{A}_{Java1.4}$ largely follows the guidelines given in Chapter 6. Its detailed definition of is not of particular interest and it can be found elsewhere [Nicholson et al. 2007].

For example, we would expect $\mathcal{A}_{Java1.4}$ to generate the finite structure depicted in Table 16 by analyzing a subset of java.util given in Program 1. If we designate the finite structure in Table 16 as $\mathfrak{F}_{util}$, then the following holds:

$$\mathcal{A}_{Java1.4}(\texttt{java.util}) = \mathfrak{F}_{util} \tag{4}$$

It is trivial to show that if all the relations in $\mathfrak{F}^*$ are decidable then $\mathcal{A}$ is also decidable.

Alternatively, $\mathrm{ANSI\text{-}CPP}$ and $\mathrm{SMALLTALK}80$ can be used to denote the sets of well-formed programs in the respective programming language, and $\mathcal{A}_{cpp}$ and $\mathcal{A}_{Smalltalk}$ can be used to denote the abstract semantics functions which map a program in each respective programming language to a finite structure.

Decidability determines that programs generating a finite structure from the source code are *possible*, but it does not guarantee that they can work in practice. The Two-Tier Programming Toolkit (§15.4) implements such a static analyzer for the $\mathcal{A}_{Java1.4}$ abstract semantics function. It is capable of analyzing the source code of any well-formed Java 1.4 program and storing the resulting finite structure in a relational database.

14.3   DESIGN MODELS

Finite structures provide us with a simplified representation of program which account for entities of dimension *0*, their properties, and the relations amongst them. Specifications, however, often contain higher dimensional terms. For example, ConcreteCollections in Codechart 39b (p. 76) is a

1-dimensional class. We may have an intuitive understanding of what `ConcreteCollections` stands for, for example, given Codechart 39a. But how is the meaning of a term determined precisely? Clearly, it is not fixed unless we provide an interpretation. Our notion of abstract semantics must therefore also provide an *interpretation* for higher dimensional terms. This motivates the notion of *design models*: structures that enrich the rudimentary notion of a finite structure with *entities of higher dimension* (namely sets of entities) and an *interpretation function*, namely a mapping from constants to entities.

Precisely put, a **design model** (Definition XII) $\mathfrak{M}$ is a triple

$$\mathfrak{M} = \langle \mathbb{U}_*, \mathbb{R}, \mathcal{I} \rangle$$

such that:

- $\mathbb{U}_* \triangleq \mathbb{U}_0 \uplus \mathbb{U}_1 \uplus \mathbb{U}_2$ is the **universe** of $\mathfrak{M}$, where each $\mathbb{U}_k$ is a finite set of entities of *dimension* k (Definition II).

- $\mathbb{R}$ is a set of unary and binary relations (Definition II).

- $\mathcal{I}$ is an **interpretation function** mapping some *constant terms* (Definition VI) to entities in $\mathbb{U}_*$.

- $\mathfrak{M}$ satisfies the *axioms of class-based programs*[3] (Definition VIII).

Given constant term τ, the entity $\mathcal{I}(\tau)$ is also called *the interpretation* of τ, where the notation <u>`entity`</u> (printed in underlined monospace typeface) stands for the interpretation of the constant `entity` (in monospace typeface).

For example, Table 17 depicts $\mathfrak{JavaUtil}$, a design model for Program 1 (p. 47).

An **entity of dimension** k is simply a uniform set of entities of dimension $k - 1$.[4] In particular, a **class of dimension** *1* is a set of classes of dimension *0*, a **signature of dimension** *1* is a set of signatures of dimension *0*, and a **method of dimension** *1* is a set of methods of dimension *0*.

For example, <u>`CollectionsHrc`</u> is a class of dimension *1*, defined in $\mathfrak{JavaUtil}$ as the set of the entities of dimension *0* representing the collection classes.

A **hierarchy of dimension** *1* (Definition IV) is a class of dimension *1* that contains a class of dimension *0* such that all other classes inherit (possibly indirectly) therefrom. For example, <u>`CollectionsHrc`</u> is a hierarchy of dimension *1*.

Table 17. $\mathfrak{JavaUtil}$. A Design Model Representing Program 1

Entities ($\mathbb{U}_*$):
$\mathbb{U}_0$: see Table 16
$\mathbb{U}_1$ contains two entities of dimension *1*:
<u>`CollectionsHrc`</u> = { <u>`Collection`</u>, <u>`List`</u>, <u>`LinkedList`</u> }
<u>`IteratorsHrc`</u> = { <u>`Iterator`</u>, <u>`ListIterator`</u>, <u>`LinkedListItr`</u> }

[3]The axioms of object-oriented design are discussed in §17.3, p.198.

[4]Since our language may only model terms of dimensions 0, 1, and 2, we are only interested in modelling entities of these dimensions. Definition II is more general, accommodating for entities of higher dimensions, if such a need does arise.

Table 17. (*Continued*)

Relations ($\mathbb{R}$): see Table 16
Interpretation function ($\mathcal{I}$):

$$\mathcal{I}(\text{object}) = \underline{\text{Object}}$$
$$\mathcal{I}(\text{collection}) = \underline{\text{Collection}}$$
$$\mathcal{I}(\text{list}) = \underline{\text{List}}$$
$$\mathcal{I}(\text{linkedList}) = \underline{\text{LinkedList}}$$
$$\mathcal{I}(\text{iterator}) = \underline{\text{Iterator}}$$
$$\mathcal{I}(\text{listIterator}) = \underline{\text{ListIterator}}$$
$$\mathcal{I}(\text{linkedlistItr}) = \underline{\text{LinkedListItr}}$$
$$\mathcal{I}(\text{newItr}) = \underline{\text{newItr()}}$$
$$\mathcal{I}(\text{next}) = \underline{\text{next()}}$$
$$\mathcal{I}(\text{CollectionsHrc}) = \underline{\text{CollectionsHrc}}$$
$$\mathcal{I}(\text{IteratorsHrc}) = \underline{\text{IteratorsHrc}}$$

The *interpretation function* maps constants to entities. For example:

$$\mathcal{I}(\text{vector}) = \underline{\text{java.util.Vector}}$$

Such statements can be used to ensure that the constant **vector** in Codechart 11 (p. 51) is interpreted correctly. The interpretation of signature constants may be less obvious; for example,

$$\mathcal{I}(\text{add}) = \underline{\text{add(Object)}}$$

The interpretation function notation is also used to indicate the mapping from higher dimensional constants to entities of higher dimension, as demonstrated in

$$\mathcal{I}(\text{ConcreteCollections}) = \underline{\text{ConcreteCollections}}$$

or to sets of entities, as demonstrated in

$$\mathcal{I}(\text{ConcreteCollections}) = \{\underline{\text{linkedList}}, \underline{\text{treeSet}}, \underline{\text{hashSet}}, \underline{\text{arrayList}}\}$$

To complete our understanding of the design model, let us define formally the superimposition operator $\otimes$ as a partial binary functional relation, defined as follows (Definition V): Let $\underline{\text{sig}}$ designate a signature of dimension 0, $\underline{\text{cls}}$ a class of dimension 0. Then $\underline{\text{sig}} \otimes \underline{\text{cls}}$ is defined as follows:

- If there exists a method of dimension 0 $\underline{\text{mth}}$ such that $\underline{\text{sig}}$ is the signature of $\underline{\text{mth}}$ and $\underline{\text{mth}}$ is a member in class $\underline{\text{cls}}$, then $\underline{\text{sig}} \otimes \underline{\text{cls}} \triangleq \underline{\text{mth}}$.
- Otherwise, if there exists a class of dimension 0 $\underline{\text{supercls}}$ such that $\underline{\text{cls}}$ inherits (possibly indirectly) therefrom and $\underline{\text{sig}} \otimes \underline{\text{supercls}}$ is defined, then $\underline{\text{sig}} \otimes \underline{\text{cls}} \triangleq \underline{\text{sig}} \otimes \underline{\text{supercls}}$.

Otherwise, $\underline{\text{sig}} \otimes \underline{\text{cls}}$ is undefined.

For entities of higher dimensions (see below), the superimposition operator is defined as follows: Let $\underline{\text{Signatures}} = \{\underline{s}_1, \dots \underline{s}_n\}$ be a signature of dimension 1, and $\underline{\text{Classes}} = \{\underline{c}_1, \dots \underline{c}_k\}$ a class of dimension d. Then we also define:

- $\underline{\text{sig}} \otimes \underline{\text{Classes}} \triangleq \{\underline{\text{sig}} \otimes \underline{c}_1, \dots, \underline{\text{sig}} \otimes \underline{c}_k\}$ iff each one of the expressions $\underline{\text{sig}} \otimes \underline{c}_1, \dots, \underline{\text{sig}} \otimes \underline{c}_k$ is defined; otherwise $\underline{\text{sig}} \otimes \underline{\text{Classes}}$ is undefined ($\underline{\text{sig}} \otimes \underline{\text{Classes}}$ is a **clan**).

- $\underline{\text{Signatures}} \otimes \underline{\text{cls}} \triangleq \{\underline{s}_1 \otimes \underline{\text{cls}}, \dots, \underline{s}_n \otimes \underline{\text{cls}}\}$ iff each one of the expressions $\underline{s}_1 \otimes \underline{\text{cls}}, \dots, \underline{s}_n \otimes \underline{\text{cls}}$ is defined; otherwise $\underline{\text{Signatures}} \otimes \underline{\text{cls}}$ is undefined ($\underline{\text{Signatures}} \otimes \underline{\text{cls}}$ is a **tribe**).

- $\underline{\text{Signatures}} \otimes \underline{\text{Classes}} \triangleq \{\underline{s}_1 \otimes \underline{\text{Classes}}, \dots, \underline{s}_n \otimes \underline{\text{Classes}}\}$ iff each one of the expressions $\underline{s}_1 \otimes \underline{\text{Classes}}, \dots, \underline{s}_n \otimes \underline{\text{Classes}}$ is defined; otherwise $\underline{\text{Signatures}} \otimes \underline{\text{Classes}}$ is undefined ($\underline{\text{Signatures}} \otimes \underline{\text{Classes}}$ is a **tribe of clans**).

The nature of class-based programs dictates some of the properties of design models. For example, no programming language allows a class to inherit, directly or indirectly, from itself. Therefore, no design models violating this property should be allowed. Such logical properties can therefore be articulated as axioms, to which we refer as the *axioms of class-based programs*, discussed in §17.3.

Unlike finite structures, design models *cannot* be adequately generated automatically from source code. One reason is because the interpretation of higher dimensional constants cannot be found in code. But design models can be defined as *expansions* of finite structures. We therefore say that a finite structure is a **submodel** of any design model that can be obtained by expanding the finite structure. For example, the design model $\mathfrak{Java Util}$ (Table 17) is an expansion of the finite structure $\mathfrak{F}_{util}$ (Table 16) with entities of higher dimension (and by introducing an interpretation function). Therefore, $\mathfrak{F}_{util}$ is a *submodel* of $\mathfrak{Java Util}$.

14.4 PROGRAM MODELLING REVISITED

In the previous section we concluded that finite structures can be generated from analyzing the source code but design models, which contain the interpretation functions and entities of higher dimensions, cannot. What, then, is the relation between a design model and a program? Presumably, a very large number of design models can be generated from expanding a finite structure, each with a different interpretation function, all of which can be thought of as appropriate representations of the original program. Therefore, a program can be appropriately represented by more than one design model. However, clearly a design model which does not expand the finite structure representing the program cannot be adequately considered an appropriate representation thereof.

Precisely put, let $\mathbb{L}$ designate the set of valid expressions in a programming language, and let $\mathcal{A}\colon\mathbb{L}\to\mathfrak{F}^{\bullet}$ designate an *abstract semantics function*. We say that design model $\mathfrak{M}$ **appropriately represents** program p if and only if $\mathcal{A}(p)$ is a *submodel* of $\mathfrak{M}$ (Definition XVI).

For example, the definition of design model $\mathfrak{Java.util}$ (Table 17) is an extension of the finite structure $\mathfrak{F}_{util}$ (Table 16). And Equation (4) (p. 174) establishes that the finite structure $\mathfrak{F}_{util}$ is the abstract semantics of Program 1 (p. 47). Therefore, we can safely conclude that the design model $\mathfrak{Java.util}$ *appropriately represents* Program 1.

Having formulated the notion of an *appropriate representation* allows us to connect the notion of abstract semantics with the activity of software modelling. Given an *abstract semantics function*, $\mathcal{A}$ and a specific program in its domain, p, we define **program modelling** as a process that results in two artefacts:

1. A design model $\mathfrak{M}=\langle\mathbb{U}_{*},\mathbb{R},\mathcal{I}\rangle$ that *appropriately represents* p

2. A set of Codecharts $\{\Psi_{1},\ldots,\Psi_{n}\}$ that $\mathfrak{M}$ *satisfies* (Chapter 15)

where the design model $\mathfrak{M}$ captures those sets of classes, methods, and signatures and the set of charts represents the manner by which they correlate. The next chapter is dedicated to the conditions under which a design model can be said to *satisfy* a chart.

Presumably, tools supporting program modelling can greatly simplify the task of generating an appropriate design model by static analysis, which generates the finite structure fully automatically. From here, the job of the software modeller is only to introduce the higher dimensional entities and their interpretations. The Two-Tier Programming Toolkit, for example, supports precisely such a process.

Chapter 15

Verification

Codecharts are specifications, or statements, that articulate expectations from programs. *Verification* [Wing 1990] is a process whose purpose is to establish whether a particular program conforms to these expectations, namely to provide an answer to the *verification question* (p. 11). More precisely, *design verification* (in short *verification*) is a process that checks whether program p *satisfies* a Codechart Ψ—or in the alternate phrasing that p *implements* Ψ. This chapter provides the precise conditions for holding such a relation, to which we shall refer to as truth conditions, and describes a tool that can check these conditions automatically.

There is a considerable body of literature on the problem of program verification. For example, Tony Hoare's [1969] approach to the problem takes each statement in the source code to be a mathematical expression which "describes with unprecedented precision and in every minutest detail the behaviour, intended or unintended, of the computer on which they are executed" [Mahoney 2002]. Hoare's logic requires us to unpack formally each and every token in the program's text. Others, like Hoare, have offered a variety of formal specification languages which make less exhaustive demands. "Program verification" is used in its strongest sense, taken to mean proving that a program behaves "correctly" and (to varying degrees) exactly as it is expected.

While the notion of program correctness is very useful, it is almost without exception[1] *undecidable* (p. 11), which means that it cannot be verified fully automatically. Had we adopted this notion of correctness, we would be forced to abandon our principle of automated verifiability (§3.4). Instead, in *design verification* we seek to ensure that programs conform to their

---

[1] Statecharts [Harel 1987] is one example.

---

specifications articulated in a design description language but which does not guarantee program correctness in the strong sense encountered elsewhere. *Correctness* in our context is therefore taken to mean consistency between programs and specifications. And since Codecharts are decidable specifications (§2.2), conformance thereto can be verified by a program. More specifically, a tool automating design verification for Codecharts can check whether program *p implements* Codechart Ψ. Such a tool must analyze the source code of a given program, take Codecharts as specifications, and at a click of a button complete the verification process within predetermined, finite bounds on time and space. Such a tool is described in the last section of this chapter.

In §14.4 we defined *program modelling* as a process which takes a program p and produces an appropriate representation (a design model $\mathfrak{M}$) and a set of Codecharts. This definition allows us to formulate the process of *design verification* as follows.

Precisely put, given a program p written in programming language $\mathbb{L}$, a fixed abstract semantics function $\mathcal{A}$ whose domain is $\mathbb{L}$, a design model $\mathfrak{M} = \langle \mathbb{U}_\bullet, \mathbb{R}, \mathcal{I} \rangle$, and a Codechart Ψ, we define **design verification** (Definition XV, in short *verification*) as that problem of determining whether the following two conditions are met:

1. $\mathfrak{M}$ *appropriately represents* p
2. $\mathfrak{M}$ *satisfies* Ψ

The question whether $\mathfrak{M}$ appropriately represents p is discussed in the previous chapter (§14.4). The remainder of this chapter is dedicated to the formal truth conditions by which the verification procedure establishes whether $\mathfrak{M}$ *satisfies* Ψ.

If both conditions are met, we say that verification was successful and that program p **implements** Ψ **according to** $\mathfrak{M}$. Given program p and specification Ψ, if there exists *some* design model $\mathfrak{M}$ such that p implements Ψ according to $\mathfrak{M}$, then we say that p **implements** Ψ (Definition XVIII) or that p **satisfies** Ψ. For example, *verification* shall provide us with the algorithm needed to establish whether a given program *implements* the Composite pattern (§15.3).

The conditions under which design models *satisfy* a specification are called **truth conditions**, a notion on a par with Tarski's truth conditions [Huth & Ryan 2000]. In mathematical logic, truth conditions are the standard criteria for establishing the relation between a structure and a well-formed formula in the predicate logic. In the remainder of this chapter, we adopt the standard notion of truth conditions to establish the "satisfies" relation $\vDash$ between a design model and a Codechart.

15.1 VERIFYING CLOSED SPECIFICATIONS

In Part I of this book we encountered two kinds of specifications: Codecharts modelling specific programs, which employ constants, versus Codecharts modelling design motifs (such as design patterns), which also include variables. We define a **closed specification** as a Codechart modelling a specific program, not a design motif. In other words, it is a chart that contains no variables, a notion on a par with a *closed formula* in the predicate logic. For example, all the Codecharts in Chapters 6 and 7 are closed specifications.

Given a closed specification Ψ and a design model $\mathfrak{M}$, the proposition $\mathfrak{M}$ **satisfies** Ψ is written using the standard symbol $\vDash$ as follows:

$$\mathfrak{M} \vDash \Psi$$

This relation is said to hold if and only if $\mathfrak{M}$ satisfies all the terms and formulas in Ψ. The truth conditions for satisfying terms in closed specifications are listed in Table 18. The truth conditions for satisfying formulas in closed specifications are listed in Table 19. The truth conditions for open specifications are discussed in the next section.

Table 18. Truth Conditions for Satisfying Closed Specifications, Part I: Terms

---

A necessary condition for a design model $\mathfrak{M}$ to satisfy a closed specification Ψ is that each one of the constant terms τ in Ψ must be in the domain of the interpretation function $\mathcal{I}$ and mapped to an entity depending on the type of the constant as follows:

- If τ is a d-dimensional class constant, then $\mathcal{I}(\tau)$ is a class of dimension d.
- If τ is a d-dimensional signature constant, then $\mathcal{I}(\tau)$ is a signature of dimension d.
- If τ is a d-dimensional hierarchy constant, then $\mathcal{I}(\tau)$ is a hierarchy of dimension d.
- If τ is a d-dimensional constant superimposition term of the form $s \otimes c$ and $\mathcal{I}(s) \otimes \mathcal{I}(c)$ is defined, then $\mathcal{I}(s \otimes c) = \mathcal{I}(s) \otimes \mathcal{I}(c)$.

Table 19. Truth Conditions for Satisfying Closed Specifications, Part 2: Formulas

---

A necessary condition for a design model $\mathfrak{M}$ to satisfy a closed specification Ψ is that each one of the formulas φ in Ψ must be satisfied by $\mathfrak{M}$, the truth conditions of which depend on φ:

- If φ is of the form $UnaryRelation(t)$, then the entity $\mathcal{I}(t)$ is in relation *UnaryRelation.*
- If φ is of the form $BinaryRelation(t_1, t_2)$, then either
  1. the pair $\langle \mathcal{I}(t_1), \mathcal{I}(t_2) \rangle$ is in relation *BinaryRelation*, or
  2. there exists some class $\underline{\textbf{sprcls}} \in \mathbb{U}_0$ such that the formulas $BinaryRelation(sprcls,\ t_2)$ and $Inherit(t_1, sprcls)$ hold, or
  3. there exists some class $\underline{\textbf{subcls}} \in \mathbb{U}_0$ such that the formulas $BinaryRelation(t_1, subcls)$ and $Inherit(subcls, t_2)$ hold.
- If φ is of the form $ALL(UnaryRelation, \tau)$, then for each entity $\underline{\textbf{e}} \in \mathcal{I}(\tau)$ [if τ is a 0-dimensional term, $\underline{\textbf{e}} = \mathcal{I}(\tau)$] the formula $UnaryRelation(\textbf{e})$ holds.
- If φ is of the form $TOTAL(BinaryRelation, \tau_1, \tau_2)$, then for each entity $\underline{\textbf{e}}_1 \in \mathcal{I}(\tau_1)$ [if τ_1 is a 0-dimensional term, $\underline{\textbf{e}}_1 = \mathcal{I}(\tau_1)$] that is not an abstract method there exists some entity $\underline{\textbf{e}}_2 \in \mathcal{I}(\tau_2)$ [if τ_2 is a 0-dimensional term, $\underline{\textbf{e}}_2 = \mathcal{I}(\tau_2)$] such that $BinaryRelation(\textbf{e}_1, \textbf{e}_2)$ holds.
- If φ is of the form $ISOMORPHIC(BinaryRelation, \tau_1, \tau_2)$, then there exists a pair of entities $\langle \underline{\textbf{e}}_1, \underline{\textbf{e}}_2 \rangle$ where $\underline{\textbf{e}}_1 \in \mathcal{I}(\tau_1)$ [if τ_1 is a 0-dimensional term, $\underline{\textbf{e}}_1 = \mathcal{I}(\tau_1)$] and $\underline{\textbf{e}}_2 \in \mathcal{I}(\tau_2)$ [if τ_2 is a 0-dimensional term, $\underline{\textbf{e}}_2 = \mathcal{I}(\tau_2)$] such that:
  1. $BinaryRelation(\textbf{e}_1, \textbf{e}_2)$ holds, unless both $\underline{\textbf{e}}_1$ and $\underline{\textbf{e}}_2$ are abstract, and
  2. $ISOMORPHIC(BinaryRelation, \tau_1 - \textbf{e}_1, \tau_2 - \textbf{e}_2)$ holds, unless both $\tau_1 - \textbf{e}_1$ and $\tau_2 - \textbf{e}_2$ are empty

  where $\mathcal{I}(\tau - \textbf{e}) = \mathcal{I}(\tau) - \mathcal{I}(\textbf{e})$.

For example, let us prove that the design model in Table 17, denoted 𝔍𝔞𝔳𝔞𝔘𝔱𝔦𝔩, *satisfies* JavaUtil (Codechart 89b, p. 148). This claim can be formulated as the following proposition:

Proposition 1. 𝔍𝔞𝔳𝔞𝔘𝔱𝔦𝔩 ⊨ JavaUtil

Proof: First, we show that each term in JavaUtil is interpreted in 𝔍𝔞𝔳𝔞𝔘𝔱𝔦𝔩 into an entity of the appropriate dimension and entity type:

- The *0*-dimensional class constant `object` is mapped to a class of dimension *0* <u>`Object`</u>.
- Each *0*-dimensional signature constant (`newItr`, `next`) is mapped to a signature of dimension *0* (<u>`newItr()`</u> and <u>`next()`</u>, respectively).
- Each *1*-dimensional hierarchy constant (`CollectionsHrc`, `IteratorsHrc`) is mapped to a hierarchy of dimension *1* (<u>`CollectionsHrc`</u>, <u>`IteratorsHrc`</u> respectively).
- The superimposition `newItr`⊗`CollectionsHrc` is interpreted as the set of methods

$$\{\underline{\texttt{Collection.newItr()}}, \underline{\texttt{LinkedList.newItr()}}\}$$

and the superimposition `next`⊗`IteratorsHrc` is interpreted as the set of methods

$$\{\underline{\texttt{Iterator.next()}}, \underline{\texttt{LinkedListItr.next()}}\}$$

Next, let us establish that 𝔍𝔞𝔳𝔞𝔘𝔱𝔦𝔩 satisfies each one of the formulas in JavaUtil:

- The assertion

𝔍𝔞𝔳𝔞𝔘𝔱𝔦𝔩 ⊨ *ISOMORPHIC*(*Produce*, `newItr`⊗`CollectionsHrc`, `IteratorsHrc`)

holds because

𝔍𝔞𝔳𝔞𝔘𝔱𝔦𝔩 ⊨ *Produce*(`newItr`⊗`linkedList`, `linkedlistItr`)

holds, in turn because

⟨<u>`LinkedList.newItr()`</u>, <u>`LinkedListItr`</u>⟩ ∈ *Produce*

- The assertion

𝔍𝔞𝔳𝔞𝔘𝔱𝔦𝔩 ⊨ *TOTAL*(*Aggregate*, `CollectionsHrc`, `object`)

holds because

𝔍𝔞𝔳𝔞𝔘𝔱𝔦𝔩 ⊨ *Aggregate*(`linkedList`, `Object`)

holds, in turn because

⟨<u>`LinkedList`</u>, <u>`object`</u>⟩ ∈ *Aggregate*

- The assertion

𝔍𝔞𝔳𝔞𝔘𝔱𝔦𝔩 ⊨ *TOTAL*(*Return*, `next`⊗`IteratorsHrc`, `Object`) holds because

$$\mathfrak{JavaUtil} \vDash Return(\text{next} \otimes \text{linkedlistItr}, \text{Object})$$

holds, in turn because

$$\langle \text{LinkedListItr.next()}, \text{Object} \rangle \in \underline{Return}$$

□

However, such lengthy, detailed proofs are rarely necessary. In any case, since they can be fully automated, they do not generally need to be carried out manually. A tool that automates this process is described in §15.4.

15.2 VERIFYING OPEN SPECIFICATIONS

In Chapter 9 we introduced variables for the purpose of modelling design motifs. We explained that variables have no fixed interpretation. Therefore, the verification of charts that contain variables, henceforth **open specifications**, is different from the verification of closed specifications.

Open specifications are on a par with *open formulas* in the predicate calculus. What is required in the verification of an open formula is to map each variable to a specific constant. *Assignments* provide such a mapping. To prove that a particular program *satisfies* a design motif, we must therefore use an assignment to turn an open specification into a closed one. In other words, *assignments* allow us to turn the problem of verifying open specifications into the problem of verifying closed specifications, solved in the previous section.

Precisely put, an **assignment** from specification Ψ into a design model $\mathfrak{M} = \langle \mathbb{U}_*, \mathbb{R}, \mathcal{I} \rangle$ is a function that maps each variable in Ψ to a constant in the domain of $\mathcal{I}$.

Let us demonstrate the notion of an *assignment* with an example. Consider an assignment g that maps each one of the variables in Codechart 90 (Iterator) to constants in the domain of the interpretation function in the design model $\mathfrak{JavaUtil}$ (Table 17), defined as follows and illustrated in Figure 15-1, where $\mathcal{I}(\text{Object}) = \{\underline{\text{Object}}\}$:

$$g(Aggregates) = \text{CollectionsHrc} \tag{5}$$

$$g(Iterators) = \text{IteratorsHrc}$$

$$g(Elements) = \text{Object}$$

$$g(createIterator) = \text{newItr}$$

$$g(next) = \text{next}$$

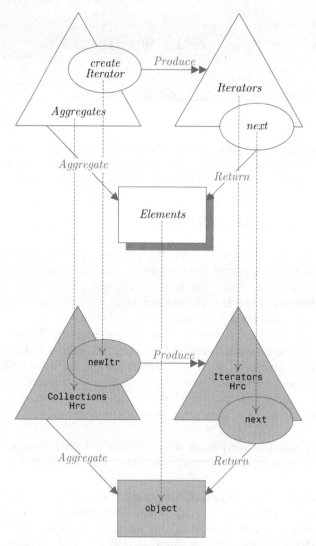

Figure 15-1. An illustration of the assignment in Equation (5) which maps each variable in the Iterator pattern (top) to a constant in the design model $\mathfrak{JavaUtil}$ (bottom)

Given a design model $\mathfrak{M} = \langle \mathbb{U}_*, \mathbb{R}, \mathcal{I} \rangle$, an (open) specification Ψ, and an assignment g, the notation

$$\Psi[\, g(\, x) \,/\, x \,]$$

stands for the chart which results from replacing all occurrences of variable x with the constant $g(\,x)$. More generally, the notation

$$\Psi[\, g(\, x_1) \,/\, x_1, \ldots, g(\, x_n) \,/\, x_n \,]$$

stands for the chart which results from the consistent replacement of all occurrences of variable x_i with the constant $g(\,x_i)$.

For example, if g stands for the assignment function defined in Equation (5), and Iterator stands for the Iterator design pattern (Codechart 90), then

Iterator[$g($ *Aggregates*$)$ / *Aggregates*,

       $g($ *Iterators*$)$ / *Iterators*,

       $g($ *Elements*$)$ / *Elements*,   **(6)**

       $g($ *createIterator*$)$ / *createIterator*,

       $g($ *next*$)$ / *next*]

            $=$ Iterator[`CollectionsHrc`/ *Aggregates*,

                     `IteratorsHrc`/ *Iterators*,

                     `object`/ *Elements*,

                     `newItr`/ *createIterator*,

                     `next`/ *next*]

            $=$ JavaUtil

where JavaUtil stands for Codechart 89b (p. 148). In other words, Equation (6) proves that JavaUtil is precisely the chart that results from the consistent replacement of each variable x in Iterator (Codechart 90) with the constant $g(x)$.

Assignments allow us to extend the notion of *satisfaction*, so far defined only for closed specifications, to open specifications. It does so as follows: Let $\mathfrak{M}$ designate a design model, let Ψ stand for an open specification, and let g designate an assignment from the variables in Ψ to constants in the domain of the interpretation function of $\mathfrak{M}$. We say that $\mathfrak{M}$ **satisfies** Ψ **under assignment** g, written

$$\mathfrak{M} \vDash_g \Psi$$

if and only if

$$\mathfrak{M} \vDash \Psi[g(x_1) / x_1, \ldots, g(x_n) / x_n]$$

In other words, $\mathfrak{M}$ satisfies open specification Ψ under assignment g if and only if $\mathfrak{M}$ satisfies the closed specification resulting from the consistent replacement of each variable x_i with the constant $g(x_i)$.

If such an assignment exists, we say that $\mathfrak{M}$ **satisfies** Ψ, written

$$\mathfrak{M} \vDash \Psi$$

For example, let us prove that design model $\mathfrak{JavaUtil}$ *satisfies* the Iterator design pattern. Let Iterator designate Codechart 90 (p. 148), and let $\mathfrak{JavaUtil}$ designate the design model in Table 17 (p. 176). A proposition to this extent can therefore be stated formally as follows:

Proposition 2. $\mathfrak{JavaUtil} \vDash$ Iterator

Proof: we must find an assignment a such that

$$\mathfrak{JavaUtil} \vDash_a \text{Iterator}$$

From Equation (6) we know that

$$\text{Iterator}[g(\textit{Aggregates}) / \textit{Aggregates}, \ldots, g(\textit{next}) / \textit{next}] = \text{JavaUtil}$$

where g is the assignment defined in Equation (5) and JavaUtil stands for Codechart 89b. From Proposition 1 (p. 182) we know that 𝔍𝔞𝔳𝔞𝔘𝔱𝔦𝔩 satisfies JavaUtil. Hence 𝔍𝔞𝔳𝔞𝔘𝔱𝔦𝔩 satisfies Iterator under assignment g.

□

15.3 VERIFYING PATTERN IMPLEMENTATIONS

In the vernacular, a program is said to "implement a pattern" if it conforms to the informal description specified by the (solution described in the) respective design pattern. Since LePUS3 provides a rigorous specification of some patterns and settles the relation between specifications and programs, we are free to render this intuitive notion (of implementing a pattern) a precise definition. Specifically, if a design pattern is taken to be represented as an open LePUS3 specification Ψ, we may show that a given program p *implements* our design pattern simply by proving that p *implements* Ψ in the sense defined in this chapter.

But what does such a proof tell us? It points out a selection of elements of the program whose representation (i.e., the respective list of entities) can be shown to *satisfy* the design pattern. The identity of these elements indicates which part of the program constitutes the implementation of said pattern.

Naturally, a pattern can be implemented as many times as we wish—or none. It is therefore convenient for us to refer to each such selection as an *instance* of the pattern. A process of **pattern mining** is therefore the process of searching for *instances* of patterns within a given program.

Precisely put, given an assignment g from variables in specification Ψ into constants in the domain of interpretation function $\mathcal{I}$ of some design model 𝔐, we say that the n-tuple $\langle \mathcal{I}(g(x_1)), \ldots, \mathcal{I}(g(x_n)) \rangle$ is an **instance** of Ψ.

In the first part of the book, we made informal claims on the implementation of several patterns. Below, we articulate them as mathematical propositions and sketch their proofs.

Proposition 3. Package `java.util` *implements* Iterator.

Proof: According to Proposition 2, the design model 𝔍𝔞𝔳𝔞𝔘𝔱𝔦𝔩 (Table 17) *satisfies* Iterator (p. 148). In §14.4 we proved that 𝔍𝔞𝔳𝔞𝔘𝔱𝔦𝔩 appropriately represents Program 1 (p. 47), which is part of `java.util`. Therefore, `java.util` *implements* Iterator. □

Proposition 4. Package `java.awt` *implements* Composite.

Proof: Let 𝔍𝔞𝔳𝔞𝔄𝔚𝔗 designate the design model whose universe consists of the classes, signatures, and methods in package `java.awt` of the Java Foundation Classes (Version. 1.4), in particular those modelled by Codechart 87a (p. 142). Let the interpretation function of 𝔍𝔞𝔳𝔞𝔄𝔚𝔗 map each one of the constants in Codechart 87a to the obvious entity, and also the higher dimensional constants in JavaAWT (Codechart 87c) as follows:

$\mathcal{I}(\text{ComponentOps}) = \{\underline{\text{numListening(long)}}, \underline{\text{countHierarchyMembers()}},$
$\underline{\text{addNotify()}}, \underline{\text{removeNotify()}}, \underline{\text{createHierarchyEvents}}$
$\underline{\text{(int,Component,Container,long,boolean)}}\}$

$\mathcal{I}(\text{CompositeOps}) = \{\underline{\text{add(Component)}}, \underline{\text{remove(Component)}}\}$

$\mathcal{I}(\text{ComponentLeaves}) = \{\underline{\text{java.awt.Button}}, \underline{\text{java.awt.Canvas}}, \underline{\text{java.awt.}}$
$\underline{\text{ScrollBar}}\}$

It is trivial to show that 𝔍𝔞𝔳𝔞𝔄𝔚𝔗 appropriately represents package
java.awt and that 𝔍𝔞𝔳𝔞𝔄𝔚𝔗 *satisfies* Codechart 87a and JavaAWT. What
remains is to define an assignment from the free variables in Composite
(Codechart 88, p. 144) to the constants in JavaAWT. Figure 15-2 illustrates
such an assignment, under which 𝔍𝔞𝔳𝔞𝔄𝔚𝔗 *satisfies* Composite.   □

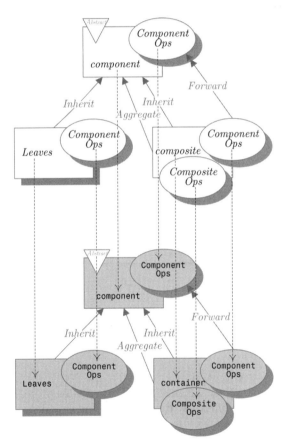

Figure 15-2. An illustration of an assignment from the Composite pattern (top) to constants in
JavaAWT (bottom)

The proof for Proposition 4 can be automated using the Two-Tier
Programming Toolkit, as demonstrated in §15.4.

In Proposition 8 (p. 207) we also prove that the Composite pattern is an *abstraction* of chart JavaAWT.

15.4 TOOL SUPPORT FOR AUTOMATED VERIFICATION

Fully automated verification of Codecharts is possible because they are *decidable* and because their truth conditions are precisely formulated. The Verifier in the Two-Tier Programming Toolkit is such a tool. For example, given a program p encoded in Java 1.4 and design model $\mathfrak{M}$ that *appropriately represents* it (§14.4), it can verify that p *implements* Ψ *according to* $\mathfrak{M}$ with a click of a button and indicate the result to the user. Below we demonstrate how the Toolkit verifies closed and open specifications using package `java.awt` and the Composite design pattern as an example.

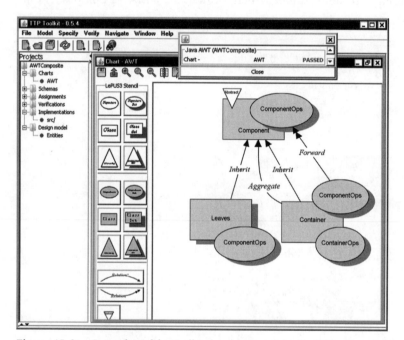

Figure 15-3.   Screenshot of the Toolkit showing the result of verifying that package `java.awt` *implements* Codechart 87c

For example, the Toolkit allows us to visually specify Codechart 87c (p. 144) and to verify that package `java.awt` *implements* it. To do so, the user first undertakes the process of *specification* by creating a new Codechart using a visual editor, as demonstrated in Figure 15-3. A panel on the left of the window (titled "LePUS3 Stencil") offers the set of visual tokens which can be clicked to create Codecharts. Next, the user indicates the set of java source code files (or in this case the folder containing them, called `src`) and have them analyzed. At the next step, the user undertakes *program modelling* (§14.4) and specifies the interpretation of higher dimensional constants such as `ComponentOps` and `Leaves` as the sets containing the respective classes and signatures. Having completed this, the user can launch the automated process of design verification simply by clicking the Verify All button. A dialogue box opens up ("Passed" in Figure 15-3), indicating that the implementation indeed conforms to the specification.

If, however, the Toolkit fails to *verify*, then it means that the specification is not satisfied by the implementation and that there is an inconsistency between the Codechart and implementation (the program does not *satisfy* the specification). For example, Figure 15-4 depicts a screenshot showing that Toolkit has discovered such an inconsistency, which in this example arises from specifying that class Component inherits from class Container, which happens to be false in package java.awt.

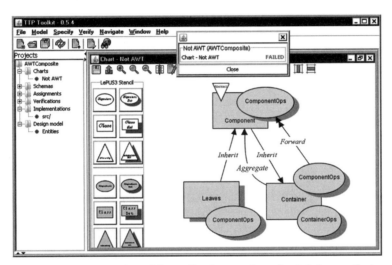

Figure 15-4. Screenshot of the Toolkit showing that it has failed to verify that a Codechart specifying that class Component inherits from class Container is satisfied by the java.awt package

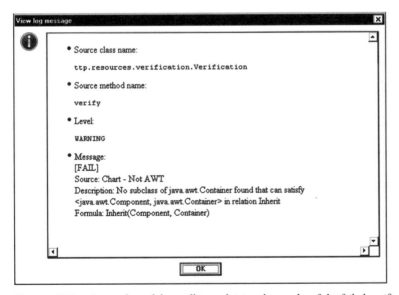

Figure 15-5. Screenshot of the toolkit explaining the results of the failed verification

To allow the programmer to resolve the inconsistency discovered between design and implementation, the Toolkit reports on the detailed nature of the violation, as demonstrated in Figure 15-5.

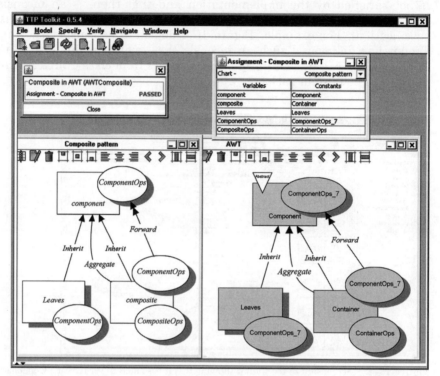

Figure 15-6. Screenshot of the Toolkit showing the successful result of verifying that java.awt *implements* the Composite pattern (Proposition 4)

The Toolkit can also verify that a program implements a pattern. For example, in Proposition 4 (p. 186) we prove that the Abstract Windowing Toolkit in Java SDK contains an implementation of the Composite design pattern. The Toolkit can be used to automate the proof to this claim, the results of which are depicted in Figure 15-6. To carry out the verification, the programmer must proceed from the previous example to specify the pattern, although in the case of the Composite pattern (as in many other Gang of Four patterns), the Toolkit already has it in its library. Finally, the user specifies the *assignment* which indicates which elements in java.awt are intended as the implementation of the pattern.[2] Verification can now commence by clicking the Verify All button, the results of which are consistent with Proposition 4.

[2]In Figure 15-5, the constant ComponentOps was renamed to ComponentOps_7 to prevent confusion with the variable *ComponentOps*.

Chapter 16

* Schemas

Symbolic transcriptions of expressions and formulas were used throughout this book for the purpose of referring to specific elements in LePUS3 Codecharts. For example, a method which is visually represented by a superimposition of an ellipse `sig` over a rectangle `cls` was symbolically represented as the expression $sig \otimes cls$. Thus, perhaps without noticing, Part I of this book has in effect introduced not one but two specification languages: the visual tokens, which constitute LePUS3, and the set of their symbolic transcriptions, to which we refer as Class-Z. The two design description languages are equally useful, each with somewhat different purposes and appealing to a different audience: where LePUS3 Codecharts capitalize on the benefits of visual languages, Class-Z schemas are designed to resemble predicate formulas in their traditional form. This chapter formally introduces this language and the notion of a *schema*.

In LePUS3, a specification is articulated as a Codechart. In Class-Z, a specification is introduced using the schema notation. For example, the two terms and the one formula in Codechart 82 (p. 129) translate to the following schema:

JavaRMI

$remoteInterface,$ `java.rmi.remote:`CLASS

$Inherit^+(remoteInterface,$ `java.rmi.remote`)

Codecharts: Roadmaps and Blueprints for Object-Oriented Programs, by Amnon H. Eden
Copyright © 2011 John Wiley & Sons, Inc.

More generally, specifications encoded in the **schema** notation consist of two compartments. The first introduces the terms in the specification, each declared with its respective type and dimension, and the second lists the formulas:

SchemaName
$$
\begin{array}{|l}
\hline
Declaration \\[4pt]
Declaration \\[4pt]
\ldots \\[4pt]
\hline
Formula \\[4pt]
Formula \\[4pt]
\ldots \\[4pt]
\hline
\end{array}
$$

Declarations introduce constant and variable terms into the specification. Each declaration consists of a comma-separated list of constant and/or variable symbols, followed by a colon and a type symbol, possibly adorned by a dimension indicator. Types are specified using either one of the symbols CLASS, SIGNATURE, or HIERARCHY. The dimension n is specified using the exponent notation $\mathcal{P}^{n}\mathbb{T}$, where $\mathcal{P}\mathbb{T}$ is shorthand for $\mathcal{P}^{1}\mathbb{T}$ and $\mathbb{T}$ is shorthand for $\mathcal{P}^{0}\mathbb{T}$. The declaration

$$x_1, \ldots, x_n \colon \mathbb{T}$$

is shorthand for the list of n declarations

$$x_1 \colon \mathbb{T}$$

$$\ldots$$

$$x_n \colon \mathbb{T}$$

As the name Class-Z suggests, the inspiration for the schema notation comes from the Z specification language [Spivey 1992]. But Class-Z is an altogether different language from Z. In particular, Z is much more expressive than Class-Z whereas Class-Z is restricted to the term declarations and formulas equivalent to their visual counterparts in LePUS3. Table 20 provides the precise rules for translating a LePUS3 chart to a Class-Z schema.

Table 20. Translating a Codechart to a Schema

Terms:

- Each d-dimensional class constant c is represented by the declaration c:$\mathcal{P}^d$CLASS.

- Each d-dimensional class variable c is represented by the declaration c:$\mathcal{P}^d$CLASS.

- Each d-dimensional signature constant s is represented by the declaration s:$\mathcal{P}^d$SIGNATURE.

- Each d-dimensional signature variable s is represented by the declaration s:$\mathcal{P}^d$SIGNATURE.

- Each d-dimensional hierarchy constant h is represented by the declaration h:$\mathcal{P}^d$HIERARCHY.

- Each d-dimensional hierarchy variable h is represented by the declaration h:$\mathcal{P}^d$HIERARCHY.

- Each superimposition of a signature term s over a class term c is represented by the term $s \otimes c$. If the term $s \otimes c$ does not appear in any one of the formulas, then it is represented by a formula (see below).

Formulas:

- Each formula consisting of a unary relation symbol marked $\mathcal{R}$ placed over the 0-dimensional term t is represented by the formula $\mathcal{R}(t)$.

- Each formula consisting of a unary relation symbol marked $\mathcal{R}$ placed over the higher dimensional term T is represented by the formula $ALL(\mathcal{R}, T)$.

- Each formula consisting of a binary relation edge marked $\mathcal{R}$ connecting the term t_1 with the term t_2 is represented by the formula $\mathcal{R}(t_1, t_2)$.

- Each formula consisting of $TOTAL$ predicate symbol $\mathcal{R}$ connecting the term T_1 with the term T_2 is represented by the formula $TOTAL(\mathcal{R}, T_1, T_2)$.

- Each formula consisting of $ISOMORPHIC$ predicate symbol $\mathcal{R}$ connecting the term T_1 with the term T_2 is represented by the formula $ISOMORPHIC(\mathcal{R}, T_1, T_2)$.

- Each superimposition term of a 0-dimensional signature term s over a 0-dimensional class term c which does not appear in any one of the formulas is represented by the formula $Method(s \otimes c)$.

- Each higher dimensional superimposition of a signature term S over a class term C which does not appear in any one of the formulas is represented by the formula $ALL(Method, S \otimes C)$.

Since converting a LePUS3 Codechart to/from a Class-Z schema is straightforward (with the obvious exception of symbol sizes and spatial locations, which in LePUS3 carry no meaning), such a conversion can be carried out by a program. The Toolkit contains a utility which performs the conversion both ways. For example, Figure16-1 depicts a screenshot demonstrating the results of converting a simple Codechart to a Class-Z schema. Additional examples are provided in the lepus.org.uk website.

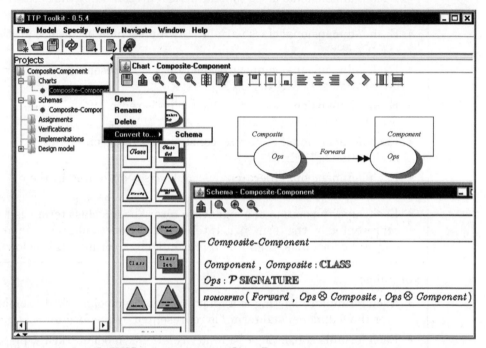

Figure 16-1. A LePUS3 Codechart and the Class-Z schema generated therefrom by the Toolkit

Given the equivalence between charts and schemes, the term **specification** may henceforth apply also to any Class-Z schema.

Chapter **17**

LePUS3 in Classical Logic

This chapter describes the relation between specifications in LePUS3 and the more general notion of specification in mathematical logic. We briefly introduce a notion of a first-order language, use it to unpack our notion of *specification*, and present the axioms of class-based programs.

17.1 LePUS3 AND CLASS-Z AS FIRST-ORDER LANGUAGES

Below we use a standard notion of a first-order predicate logic (FOPL) language. The set of *logical symbols* includes the logical connectives $\wedge$ (conjunction), $\vee$ (disjunction), $\Rightarrow$ (implication), $\Leftrightarrow$ (biconditional), the quantifiers $\forall$ (universal), $\exists$ (existential), and the symbols for set $\{\}$, set membership $\in$ and non membership $\notin$, equation $=$, and inequation $\neq$. The set of nonlogical symbols includes the binary superimposition operator $\otimes$ and set subtraction $-$. *Terms* include unary (*Abstract*), binary (*Inherit*), and transitive binary (*Inherit⁺*) relation symbols, *constants* (`linkedList`), and *variables* (*factoryMethod*). If t, t_1, t_2 are terms, then 2^t, $t_1 - t_2$, and $t_1 \otimes t_2$ are also terms. If t_1, t_2 are terms, then $t_1 \neq t_2$ and $t_1 \in t_2$ are *well-formed formulas* (wff). Given the wffs φ and ψ and term t; then $\varphi \wedge \psi$, $\varphi \vee \psi$, $\varphi \Rightarrow \psi$, $\forall x \in t \bullet \varphi$, $\exists x \in t \bullet \varphi$ are also wffs. In Table 12 we sketch how to articulate in such a language some of the declarations and formulas of Class-Z.

The semantics of our FOPL language require a *design model*, a straight forward adaptation of our notions of a *finite structure* (§14.1), and an *interpretation function* (§14.3). The term $2^{\underline{relation}}$ is interpreted as the set of all nonempty subsets of tuples in the interpretation of *Relation*. Given a higher dimensional term T, the term $\mathsf{T} - \mathsf{t}$ is interpreted as $\mathcal{I}(\mathsf{T}) - \{\mathcal{I}(\mathsf{t})\}$, that is, the set of entities that is the interpretation of T minus the set containing only the interpretation of t. Superimposition terms are interpreted as specified in the

Codecharts: Roadmaps and Blueprints for Object-Oriented Programs, by Amnon H. Eden
Copyright © 2011 John Wiley & Sons, Inc.

first part of the book (also formulated in Definition V). Beyond these, Tarski's standard truth conditions for the usual quantifiers and connectives (e.g., [Huth & Ryan 2000]) apply.

Table 21.   Unpacking Some LePUS3/Class-Z Declarations and Formulas in the First-Order Predicate Logic

c:CLASS	$\triangleq$	$c \in \underline{Class}$
s:$\mathcal{P}$SIGNATURE	$\triangleq$	$s \in 2^{\underline{Signature}}$
Hrc:HIERARCHY	$\triangleq$	$Hrc \in 2^{\underline{Class}} \wedge \exists\, root \in Hrc \bullet$
		$\forall\, c \in Hrc \bullet (\, c \neq root \Rightarrow \langle c, root \rangle \in \underline{Inherit}^{+}\,)$
$Relation(x, y)$	$\triangleq$	$(\langle x, y \rangle \in \underline{Relation}) \vee$
		$(\exists\, sup \bullet Relation(\, sup, y)$
		$\wedge\, Inherit(x, sup)\,) \vee$
		$(\exists\, sub \bullet Relation(x, sub)$
		$\wedge\, Inherit(\, sub, y)\,)$
$ALL(\, Unary, X)$	$\triangleq$	$\forall x \in X \bullet x \in \underline{Unary}$
$TOTAL(\, Relation, X, Y)$	$\triangleq$	$\forall x \in X \bullet$
		$(\, x \in \underline{Method} \wedge x \in \underline{Abstract}) \vee$
		$(\exists\, y \in Y \bullet Relation(\, x, y)\,)$
$ISOMORPHIC(\, Relation, X, Y)$	$\triangleq$	$\forall x \in X\, \exists\, y \in Y \bullet$
		$(\,\underline{Relation}(\, x, y) \vee x, y \in \underline{Abstract})\,) \wedge$
		$ISOMORPHIC(\, Relation, X - x, Y - y)$

Note: Predicates are defined for *1*-dimensional terms; the unpacking of predicates for arguments of higher dimensions is a natural extension

17.2 SPECIFICATIONS IN THE PREDICATE LOGIC

Complete LePUS3 specifications can also be unpacked in the FOPL. To do so we turn to "The Foundations of Specification" [Turner 2005], in which the context is set for a discussion in the mathematical properties of specification languages. Turner develops a core specification theory (CST) and shows that his general account adequately unpacks statements in many formal specification languages. Turner's analysis provides us with a general and well-defined notion of a *specification*, which can be paraphrased as follows. Having unpacked in our FOPL the truth conditions for individual formulas in our specification languages (Table 21), we may now move to unpack complete LePUS3 and Class-Z specifications as sentences in the FOPL.

In Chapter 15 we distinguished between *open specifications* (a specification with variables) and *closed specifications*. We shall employ this distinction in the discussion in the translation of LePUS3 specifications to FOPL. We say that the variable x is *free* in the FOPL wff φ if at least one of its occurrences in φ is not bound by any quantifier within φ. A wff is *closed* if and only if it contains no free variables.

Let Ψ designate a closed specification whose set of declarations and formulas are equivalent (by Table 21) to the set of k closed FOPL wffs $\psi_1, \ldots, \psi_k$. Then Ψ introduces a new predicate Ψ as follows:

$$\Psi \triangleq \psi_1 \wedge \ldots \wedge \psi_k$$

For example, consider the closed schema ItrNextReturnsObject (equivalent to Codechart 25, p. 61):

ItrNextReturnsObject

> object, arrayListItr : CLASS
> next : SIGNATURE
>
> ---
>
> *Return*(next ⊗ arrayListItr, object)

Schema ItrNextReturnsObject is unpacked in the FOPL to introduce the predicate *ItrNextReturnsObject* as follows:

ItrNextReturnsObject $\triangleq$

> object $\in$ *Class* $\wedge$
>
> arrayListItr $\in$ *Class* $\wedge$
>
> next $\in$ *Signature* $\wedge$
>
> (((⟨ next ⊗ arrayListItr, object ⟩) $\in$ *Return*) $\vee$
>
> ($\exists$ *sub* • *Return*(next ⊗ arrayListItr, *sub*) $\wedge$ *Inherit*(*sub*, object)))

We may generalize this description to open specifications as follows. Let Ψ designate a LePUS3 specification with n variables $x_1, \ldots, x_n$ where n is a natural number. (When $n = 0$, Ψ is a closed specification). Let $\psi_1[x_1, \ldots, x_n], \ldots, \psi_k[x_1, \ldots, x_n]$ designate the list of FOPL wffs, each of which represents the unpacking of exactly one declaration or Class-Z formula in Ψ as indicated by Table 21, where the set of free variables for each ψ_i is a (possibly empty) subset of $\{x_1, \ldots, x_n\}$. Then Ψ introduces the n-ary predicate symbol $\Psi[x_1, \ldots, x_n]$ into the language as follows:

$$\Psi[x_1, \ldots, x_n] \triangleq \psi_1[x_1, \ldots, x_n] \wedge \ldots \wedge \psi_k[x_1, \ldots, x_n]$$

For example, the open schema CompositeComponent schema (Figure 16-1, p. 194) is unpacked in the FOPL as a definition that introduces the ternary predicate symbol CompositeComponent [*composite, component, Ops*] defined as follows:

CompositeComponent[*composite, component, Ops*] $\triangleq$
    Composite $\in$ *Class* $\wedge$

$Component \in \underline{Class} \wedge$

$Ops \in Set(\underline{Signature}) \wedge$

$(\forall orig \in (Ops \otimes composite) \bullet$

$(orig \in \underline{Method} \wedge orig \in \underline{Abstract}) \vee$

$(\exists dest \in (Ops \otimes component) \bullet \langle orig, dest \rangle \in \underline{Forward}))$

17.3   THE AXIOMS OF CLASS-BASED PROGRAMS

The abstract semantics for LePUS3 were defined in Chapter 14 in terms of *finite structures* and *design models*. Among the conditions imposed on design models in Chapter 14 is the requirement that they satisfy the *axioms of class-based programs* (Definition VIII). What are these axioms and why are they necessary?

By *axiomatization* we refer to the process of articulating formally the constraints imposed on a particular collection of model-theoretic structures. The axioms of class-based programs articulate some of the basic conditions that any design model that appropriately represents a valid program must satisfy by virtue of the properties of class-based programming languages. In other words, these axioms restrict the abstract semantics to exclude many of the models that under no circumstances may appropriately represent a valid program.

Consider, for example, the constraint imposed by all class-based programming languages that a class may not inherit from itself, directly or indirectly. Axiom 2 holds because design models are the abstract semantics *only* for well-formed programs, and because all well-formed programs satisfy this condition. In other words, Axiom 2 captures and makes explicit a constraint that the syntactic and semantic rules of class-based programming languages impose on the manner by which inheritance relations can be defined in well-formed programs.

Ideally, the combination of these axioms would be complete: It would guarantee that every design model that satisfies them appropriately represents (§14.3, p. 175) some program. Unfortunately, they are not. One of the reasons for this is because class-based programming languages vary by the set of constraints they impose.

Axiom 1. No two methods with the same signature are members of the same class:

$\forall sig \in \underline{Signature} \ \forall cls \in \underline{Class} \ \forall mth_1, mth_2 \in \underline{Method} \bullet$

$\quad (\langle sig, mth_1 \rangle \in \underline{SignatureOf} \wedge$

$\quad\quad \langle mth_1, cls \rangle \in \underline{Member} \wedge$

$\quad\quad \langle sig, mth_2 \rangle \in \underline{SignatureOf} \wedge$

$\quad\quad \langle mth_2, cls \rangle \in \underline{Member})$

$\quad\quad \Rightarrow mth_1 = mth_2$

The first axiom represents a rule that is enforced by the compilers of every class-based program language, in particular Java, C++, Smalltalk, and C#, on the relation between methods and classes.[1]

Note that we do *not* require that every method is a member of exactly one class. Although this is true in the Java programming language, it is not true for C++, which allows for methods ("global functions") that are not members of any class. This is neither true in CLOS, which supports multiple dispatch [Craig 2000], a mechanism which associates each method with any (fixed) number of classes.

Axiom 2. (Asymmetry of Transitive Closure of Relation *Inherit*). There are no cycles in the inheritance graph:

$$\forall\, cls_1 \in \underline{Class}\ \forall\, cls_2 \in \underline{Class}\ \bullet$$
$$\langle\, cls_1, cls_2 \rangle \notin \underline{Inherit}^+ \vee \langle\, cls_2, cls_1 \rangle \notin \underline{Inherit}^+$$

The second axiom requires that a class may not, directly or indirectly, inherit from itself:

Axiom 3. Every method has exactly one signature.

$$\forall\, mth \in \underline{Method}\ \exists\, sig \in \underline{Signature}\ \bullet \langle\, sig, mth \rangle \in \underline{SignatureOf} \wedge$$
$$(\forall\, sig_2 \in \underline{Signature}\ \bullet \langle\, sig_2, mth \rangle \in \underline{SignatureOf} \Leftrightarrow sig_2 = sig)$$

The third axiom requires that the notion of a signature is unique for each method. Indeed, a method signature is uniquely defined in the program by the method's name and argument types. It would therefore be meaningless to associate a method with more than one signature.

Axiom 4. Certain relations imply other relations:

$$\forall\, mth \in \underline{Method}\ \forall\, cls \in \underline{Class}\ \bullet$$
$$\langle\, mth, cls \rangle \in \underline{Produce} \Rightarrow$$
$$\langle\, mth, cls \rangle \in \underline{Create} \wedge \langle\, mth, cls \rangle \in \underline{Return}$$
$$\forall\, mth_1, mth_2 \in \underline{Method}\ \bullet$$
$$\langle\, mth_1, mth_2 \rangle \in \underline{Forward} \Rightarrow \langle\, mth_1, mth_2 \rangle \in \underline{Call}$$
$$\forall\, cls_1, cls_2 \in \underline{Class}\ \bullet$$
$$\langle\, cls_1, cls_2 \rangle \in \underline{Aggregate} \Rightarrow \langle\, cls_1, cls_2 \rangle \in \underline{Member}$$

The fourth axiom requires that the notions of some relations fit our intuitive expectations. For example, if one method is said to forward the call to another, we expect it to be true to say that the first method *calls* the second.

---

[1]Method "overloading" allows several methods with the same "name" to be defined in the same class, as long as their signatures are sufficiently distinct.

Chapter 18

Reasoning About Charts

Visual representations of evidence should be governed by principles of reasoning...
Clear and precise seeing becomes as one with clear and precise thinking.

—Edward R. Tufte

In this chapter we examine some simple means for reasoning about Codecharts. Having formalized the relation between charts and programs, we revisit the problem of *abstraction* (Chapter 1) and introduce a set of abstraction operators which allow us to reason rigorously about Codecharts. This shall allow us to formulate precisely the relation between charts that are similar in some sense and draw sound conclusions on the relations between design patterns.

In the first part of this book we made informal claims of the form "chart Ψ is an *abstraction* of chart Φ" and "chart Φ is a special case of chart Ψ". One way of understanding such claims is that "every program that implements Φ also implements Ψ." The formal definitions provided in this part of the book allow us to make this intuitive notion precise with relative ease.

Precisely put, given specifications Φ and Ψ, we say that Φ **semantically entails** Ψ (Definition XIX), written

$$\Phi \vDash \Psi$$

if and only if every design model that *satisfies* Φ also *satisfies* Ψ.

Corollary 1. The *semantic entailment* relation is transitive: If $\Phi \vDash \Psi$ and $\Psi \vDash \Delta$, then $\Phi \vDash \Delta$.

Semantic entailment captures much of the intuitive notion of *abstraction* discussed in Chapter 1 and throughout the first part of this book. Let us illustrate this definition and the intuition behind it.

Abstraction Lemma. If chart Ψ results from one or more of the following operations on Φ, then $\Phi \vDash \Psi$:

- Consistent removal of formula or a term[1] from Ψ ("abstraction viz. information neglect")
- Replacing an *ISOMORPHIC* with a *TOTAL* formula ("abstraction viz. predicate weakening")
- Consistently replacing a constant with a variable of the same type ("abstraction viz. generalization")
- Consistently replacing a variable of type $\mathcal{P}^d\mathbb{T}$ with a variable of type $\mathcal{P}^{d+1}\mathbb{T}$ ("abstraction viz. exponentiation")

Proof: By induction on the number of formulas in Φ. The proof for the last leg of the induction for each abstraction step is demonstrated in the propositions below as follows:

- For the abstraction viz. information neglect step, it follows Proposition 5.
- For the abstraction viz. predicate weakening step, it follows Proposition 6.
- For the abstraction viz. generalization step, it follows Proposition 7.
- For the abstraction viz. exponentiation step, it follows Proposition 10. □

An interesting consequence from the notion of semantic entailment is the following corollary, which simply states the intuitive expectation that, if a specification Ψ is an abstraction of Φ ($\Phi \vDash \Psi$), then every program that *implements* (Definition XVIII) Φ also implements Ψ:

Corollary 2. If program p *implements* Φ and $\Phi \vDash \Psi$, then p also *implements* Ψ.

Abstraction viz. Information Neglect

Abstraction viz. information neglect refers to the process of abstracting a chart in either one of the following ways:

- By removing an edge
- By removing all occurrences of a term t and all the formulas containing it

For example, compare the specifications Iterator (Codechart 105a) with FactoryMethod (Codechart 105b), representing the respective design patterns (presented in Chapter 11). Note that FactoryMethod can result from performing the following operations on Iterator:[2]

1. Removing the edge corresponding to the formula

$$TOTAL(\ Aggregate, Aggregates, Elements)$$

---

[1]A consistent removal of a term t is defined as the removal of all occurrences of t and of all the formulas containing it from the specification.

[2]The difference between the chart resulting from these operations and Codechart 94 is merely in the names of the variables, which, if consistent, is insignificant.

2. Removing the edge corresponding to the formula

$$TOTAL(\ Return, next \otimes Iterators, Elements)$$

3. Removing the terms *Elements, next* , and *next⊗ Iterators*

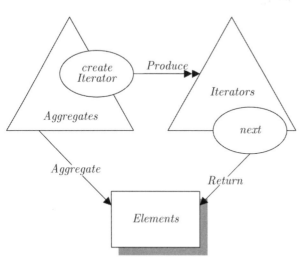

Codechart 105a.   Iterator

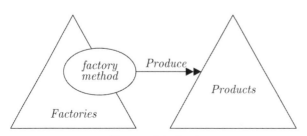

Codechart 105b.   FactoryMethod

Clearly, any set of entities that satisfy the requirements imposed by Iterator also satisfy the requirements imposed by FactoryMethod. More generally, abstraction viz. information neglect removes some of the implementation constraints imposed by a chart. It is only natural to expect that a design model that satisfies the more restricting specification (e.g., Iterator), namely a special case, also satisfies the less restrictive chart (FactoryMethod), namely the more general case.

Proposition 5. Iterator ⊨ FactoryMethod.

Proof: Follows immediately from the truth conditions for LePUS3.   □

As a consequence, we conclude that every implementation of the Iterator pattern is an implementation of the Factory Method pattern. This allows us to prove that the package `java.util` (Programs 1 and 10) also implements the Factory Method pattern (Proposition 12).

Abstraction viz. Predicate Weakening

Abstraction viz. predicate weakening refers to the process of abstracting a chart by replacing an *ISOMORPHIC* edge with a *TOTAL* edge. For example, the specification TotalNumbers (Codechart 106a) results from replacing the edge representing an isomorphic predicate formula in IsoNumbers (Codechart 106b) with an edge representing the respective total predicate formula. Both Codecharts model Program 14 (p. 98).

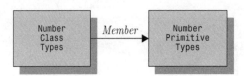

Codechart 106a.   TotalNumbers

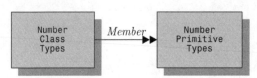

Codechart 106b.   IsoNumbers

These charts differ only in one predicate and impose slightly different conditions. The isomorphic predicate formula

$$ISOMORPHIC(\ Member, \texttt{NumberClassTypes}, \texttt{NumberPrimitiveTypes})$$

in IsoNumbers requires that each number class type has a field of a *unique* primitive type, whereas the total predicate formula

$$TOTAL(\ Member, \texttt{NumberClassTypes}, \texttt{NumberPrimitiveTypes})$$

in TotalNumbers requires only that each number class type has a field of *some* primitive type.[3] Since every isomorphic relation (§7.4) is also a total relation (§7.2), IsoNumbers imposes a requirement that is strictly stronger than the

---

[3]Since no abstract classes belong to the two sets, they are excluded from this example.

requirement imposed by TotalNumbers. The following conclusion should therefore come as no surprise.

Proposition 6. IsoNumbers ⊨ TotalNumbers.

Proof: Follows immediately from the truth conditions for formulas with the *TOTAL* (Definition XII) and *ISOMORPHIC* (Definition XIII) predicates. □

More generally, predicate weakening is an abstraction operator because isomorphic predicate formulas articulate a special case of total predicate formulas. Therefore, when an isomorphic edge is replaced by a total edge, the result is a more general specification.

Abstraction viz. Generalization

Abstraction viz. generalization refers to the process of abstracting a chart by replacing a constant with a variable of the same type. Abstraction viz. generalization is the inverse process to that designated by the *assignment* (§15.2) notation $\Psi[g(x)/x]$ referring to the consistent replacement of each variable x with the constant $g(x)$.

Compare, for example, the specification JavaRMIImp (Codechart 107a), modelling an implementation of the Java RMI framework, with JavaRMI (Codechart 107b), modelling the application framework itself (Chapter 10). Note that JavaRMI results from replacing the *0*-dimensional class constant remoteInterface with the *0*-dimensional variable constant *RemoteInterface* in JavaRMIImp. Evidently JavaRMIImp is "a special case" of JavaRMI because every program which satisfies the constraints imposed by JavaRMIImp (remoteInterface inherits from java.rmi.Remote) implements the more generic specification JavaRMI (i.e., there exists a remote interface which inherits from java.rmi.Remote.)

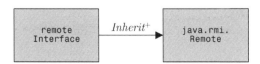

Codechart 107a. JavaRMIImp. An implementation of Java RMI

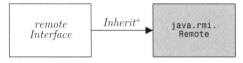

Codechart 107b. The generic Java RMI design Motif

Our intuition about the relation between these charts can be recast in formal terms using the semantic entailment notation as follows:

Proposition 7. JavaRMIImp ⊨ JavaRMI.

Proof: Let $\mathfrak{M}$ designate a design model that satisfies JavaRMIImp. Let g stand for an assignment such that $g(RemoteInterface)$=RemoteInterface. Clearly, JavaRMIImp=JavaRMI[RemoteInterface/$RemoteInterface$], and therefore JavaRMIImp ⊨ $_g$JavaRMI. By definition, also $\mathfrak{M}$ ⊨ $_g$JavaRMI(Definition XV). □

More generally, this method can be used to prove that, if there exists an assignment g from the variables $x_1, \ldots, x_n$ in an open chart Ψ into the constants in a closed chart Φ such that $\Phi = \Psi[g(x_1)/x_1, \ldots, g(x_n)/x_n]$, then $\Phi \vDash \Psi$. This method can be used to demonstrate that a particular chart models an instance of a design pattern.

Compare, for example, JavaAWT (Codechart 108a) with Composite (Codechart 108b) and observe that Composite results from the consistent replacement of each of the constants in JavaAWT with a variable of the same type and dimension.

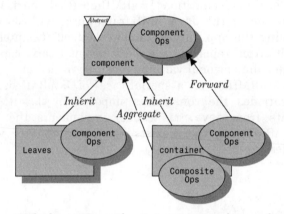

Codechart 108a. Class Component and some of its subclasses in java.awt

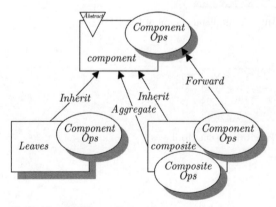

Codechart 108b. Composite pattern

Proposition 8. JavaAWT ⊨ Composite.

Proof: Similar to the proof of Proposition 7 except that assignment *g* maps the variables in Composite into the constants in JavaAWT, as illustrated in Figure 15-2 (p. 187). □

The same relationship can be demonstrated between the specifications WidgetFactory (Codechart 95, p. 155) and AbstractFactory (Codechart 96), illustrated in Figure 18-1 as an assignment from the variables in AbstractFactory to constants in WidgetFactory:

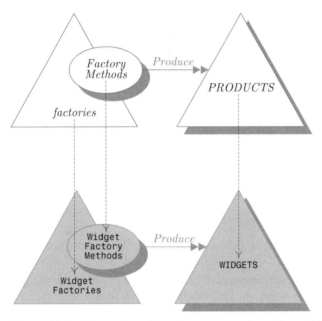

Figure 18-1. Illustration of an assignment mapping each variable in the Abstract Factory pattern (top) to a constant in the Widget Factory (bottom)

Proposition 9. WidgetFactory ⊨ AbstractFactory.

Proof: Similar to the proof of Proposition 7 except that assignment *g* is as illustrated in Figure 18-1. □

Abstraction viz. Exponentiation

Abstraction viz. exponentiation refers to the process of abstracting a specification by replacing a variable of type $\mathcal{P}\,^d\mathbb{T}$ with a variable of type $\mathcal{P}\,^{d+1}\mathbb{T}$, namely with a variable representing a set of entities of the type of the first variable. Visually, abstraction viz. exponentiation amounts to "shadowing" a non shadowed shape.

Compare, for example, the specifications for the Factory Method design pattern (FactoryMethod, Codechart 109a) with the Abstract Factory design pattern (AbstractFactory, Codechart 109b).

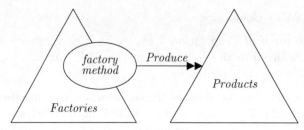

Codechart 109a. FactoryMethod

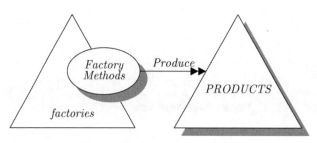

Codechart 109b. AbstractFactory

Observe two differences between the charts:

- *factorymethod* is a *0*-dimensional variable in FactoryMethod whereas *FactoryMethods* is a *1*-dimensional variable in AbstractFactory

- *Products* is a *1*-dimensional variable in FactoryMethod whereas *PRODUCTS* is a *2*-dimensional variable in AbstractFactory.

Evidently the Abstract Factory is a generalization of the Factory Method. This intuition can be articulated using semantic entailment as demonstrated in the following proposition.

Proposition 10. FactoryMethod $\vDash$ AbstractFactory.

Proof: Let $\mathfrak{M}$ denote a design model that *satisfies* FactoryMethod. By definition of the *satisfies* relation for open specifications (§15.2), there exists an assignment g such that $\mathfrak{M} \vDash_g$ FactoryMethod. Let us define a new assignment h as follows:

$$h(\textit{Factories}) = g(\textit{Factories})$$

$$h(\textit{FactoryMethods}) = \{ g(\textit{factorymethod}) \} \tag{7}$$

$$h(\textit{PRODUCTS}) = \{ g(\textit{Products}) \}$$

where $\mathcal{I}(\{\mathsf{x}\}) = \{\mathcal{I}(\mathsf{x})\}$. Clearly, $\mathfrak{M} \vDash_h$ AbstractFactory, and hence $\mathfrak{M} \vDash$ Abstract Factory. $\qquad\square$

Reasoning About Patterns

The abstraction lemma provides us with a powerful means of reasoning on patterns and their implementations in programs. Pattern implementations can simply be recognized by performing a number of abstraction steps on a Codechart. Below we demonstrate how this can be done with a number of the Codecharts provided in this book.

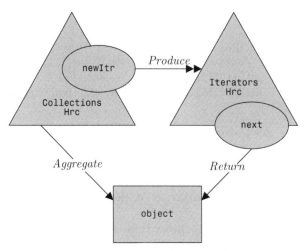

Codechart 110a. Elements of `java.util`

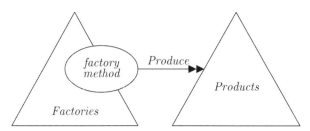

Codechart 110b. FactoryMethod

For example, Proposition 11 articulates the claim that JavaUtil (Codechart 110a), the Codechart modelling package `java.util`, indeed depicts an instance of the Factory Method design pattern (Codechart 110b).

Proposition 11. JavaUtil ⊨ FactoryMethod.

Proof: FactoryMethod results from two *abstraction* steps:

1. Removing the terms **object**, **next**, and all related edges (abstraction viz. information neglect) from JavaUtil

2. Replacing each remaining constant in JavaUtil with a variable of the same type (abstraction viz. generalization).

That which was to be proved follows immediately from the abstraction lemma. □

Proving Proposition 11 allows us to prove that package java.util indeed implements the Factory Method pattern, as implied by the visual similarity of their Codecharts.

Proposition 12. Package java.util *implements* FactoryMethod

Proof: Clearly, 𝔍𝔞𝔳𝔞𝔘𝔱𝔦𝔩 (p. 176) *appropriately represents* package java.util (p. 47 and 72). According to Proposition 1 (p. 182), 𝔍𝔞𝔳𝔞𝔘𝔱𝔦𝔩 *satisfies* JavaUtil. By Proposition 11, 𝔍𝔞𝔳𝔞𝔘𝔱𝔦𝔩 also *satisfies* FactoryMethod. Therefore, package java.util *implements* FactoryMethod according to 𝔍𝔞𝔳𝔞𝔘𝔱𝔦𝔩 (Definition XVIII). □

Our formalization of design patterns as Codecharts (Chapter 11) of the various *abstraction* operators (the abstraction lemma) equips us with potent means of reasoning about the relations between design patterns. In particular, they allow us to conclude that one pattern is a special case of another—and conversely that the latter is a generalization (namely an *abstraction*) of the former.

For example, Proposition 5 (p. 203) shows that the Factory Method design pattern is an abstraction of the Iterator pattern, or that the Iterator is a special case of the Factory Method. And Proposition 10 (p. 208) shows that the Abstract Factory design pattern is an abstraction of the Factory Method pattern, or that the Factory Method is a special case of the Abstract Factory. Since the semantic entailment relation that formulates the *abstraction* relation is transitive (Corollary 1), these suggest that the Abstract Factory is an abstraction of the Iterator pattern. It is easy to prove a formalization of this claim.

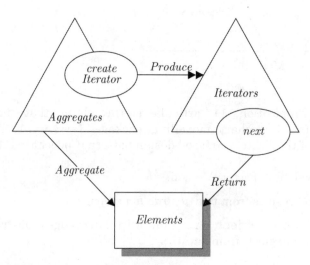

Codechart 111a. Iterator

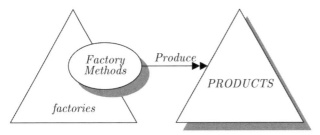

Codechart 111b.   AbstractFactory

Proposition 13. Iterator ⊨ AbstractFactory.

Proof: According to Proposition 5 (p. 203), Iterator ⊨ FactoryMethod, and according to Proposition 10 (p. 208), FactoryMethod ⊨ AbstractFactory. By the transitivity of semantic entailment (Corollary 1), Iterator ⊨ AbstractFactory. □

   Thanks to the abstraction lemma, most such proofs are not necessary. Indeed, LePUS3 is sufficiently simple so that, if patterns are modelled visually, reasoning about them most commonly becomes a matter of simple operations such as removing formulas or terms (abstraction viz. information neglect) and shading (abstraction viz. exponentiation).

Appendix I

The Gang of Four Companion

This appendix demonstrates how informal specifications of some of the design patterns in the seminal Gang of Four catalogue [Gamma et al 1995] can be specified formally using Codecharts. Each section contains a brief description of the pattern, followed by a UML class diagram of the pattern's structure and a Codechart.

ABSTRACT FACTORY

See §11.4.

ADAPTER

Intent Convert a class's interface to one that a client expects.
Participants

- Target: Defines the interface that Client uses.
- Client: Collaborates with objects conforming to the Target interface.
- Adaptee: Defines an existing interface that needs adapting.
- Adapter: Adapts the interface of Adaptee to the Target interface.

Collaborations Clients call operations on an Adapter instance. In turn, the adapter calls Adaptee operations that carry out the request. The collaboration can take in either one of two forms: In the Adapter (class) variation, the Adapter class inherits from the Adaptee class, and in the Adapter (object) variation, the Adapter class holds a member (field) instance of the Adaptee class.

Codecharts: Roadmaps and Blueprints for Object-Oriented Programs, by Amnon H. Eden
Copyright © 2011 John Wiley & Sons, Inc.

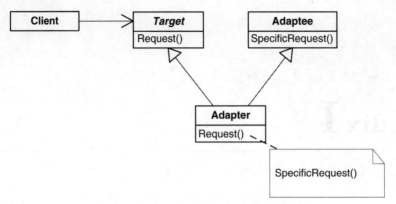

Figure I-1. UML Class diagram of the structure of the Adapter (class) pattern (adapted from [Gamma et al. 1995] by conversion from the OMT notation)

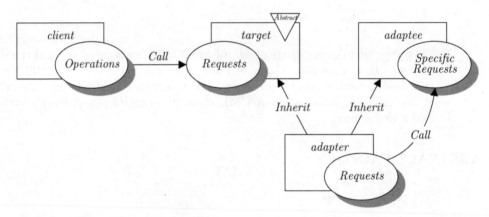

Codechart 112. Adapter (class) pattern

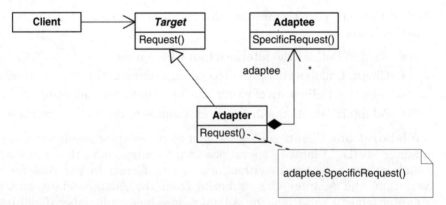

Figure I-2. UML Class diagram of the structure of the Adapter (object) pattern

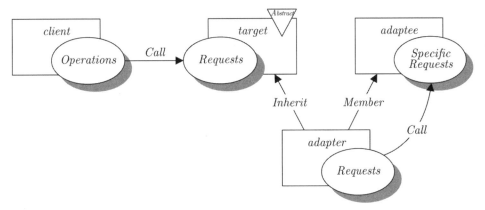

Codechart 113.   Adapter (object) pattern

BRIDGE

Intent Decouple an abstraction from its implementation so that the two can vary independently.

Participants

- Abstraction: Defines the abstraction interface and stores a reference to an Implementor instance.
- RefinedAbstraction: Extends the interface defined by Abstraction.
- Implementor: Defines the interface to the implementation, which is often different from the Abstraction's interface. Typically the Implementor interface provides only primitive operations, and Abstraction defines higher level operations based on these primitives.
- ConcreteImplementor: Implements the Implementor interface and defines its concrete implementation.

Collaborations Abstraction forwards client requests to its Implementor object.

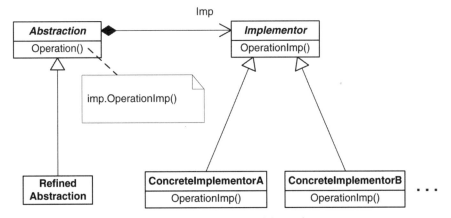

Figure I-3.   UML Class diagram of the structure of the Bridge pattern

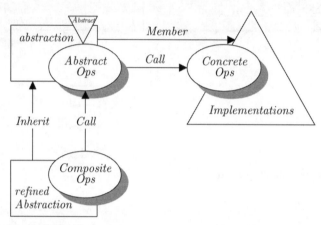

Codechart 114. Bridge pattern

COMPOSITE

See §11.1.

DECORATOR

Intent Dynamically attach additional behaviour and properties to an object, providing a flexible method of extending functionality.

Participants

- Component: Defines the interface for objects that can have responsibilities added to them.
- ConcreteComponent: Defines an object to which additional responsibilities can be attached.
- Decorator: Has a reference to a Component object and defines an interface that conforms to Component's interface.
- ConcreteDecorator: Adds responsibilities to the component.

Collaborations Decorator forwards requests to its Component object. It may optionally perform additional operations before and after forwarding the request.

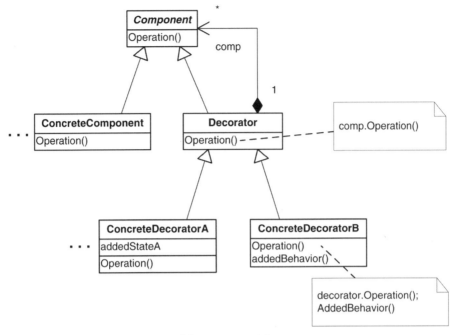

Figure I-4. UML Class diagram of the structure of the Decorator pattern

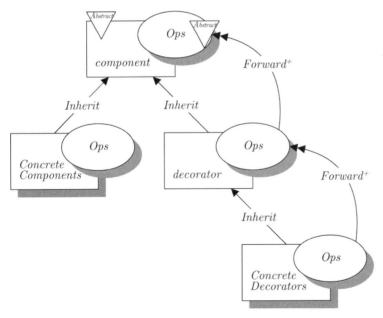

Codechart 115. Decorator pattern

FAÇADE

Intent Unify a set of low-level interfaces in one higher level interface.
Participants

- Facade: Knows which classes are responsible for a request, delegating requests appropriately.
- Subsystem classes: Provide low-level functionality. Should not have any knowledge of the Facade; that is, they keep no references to it.

Collaborations Clients communicate with the subsystem via the Facade, which may have to translate its interface to the subsystem interfaces. Clients that use the facade don't have to access its subsystem objects directly.

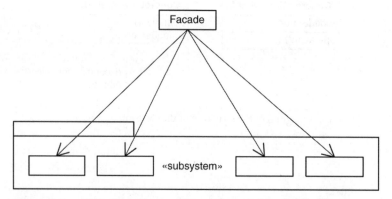

Figure I-5. UML Class diagram of the structure of the Façade pattern

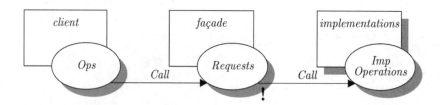

Codechart 116. Façade pattern

FACTORY METHOD

See §11.3

FLYWEIGHT

Intent Efficiently share large numbers of simple objects.

Participants

- Flyweight: Declares an interface through which flyweights can receive and act on extrinsic state.
- ConcreteFlyweight: Implements the Flyweight interface and adds (possibly stores) an intrinsic (independent of the context in which it is used) state. A ConcreteFlyweight object must be sharable but may not be shared at any given time.
- FlyweightFactory: Creates and manages Flyweight objects; when a client requests a Flyweight, the FlyweightFactory object supplies an existing instance or creates one if none exists.
- Client: Maintains a reference to Flyweight(s) and computes (or stores) their extrinsic state.

Collaborations Clients must obtain ConcreteFlyweight objects exclusively from the FlyweightFactory object to ensure they are shared properly.

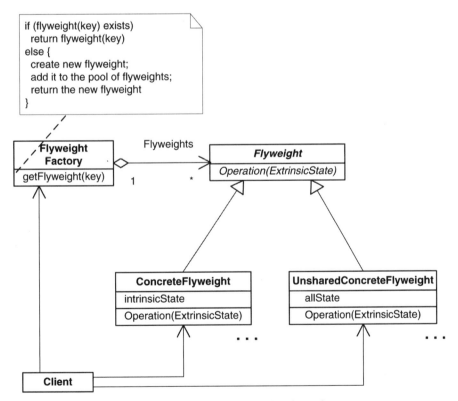

Figure I-6. UML Class diagram of the structure of the Flyweight pattern

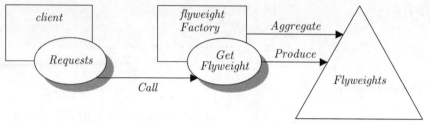

Codechart 117. Flyweight pattern

ITERATOR

See §11.2.

OBSERVER

Intent Define a one-to-many dependency between objects so that when one object changes state, all its dependents are notified and updated automatically.

Participants

- Subject: Knows its observers. Provides an interface for attaching and detaching observers.

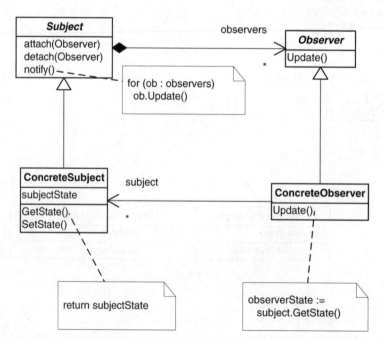

Figure I-7. UML Class diagram of the structure of the Observer pattern

- Observer: Defines an interface for objects that should be notified of changes in a subject.
- ConcreteSubject: Defines objects of interest to ConcreteObserver objects. Notifies its observers when its state changes.
- ConcreteObserver: References a ConcreteSubject object. Maintains a state that should remain consistent with the subject's by implementing the Observer interface appropriately.

Collaborations A ConcreteSubject notifies its observers whenever its state changes. Once notified, a ConcreteObserver object may query the subject for information.

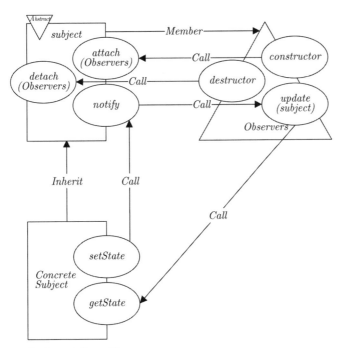

Codechart 118. Observer pattern

PROXY

Intent Provide a placeholder for another object which controls access to it.
Participants

- Proxy: Maintains a reference that lets the proxy access the real subject. Provides an interface identical to Subject's so that a proxy can be substituted for the real subject. Controls access to the real subject and may be responsible for creating and deleting it; other responsibilities depend on the kind of proxy (which we shall not discuss here).

- Subject: Defines the common interface for RealSubject and Proxy objects.
- RealSubject: Defines the real object that the proxy represents.

Collaborations Proxy forwards requests to a RealSubject when appropriate.

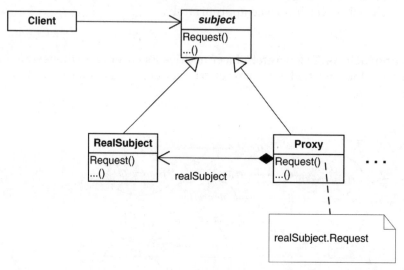

Figure I-8. UML Class diagram of the structure of the Proxy pattern

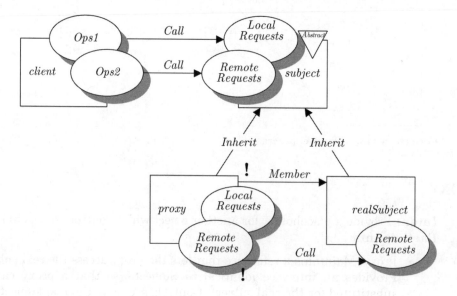

Codechart 119. Proxy pattern

STATE

Intent Define an object which adapts its behaviour according to its internal state.

Participants

- Context: Defines the interface of interest to clients and maintains an instance of a state that defines the current state.
- State: Encapsulates the behaviour associated with a particular state of the Context.
- ConcreteStates: Each subclass implements behaviors associated with a state of the Context.

Collaborations The Context serves as the interface for clients, and it delegates all messages to which its response is state dependent to the current ConcreteState object.

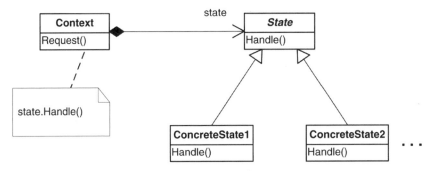

Figure I-9. UML Class diagram of the structure of the State pattern

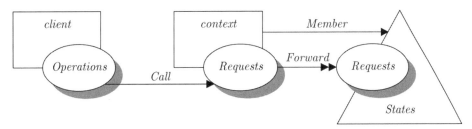

Codechart 120. State pattern

STRATEGY

Intent Allow algorithms to vary independently from clients by encapsulating them.

Participants

- Strategy: Declares a common algorithm interface used by a Context to call the current ConcreteStrategy.
- ConcreteStrategy: Implements the algorithm using the Strategy interface.
- Context: Maintains a reference to a Strategy object and may allow callbacks.

Collaborations A context forwards requests from clients to the strategy object. Some external object usually creates an instance of a ConcreteStrategy from a family of such classes and passes a ConcreteStrategy object to the context; thereafter, clients interact with the context exclusively.

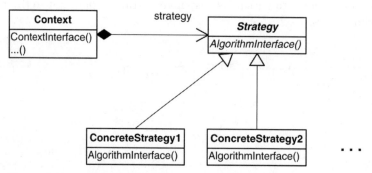

Figure I-10. UML Class diagram of the structure of the Strategy pattern

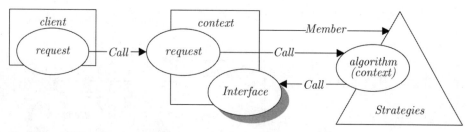

Codechart 121. Strategy pattern

TEMPLATE METHOD

Intent Define the skeleton of an algorithm in an abstract class, deferring some steps to its subclasses. This allows subclasses to redefine certain steps of an algorithm without changing the algorithm's skeleton.

Participants

- AbstractClass: Defines abstract primitive operations, and a ("template") method which specifies the skeleton of an algorithm.
- ConcreteClass: Implements the primitive operations that flesh out the algorithm.

Collaborations The AbstractClass relies on each one of the ConcreteClass implementations to flesh out the algorithm.

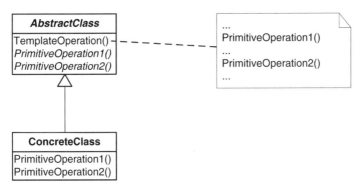

Figure I-11.   UML Class diagram of the structure of the Template Method pattern

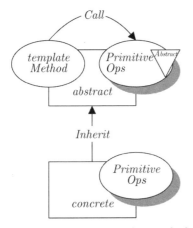

Codechart 122.   Template Method pattern

VISITOR

Intent Represent a set of operations to be performed on the elements of an object structure. The Visitor pattern lets you define a new operation without changing the elements of the object structure on which it operates.

Participants

- Visitor: Declares a Visit operation for the elements of the object structure and an algorithm to navigate it. The operation's signature identifies the class that it deals with, which accesses the element directly through its particular interface.
- ConcreteVisitor: Implements the Visitor interface, providing the context for the visiting algorithm and stores its local state.
- Element: Defines an abstract Accept operation that takes a visitor as an argument.
- ConcreteElement: Implements an Accept operation that takes a visitor as an argument.
- ObjectStructure: Can enumerate its elements and may provide a high-level interface to allow the visitor to visit its elements.

Collaborations A client must create a ConcreteVisitor object and then call its Visit operation in order to traverse the object structure.

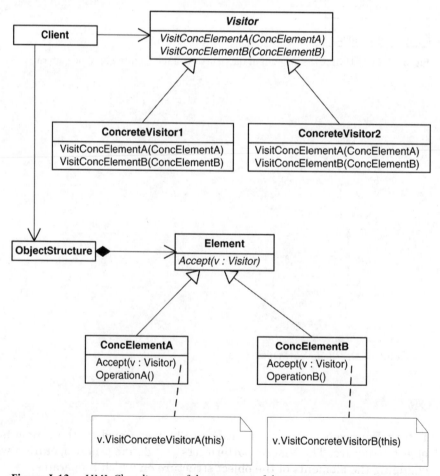

Figure I-12.   UML Class diagram of the structure of the Visitor pattern

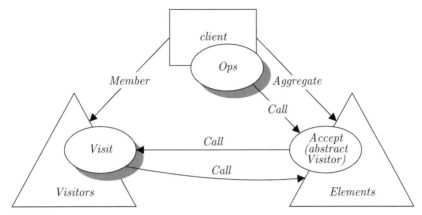

Codechart 123.   Visitor pattern

Appendix II

Formal Definitions

The secret of being boring is to say everything.

—Voltaire

For notational conventions please refer to page 168.

Definition I. A **finite structure** is a pair $\mathfrak{F} = \langle \mathbb{U}_0, \mathbb{R} \rangle$ such that:

- $\mathbb{U}_0$ is a set of primitive elements or **entities of dimension** 0 called the **universe** *of* $\mathfrak{F}$
- $\mathbb{R}$ is a finite set of relations (Definition II)

Definition II. A **unary (binary) relation** is a set of 1-tuples [2-tuples, or *pairs*] of entities of dimension 0. A **class (method, signature) of dimension** 0 is an entity in the relation *Class* (*Method*, *Signature*). A **class (method, signature) of dimension** d is a set of classes (methods, signatures) of dimension $d - 1$.

Definition III. Given a binary relation *BinaryRelation*, the **transitive closure** of *BinaryRelation*, written *BinaryRelation*$^+$, is that set of pairs $\langle x, y \rangle$ such that at least one of the following conditions hold:

- $\langle x, y \rangle \in$ *BinaryRelation*
- There exists an element z in $\mathbb{U}$ such that $\langle x, z \rangle \in$ *BinaryRelation* and $\langle z, y \rangle \in$ *BinaryRelation*$^+$

Definition IV. A class of dimension 1 (Definition II) Hrc is also called a **hierarchy of dimension** 1, or simply a **hierarchy** iff the following conditions hold:

1. Hrc contains at least two classes of dimension 0

Codecharts: Roadmaps and Blueprints for Object-Oriented Programs, by Amnon H. Eden
Copyright © 2011 John Wiley & Sons, Inc.

2. $\underline{\text{Hrc}}$ contains a class of dimension 0 $\underline{\text{root}}$ such that, for all other classes x in $\underline{\text{Hrc}}$, $\langle x, \underline{\text{root}} \rangle \in \textit{Inherit}^+$

Definition V. The **superimposition operator** $\otimes$ is a binary partial-functional relation. Let $\underline{\text{sig}}$ designate a signature of dimension 0, $\underline{\text{cls}}$ a class of dimension 0 (Definition II); then:

- If there exists $\underline{\text{mth}}$ a method of dimension 0 such that $\langle \underline{\text{sig}}, \underline{\text{mth}} \rangle \in \textit{SignatureOf}$ and $\langle \underline{\text{cls}}, \underline{\text{mth}} \rangle \in \textit{Member}$, then $\underline{\text{sig}} \otimes \underline{\text{cls}} \triangleq \underline{\text{mth}}$.
- Otherwise, if there exists a $\underline{\text{supercls}}$ class of dimension 0 where $\langle \underline{\text{cls}}, \underline{\text{supercls}} \rangle \in \textit{Inherit}$ such that $\underline{\text{sig}} \otimes \underline{\text{supercls}}$ is defined, then $\underline{\text{sig}} \otimes \underline{\text{cls}} \triangleq \underline{\text{sig}} \otimes \underline{\text{supercls}}$.
- Otherwise, $\underline{\text{sig}} \otimes \underline{\text{cls}}$ is undefined.

Let $\underline{\text{Signatures}} = \{\underline{s}_1, \ldots, \underline{s}_n\}$ be signature of dimension 1, and $\underline{\text{Classes}} = \{\underline{c}_1, \ldots, \underline{c}_k\}$ a class of dimension d (Definition II). Then we also define:

- $\underline{\text{sig}} \otimes \underline{\text{Classes}} \triangleq \{\underline{\text{sig}} \otimes \underline{c}_1, \ldots, \underline{\text{sig}} \otimes \underline{c}_k\}$

($\underline{\text{sig}} \otimes \underline{\text{Classes}}$ is a **clan**)

- $\underline{\text{Signatures}} \otimes \underline{\text{cls}} \triangleq \{\underline{s}_1 \otimes \underline{\text{cls}}, \ldots, \underline{s}_n \otimes \underline{\text{cls}}\}$

($\underline{\text{Signatures}} \otimes \underline{\text{cls}}$ is a **tribe**)

- $\underline{\text{Signatures}} \otimes \underline{\text{Classes}} \triangleq \{\underline{s}_1 \otimes \underline{\text{Classes}}, \ldots, \underline{s}_n \otimes \underline{\text{Classes}}\}$

($\underline{\text{Signatures}} \otimes \underline{\text{Classes}}$ is a **tribe of clans**)

Definition VI. **Constants** (x) and **variables** (y) are terms in the language such that:

- A d-dimension class is a term of type $\mathcal{P}^d\text{CLASS}$
- A d-dimension signature is a term of type $\mathcal{P}^d\text{SIGNATURE}$
- A d-dimension hierarchy is a term of type $\mathcal{P}^d\text{HIERARCHY}$ and also of type $\mathcal{P}^{d+1}\text{CLASS}$
- If $\textit{cls}$ is a c-dimension class, and $\textit{sig}$ is an s-dimension signature, then $\textit{sig} \otimes \textit{cls}$ is a term of type $\mathcal{P}^{c+s}\text{METHOD}$. If either $\textit{cls}$ or $\textit{sig}$ are variables, then so too is $\textit{sig} \otimes \textit{cls}$.

Finally, a term of type $\mathcal{P}^d\mathbb{T}$ is called a d-**dimensional term**. $\mathcal{P}\mathbb{T}$ is shorthand for type $\mathcal{P}^1\mathbb{T}$ and $\mathbb{T}$ is shorthand for type $\mathcal{P}^0\mathbb{T}$.

Definition VII. A **design model** is a triple $\mathfrak{M} = \langle \mathbb{U}_*, \mathbb{R}, \mathcal{I} \rangle$ such that:

- $\mathbb{U}_* \triangleq \mathbb{U}_0 \uplus \mathbb{U}_1 \uplus \ldots \uplus \mathbb{U}_d$ is the **universe** of $\mathfrak{M}$ where each $\mathbb{U}_k$ is a finite set of entities of $\textit{dimension}$ k (Definition II) and d is some small natural number (usually no greater than 3).
- $\mathbb{R}$ is a set of relations (Definition II) including the unary relations $\textit{Class}$, $\textit{Method}$, $\textit{Signature}$, and $\textit{Abstract}$ and the binary relations $\textit{Inherit}$, $\textit{Member}$, $\textit{Produce}$, $\textit{Call}$, $\textit{Return}$, $\textit{Forward}$, and $\textit{SignatureOf}$.

- $\mathcal{I}$ is an **interpretation function** which maps some constant terms (Definition VI) to entities in $\mathbb{U}_*$. If the superimposition (Definition V) $\mathcal{I}(t_1) \otimes \mathcal{I}(t_2)$ is defined, then $\mathcal{I}(t_1 \otimes t_2) \triangleq \mathcal{I}(t_1) \otimes \mathcal{I}(t_2)$. $\mathcal{I}(\tau)$ is also called the interpretation of τ.
- $\mathfrak{M}$ satisfies the *axioms of class-based programs* (Definition VIII).

Definition VIII. The **axioms of class-based programs** are the following:

Axiom 1: No two methods with the same signature are members of the same class.

Axiom 2: There are no cycles in the inheritance graph.

Axiom 3: Every method has exactly one signature.

Axiom 4: If a method "produces" instances of a class, it also creates it and returns it; if one method forwards the call to another, it can be said to call it; and if one class holds an aggregate of another, it can also be said to hold a member of it.

Definition IX. A unary relation symbol marked *UnaryRelation* placed over a term t stands for the **ground formula** *UnaryRelation*(t). A binary relation symbol marked *BinaryRelation* connecting t_1 to t_2 stands for the ground formula *BinaryRelation*(t_1, t_2). An All predicate symbol (Appendix I) marked *UnaryRelation* placed over τ stands for the **predicate formula** *ALL*(*UnaryRelation*,τ). A Total predicate symbol (Appendix I) marked *BinaryRelation* connecting τ_1 with τ_2 stands for the predicate formula *TOTAL*(*BinaryRelation*,τ_1,τ_2). An Isomorphic predicate symbol (Appendix I) marked *BinaryRelation* connecting τ_1 and τ_2 stands for the formula *ISOMORPHIC*(*BinaryRelation*,τ_1,τ_2). A **well-formed formula** (in short **formula**) is either a *ground formula* or a *predicate formula*.

Definition X. A design model $\mathfrak{M}$ **satisfies the ground formula** *Unary Relation*(t) iff $\mathcal{I}(t) \in$ *UnaryRelation*. It **satisfies the ground formula** *BinaryRelation*(t_1, t_2) if

- $\langle \mathcal{I}(t_1), \mathcal{I}(t_2) \rangle \in$ *BinaryRelation*, or
- there exists some class *sprcls*$\in \mathbb{U}_0$ such that *BinaryRelation*(*sprcls*,t_2) and *Inherit*(t_1,*sprcls*), or
- there exists some class *subcls*$\in \mathbb{U}_0$ such that *BinaryRelation*(t_1,*subcls*) and *Inherit*(*subcls*,t_2)

Definition XI. A design model $\mathfrak{M}$ **satisfies an All predicate formula** *ALL*(*UnaryRelation*,τ) iff for each entity $\underline{\mathbf{e}} \in \mathcal{I}(\tau)$ [if τ is a *0*-dimensional term, $\underline{\mathbf{e}} = \mathcal{I}(\tau)$] $\mathfrak{M} \vDash$ *UnaryRelation*(**e**).

Definition XII. A design model $\mathfrak{M}$ **satisfies a Total predicate formula** *TOTAL*(*BinaryRelation*,τ_1,τ_2) iff for each entity $\underline{\mathbf{e}}_1 \in \mathcal{I}(\tau_1)$ [if τ_1 is a *0*-dimensional term, $\underline{\mathbf{e}}_1 = \mathcal{I}(\tau_1)$] that is not an abstract method there exists some entity $\underline{\mathbf{e}}_2 \in \mathcal{I}(\tau_2)$ [if τ_2 is a *0*-dimensional term, $\underline{\mathbf{e}}_2 = \mathcal{I}(\tau_2)$] such that $\mathfrak{M} \vDash$ *BinaryRelation*(**e**$_1$,**e**$_2$).

Definition XIII. A design model $\mathfrak{M}$ **satisfies an Isomorphic predicate formula** *ISOMORPHIC(BinaryRelation,τ_1,τ_2)* iff there exists a pair of entities $\langle \underline{e}_1, \underline{e}_2 \rangle$ where $\underline{e}_1 \in \mathcal{I}(\tau_1)$ [if τ_1 is a *0*-dimensional term, $\underline{e}_1 = \mathcal{I}(\tau_1)$] and $\underline{e}_2 \in \mathcal{I}(\tau_2)$ [if τ_2 is a *0*-dimensional term, $\underline{e}_2 = \mathcal{I}(\tau_2)$] such that both conditions hold:

- $\mathfrak{M} \vDash BinaryRelation(\underline{e}_1, \underline{e}_2)$ unless both $\underline{e}_1$ and $\underline{e}_2$ are abstract and
- *ISOMORPHIC(BinaryRelation,$\tau_1 - \underline{e}_1$,$\tau_2 - \underline{e}_2$)*, unless both $\tau_1 - \underline{e}_1$ and $\tau_2 - \underline{e}_2$ are empty,

where $\mathcal{I}(\tau - \underline{e}) = \mathcal{I}(\tau) - \mathcal{I}(\underline{e})$.

Definition XIV. An **assignment** from specification Ψ into a design model $\mathfrak{M}$ is a function g mapping each variable in Ψ to a constant in the domain of $\mathcal{I}$. The notation $\Psi[g(x)/x]$ stands for the chart which results from replacing all occurrences of variable x with the constant $g(x)$ in Ψ. The notation $\Psi[g(x_1)/x_1, \ldots, g(x_n)/x_n]$ stands for the chart which results from consistent replacement of all occurrences of each variable x_i with the constant $g(x_i)$ in Ψ.

Definition XV. We say that design model $\mathfrak{M}$ **satisfies** closed specification Ψ, written $\mathfrak{M} \vDash \Psi$, iff each one of the terms of Ψ has an interpretation and each one of the formulas is *satisfied* (Definition X to Definition XIII). We say that a design model $\mathfrak{M}$ **satisfies** open specification Φ **under** assignment g, written $\mathfrak{M} \vDash_g \Phi$, iff g maps each variable in Φ to a constant in the domain of $\mathcal{I}$ such that $\mathfrak{M}$ *satisfies* the closed specification $\Phi[g(x_1)/x_1, \ldots, g(x_n)/x_n]$. We say that $\mathfrak{M}$ **satisfies** open specification Φ, written $\mathfrak{M} \vDash \Phi$, iff there exists some mapping g such that $\mathfrak{M} \vDash_g \Phi$.

Definition XVI. We say that a finite structure (Definition I) $\mathfrak{F} = \langle \mathbb{U}_0, \mathbb{R} \rangle$ is a **submodel** of design model (Definition VII) $\mathfrak{M}$ if $\mathfrak{M} = \langle \mathbb{U}_0 \uplus \ldots, \mathbb{R}, \mathcal{I} \rangle$.

Definition XVII. Given an abstract semantics function $\mathcal{A}$ and a program p in the domain of $\mathcal{A}$, we say that *design model* (Definition VII) $\mathfrak{M}$ **appropriately represents** p if $\mathcal{A}(p)$ is a *submodel* (Definition XVI) of $\mathfrak{M}$.

Definition XVIII. Given a program p written in programming language $\mathbb{L}$, abstract semantics function $\mathcal{A}: \mathbb{L} \to \mathfrak{F}^*$, a design model $\mathfrak{M}$, and chart Ψ, we say that p **implements** Ψ **according to** $\mathfrak{M}$ iff

1. $\mathfrak{M}$ *appropriate represents* (Definition XVII) p
2. $\mathfrak{M}$ *satisfies* (Definition XV) Ψ

Given program p and specification Ψ, p **implements** Ψ iff there exists some design model $\mathfrak{M}$ such that p *implements* Ψ *according to* $\mathfrak{M}$.

Definition XIX. Given specifications Φ and Ψ, we say that Φ **semantically entails** Ψ, written $\Phi \vDash \Psi$, iff every design model that *satisfies* Φ also *satisfies* Ψ.

Appendix III

UML Quick Reference

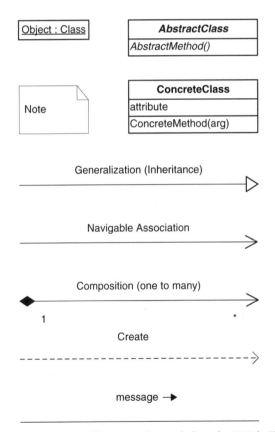

Figure III-1. Glossary to the symbols in the UML's Class Diagrams and collaboration diagrams notations

Codecharts: Roadmaps and Blueprints for Object-Oriented Programs, by Amnon H. Eden
Copyright © 2011 John Wiley & Sons, Inc.

References

A. Abran, J. W. Moore (2004). *Guide to the Software Engineering Body of Knowledge.* Washington, DC: IEEE Computer Society.

J. -R. Abrial (1996). *The B-Book: Assigning Programs to Meanings.* Cambridge: Cambridge University Press.

ACM/IEEE Joint Task Force (2004). "Software Engineering 2004: Curriculum Guidelines for Undergraduate Degree Programs in Software Engineering." ACM *Computing Curricula Series,* pp. 1–128.

C. Alexander (1996). "The Origins of Pattern Theory: the Future of the Theory, and the Generation of a Living World." *Software, IEEE,* 16(5), 71–82.

K. Beck (1996). *Smalltalk Best Practice Patterns.* Englewood Cliffs, NJ: Prentice Hall.

A. E. Bell (2004). "Death by UML Fever: Self-Diagnosis and Early Treatment Are Crucial in the Fight Against UML Fever." *Queue,* 2(1), 72–80.

A. E. Bell (2005). "UML Fever: Diagnosis and Recovery." *Queue,* 3(2), 48–56.

G. Booch (1993). *Object-Oriented Analysis and Design with Applications,* 2nd ed. Reading, MA: Addison-Wesley Professional.

E. Börger, R. Stärk (2003). *Abstract State Machines: A Method for High-Level System Design and Analysis.* Berlin: Springer.

F. P. Brooks II. (1987). "No Silver Bullet: Essence and Accidents of Software Engineering." *IEEE Computer,* 20(4), 10–19.

N. G. Carr (2004). *Does IT Matter? Information Technology and the Corrosion of Competitive Advantage.* Boston: Harvard Business School Press.

J. O. Coplien (1991). *Advanced C++ Programming Styles and Idioms.* Reading, MA: Addison-Wesley Professional.

J. O. Coplien, D. C. Schmidt (Eds., 1995). *Pattern Languages of Program Design.* Reading, MA: Addison Wesley.

I. Craig (2000). *The Interpretation of Object-Oriented Programming Languages.* London: Springer.

R. A. DeMillo, R. J. Lipton, A. J. Perlis (1979). "Social Processes and Proofs of Theorems and Programs." *Communications of the ACM* 22 (5), 271–280.

A. H. Eden (1998). "Giving 'The Quality' a Name." *Journal of Object Oriented Programming,* 11(3), 5–11.

A. H. Eden (2000). "Precise Specification of Design Patterns and Tool Support in Their Application." PhD dissertation. Department of Computer Science, Tel-Aviv University.

A. H. Eden (2005). "Strategic Versus Tactical Design." *Proc. 38th Annual Hawaii Int'l Conf. System Sciences—HICSS' OS,* Honolulu, HI, USA (Vol. 9), 3–6 Jan.

A. H. Eden, E. Gasparis, J. Nicholson (2007). "LePUS3 and Class-Z Reference Manual." Tech. Rep. CSM-474. Department of Computer Science, University of Essex, Available: http://www.lepus.org.uk/ref/refman/refman.xml.

A. H. Eden, E. Gasparis (2009). "Three Controlled Experiments in Software Engineering with the Two-Tier Programming Toolkit: Final Report." Tech. Rep. CES-496. School of Computer Science and Electronic Engineering, University of Essex. Available: http://ttp.essex.ac.uk/main/experiment.

A. H. Eden, R. Kazman (2003). "Architecture, Design, Implementation." *Proc. 25th Int'l Conf. Software Engineering*, Portland, OR. Washington, DC: IEEE Computer Society, pp. 149–159.

M. Fayad, D. C. Schmidt (1997). "Object-Oriented Application Frameworks." *Communications of the ACM*, 40(10), 32–38.

M. Fowler (2004). *UML Distilled: A Brief Guide to the Standard Object Modelling Language*, 3rd ed. Boston: Addison-Wesley.

E. Gamma, R. Helm, R. Johnson, J. Vlissides (1995). *Design Patterns: Elements of Reusable Object-Oriented Software*. Boston, MA: Addison-Wesley Longman.

D. Garlan, M. Shaw (1993). "Introduction to Software Architecture." In V. Ambriola, G. Tortora (Eds.), *Advances in Software Engineering and Knowledge Engineering*. Hackensack, NJ: World Scientific Publishing Company.

E. Gasparis (2004). "Definition of the Visual Formalism and Grammar of LePUS." MSc dissertation. Department of Computer Science, University of Essex.

E. Gasparis (2006). "LePUS2 User Guide." Tech. Rep. CSM-436. Department of Computer Science, University of Essex.

E. Gasparis (2009). "Design Navigation: Recovering Design Charts from Object-Oriented Programs." PhD dissertation, School of Computer Science and Electronic Engineering, University of Essex.

E. Gasparis, A. H. Eden, J. Nicholson, R. Kazman (2008). "The Design Navigator: Charting Java Programs." In *Companion, 30th Int'l Conf. for Software Engineering—ICSE*, Leipzig, Germany.

W. W. Gibbs (1994). "Software's Chronic Crisis." *Scientific American*, 271(3), 86–95.

J. Gosling, B. Joy, G. Steele (1996). *The Java Language Specification,* 1st ed. Reading, MA: Sun Microsystems.

J. V. Guttag, J. J. Horning (1993). *Larch: Languages and Tools for Formal Specification.* New York: Springer-Verlag.

M. Hall, L. Brown (2003). *Core Servlets and Java Server Pages*, Java 2 Platform, Enterprise Edition Series. Upper Saddle River, NJ: Prentice Hall.

D. Harel (1987). "Statecharts: A Visual Formalism for Complex Systems." *Science of Computer Programming,* 8(3), 231–274.

C. A. R. Hoare (1969). "An Axiomatic Basis for Computer Programming." *Communications of the ACM,* 12(10), 576–580.

C. A. R. Hoare (1975). "Software Design: A Parable." *Software World,* 5(9–10), 53–56.

C. A. R. Hoare (1978). "Communicating Sequential Processes." *Communications of the ACM* 21(8), 666–677.

C. A. R. Hoare (1983). "Programming is an Engineering Profession." In J. L. E. Wallis (Ed.), *Software Engineering: Developments.* State of the Art Report 11 (Vol. 3), Devonshire: Pergamon Infotech, pp. 77–84.

M. Huth, M. Ryan (2000). *Logic in Computer Science: Modelling and Reasoning about Systems.* Cambridge: Cambridge University Press.

O. A. Iyaniwura (2003). "Software Evolution Coordination: A Verification Tool for Object-Oriented Programs." MSc dissertation, Department of Computer Science, University of Essex.

jGuru (2000). "Enterprise JavaBeans Fundamentals." Available: http://java.sun.com/developer/onlineTraining/EJBIntro/EJBIntro.html.

R. Kazman, H.-M. Chen (2009). "The Metropolis Model: A New Logic for Development of CrowdSourced Systems." *Communications of the ACM,* 52(7), 76–84.

L. Lamport (1994). "The Temporal Logic of Actions." *ACM Trans. Program. Lang. Syst.,* 16(3), 872–923.

M. M. Lehman (1996). "Laws of Software Evolution Revisited." Proc. 5th European Workshop Software Process Technology—EWSPT'96, Nancy, France.

M. S. Mahoney (2002). "Software As Science: Science As Software." *Proc. Int'l conf. on History of Computing: Software Issues.* Paderborn, Germany: Springer-Verlag, pp. 25–48.

G. Malcolm, J. A. Goguan (1996). "An Executable Course in the Algebraic Semantics of Imperative Programs." In D. C. Neville, M. G. Hinchey (Eds.), *Teaching and Learning Formal Methods.* San Deigo, CA: Academic Press, inc.

C. Maniati (2008). "Empirical Evaluation of the Design Navigator as a Reverse Engineering Tool for Java Programs." MSc dissertation, Department of Computing and Electronic Systems, University of Essex.

J. C. Martin (1991). *Introduction to Languages and the Theory of Computation.* New York: McGraw-Hill.

V. Matena, M. Hapner (1999). *Enterprise JavaBeans™ Specification,* version 1.1. Palo Alto: Sun Microsystems.

B. Meyer (1997). "UML: The Positive Spin." *American Programmer,* 10(3), 37–41.

Microsoft Inc. (2005). *Visual C++ Developers Kit.* Redmond: Microsoft.

R. Milner (1982). *A Calculus of Communicating Systems.* Secaucus, NJ: Springer-Verlag.

R. Milner (1986). "Is Computing an Experimental Science? Inaugural Lecture for the Laboratory for Foundations of Computer Science." Department of Computer Science, University of Edinburgh, Tech. Rep ECS-LFCS-86-1.

R. Monson-Haefel (2001). *Enterprise JavaBeans,* 3rd ed, Sebastopol, CA: O'Reilly.

T. Murata (1989). "Petri Nets: Properties, Analysis and Applications." *Proc. IEEE,* 77(4), 541–580.

P. Naur, B. Randell (Eds., 1969). "Software Engineering: Report of a Conference Sponsored by the NATO Science Committee." Garmisch, Germany (7–11 Oct. 1968).

J. Nicholson, A. H. Eden, E. Gasparis (2007). "Verification of LePUS3/Class-Z Specifications: Sample Models and Abstract Semantics for Java 1.4." Technical Report CSM-471, Department of Computer Science, University of Essex. Available: http://lepus.org.uk/ref/verif/verif.pdf.

Object Management Group (OMG) (2004). "CWM Metadata Interchange Patterns Specification." Available: http://www.omg.org/docs/formal/04-03-25.pdf.

Object Management Group (OMG) (2005). "Unified Modeling Language (UML), version 2.0." Available: http://www.omg.org/cgi-bin/apps/doc?formal/05-07-04.pdf.

G. Odenthal, K. Quibeldey-Cirkel (1997). "Using Patterns for Design and Documentation." *Proc. 11th European Conf. Object Oriented Programming—ECOOP,* Jyväskylä, Finland. Lecture Notes in Computer Science. Berlin: Springer Verlag.

D. E. Perry, A. L. Wolf (1992). "Foundations for the Study of Software Architecture." *ACM SIGSOFT Softw. Eng. Notes,* 17(4), 40–52 .

J. Rumbaugh, M. R. Blaha, W. Lorensen, F. Eddy, W. Premerlani (1990). *Object-Oriented Modeling and Design.* Englewood Cliffs, NJ: Prentice Hall.

D. Schmidt, R. E. Johnson, M. Fayad (1996). "Software Patterns." *Communications of the ACM,* Special Issue on Patterns and Pattern Languages, 39(10), 37–39.

D. C. Schmidt, M. Stal, H. Rohnert, F. Buschmann (2000). *Pattern-Oriented Software Architecture,* Vol. 2: *Patterns for Concurrent and Networked Objects.* Hoboken, NJ: Wiley.

M. Shermer (2005). "The Feynman-Tufte Principle: A Visual Display of Data Should Be Simple Enough to Fit on the Side of a Van." *Scientific American,* 292(4), 38.

M. Sipser (1997). *Introduction to the Theory of Computation.* Boston: PWS Publishing Co.

J. M. Spivey (1992). *The Z Notation: A Reference Manual.* Hertfordshire: Prentice-Hall.

B. Stroustrup (2000). *The C++ Programming Language,* Special ed., Englewood Cliffs, Addison Wesley.

Sun Microsystems (1999). *Java™ Remote Method Invocation (RMI),* J2SE 1.3 version. Available: http://java.sun.com.

Sun Microsystems (2003). *Java Software Development Kit* (SDK)—J2SE 1.4.2 version. Available: http://java.sun.com.

C. A. Szyperski (2002). *Component Software—Beyond Object-Oriented Programming,* 2nd ed., Readings MA: Addison-Wesley.

T. Taibi (Ed., 2007). *Design Patterns Formalization Techniques.* Hershey, PA: Idea Group.

A. Taivalsaari (1996). "On the Notion of Inheritance." *ACM Computing Surveys,* 28(3), 438–479.

R. Turner (2005). "The Foundations of Specification." *Journal of Logic and Computation,* 15(5), 623–663.

J. M. Wing (1990). "A Specifier's Introduction to Formal Methods." *Computer,* 23(9), 8–23.

R. Wirfs-Brock, B. Wilkerson, L. Wiener (1990). *Designing Object-Oriented Software.* Englewood Cliffs, NJ: Prentice Hall.

E. S. Yudkowsky (2002). "Levels of Organization in General Intelligence." In B. Goertzel, C. Pennachin (Eds.), *Artificial General Intelligence,* Berlin: Springer.

Index

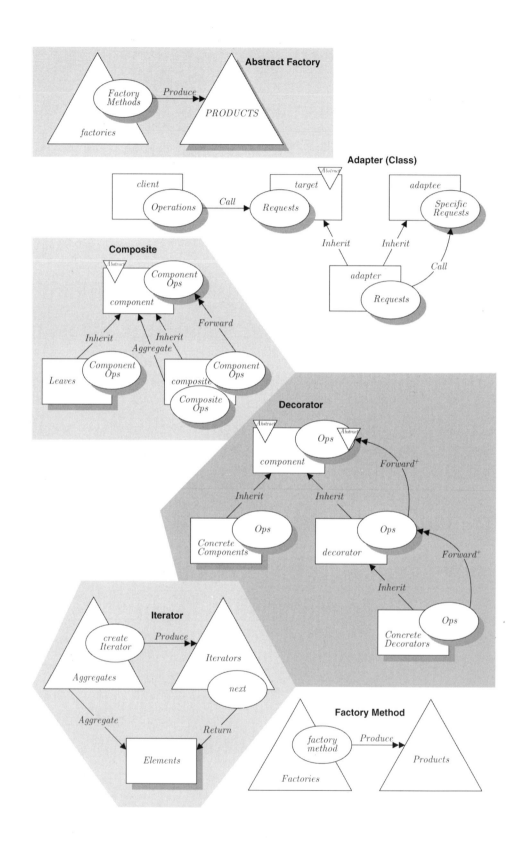